The Sexual and Gender Development of Young Children: The Role of the Educator

The Sexual and Gender Development of Young Children: The Role of the Educator

This publication was made possible by a grant from the Rosenberg Foundation, San Francisco

Edited by
Evelyn K. Oremland, M.S.W.
Jerome D. Oremland, M.D.

Ballinger Publishing Company • Cambridge, Massachusetts
A Subsidiary of J.B. Lippincott Company

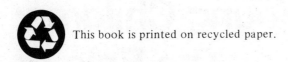
International Standard Book Number: 0-88410-169-X

Library of Congress Catalog Card Number: 77-5005

Printed in the United States of America

Library of Congress Cataloging in Publication Data
Main entry under title:

The Sexual and gender development of young children.

   Selected papers and discussions from a symposium held in San Francisco,
November, 1974, and co-sponsored by the Extension Division of the San Fran-
cisco Psychoanalytic Institute, et. al.
   Includes bibliographical references.
   1. Sex role—Congresses. 2. Sex (Psychology)—Congresses. 3. Sex instruction—
Congresses. 4. Child psychology—Congresses. I. Oremland, Evelyn K. II. Orem-
land, Jerome D. III. San Francisco Psychoanalytic Institute. Extension Division.
BF723.S42S49   155.4'18   77-5005
ISBN 0-88410-169-X

Contents

Preface

Among the farthest reaching of the vast social upheavals characterizing the past decade has been the emergence of new considerations about sex roles, gender, and sexuality itself. Every aspect of the study of this subject reveals more clearly how multitudinous, early, and largely unrecognized are the crucial factors affecting this important aspect of human development.

Perhaps no area of human functioning represents more the interface of genetic, anatomical, physiological, biochemical, psychological, and cultural influences. Reflecting the complexity of the subject is this multidisciplinary volume organized around the central theme of the role of the educator as an influence on the emerging sexual and gender development of young children.

It is no accident that in order to direct efforts toward providing educators with the greatest amount of information available in what has been a somewhat neglected area, we had to enlist contributions from nearly all of the great disciplines of behavioral science—psychology, psychoanalysis, sociology, social work, anthropology, law, and education. The teacher as the personification of the application of these fields is at once psychologist, sociologist, social worker, anthropologist, advocate, and parent in the classroom. In the teacher's work is potential for social change more powerful than the administrations of all of these disciplines combined. It is a stunning fact, the significance of which we often must remind ourselves, that *by law*, every child in this country, and indeed in every modern nation, must be exposed to the schools' collective influence from

early in life to adolescent maturity, and that the age at which this influence begins is becoming earlier, at more crucial developmental periods. The school as the great promulgator, mediator, and developer of society's values is second only to the family itself in influencing children.

This volume was prompted by an enthusiastic response to a symposium, The Sexual and Gender Development of Young Children: The Role of Education, held in San Francisco in November, 1974. The symposium was cosponsored by the Extension Division of the San Francisco Psychoanalytic Institute; The Department of Child Psychiatry, Mt. Zion Hospital and Medical Center; The Department of Psychology, San Francisco State University; and the Sex Information Education Council of the United States (SIECUS). This book consists of edited selected papers and discussions from that conference augmented by invited additional contributions that elaborate and further develop the significant themes.

The topic is complex and we are clearly aware that isolating one aspect of life can be misleading if we fail to recognize how that "slice of life" is integrated into whole patterns of personality, behavior, and social relationships. Even though our discussions of influences on the child focus on the school, it is not implied that the child comes from nowhere or is reborn on entering school. Repeatedly the symposium emphasized that the child's sexuality and gender identity, like every aspect of his developing personality, have origins very early in life, before society's formal institutions directly take hold. When the child comes to school, the still developing personality and the problems quickly become a part of a matrix, a highly complex social system.

The basis for a rational approach to children's needs is understanding development. Although development is characteristically described as sequential phasings, every child's idiosyncratic needs and reactions must be sensitively acknowledged and evaluated. The developmental orientation is the predominant framework of most of the presentations, discussions, and conclusions that follow. This developmental approach, described as a universal "road map,"[1] becomes a guide for evaluating children's directions, their interesting side roads, or paths that may lead to dangerous terrain or dead ends. To carry the metaphor further, when the itinerary indicates danger, alert stand-by crews are essential.

Selma Fraiberg's *The Magic Years*, still widely used in schools of education, clarifies the relationship between sex education and children's development.

The trouble with the straight story is that it is more fantastic to the mind of the small child than his own theories. . . . It is necessary to understand [the] sexual theories of a small child in order to give sex instructions. . . . If we fully understand, we modify sex instruction techniques according-ly. . . . Sex instruction *per se* is successful when it strengthens the child's satisfaction in his own sexual role. . . . Even with the best education the child cannot be completely educated because his child's body and his child's experience cannot provide him with the means for complete understanding. . . . The aim of sex education is not only to teach facts, but create desirable attitudes toward his own body and role, now and in the future.[2]

Discussion of sexual and gender development of children requires additional caution, for sexual education and its related implications are highly controversial. (Still smarting ten years later from a public attack and legal battle over sex education programming, one superintendent of a large county school office had to interview personally the symposium's program coordinator and evaluate the "credentials" of the symposium's major sponsoring organization before permitting staff participation.) Even in the symposium, designed to bring together the scientific thinking of diversified points of view from a variety of disciplines and professions, the political nature of the issues sometimes became evident and disruptive. At times, a force reminiscent of religious fervor was introduced to further particular interests.

Although it is obviously timely to reevaluate the role of education, the curriculum, and the very structure of the class itself in terms of the potentials and possible perils in the sexual and gender development of young children, the symposium clearly indicated that with all that the related disciplines know, there is much still to be learned. Though the mutual aim of all of the disciplines is to enable children to develop into men and women more able to meet and profit from the challenges presented by the accelerating changes in social patterns, the methods proposed and the emphases varied widely.

Nonetheless, the consensus was that it is essential that speculations based on our knowledge be proposed and tested. New programs, careful evaluation, and planned follow-up are initial and often courageous steps toward enlarging theory and creating the possibility for more effective interventions. It is hoped that such programs oriented toward the enhancement of basic understanding of sexual and gender development of young children will be encouraged by the pages that follow.

A preface to this book could not conclude without special

mention of the efforts, support, and contributions of those whose papers and discussions appear here. In addition, the stimulating ideas and encouragement, though regrettably often not specifically annotated, of Albert Ackerman, M.D.; Mildred Ash, M.D.; Gay Austin; Lonnie Barbach, Ph.D.; Elaine Barnes, Ed.D.; Lyn Berry, B.A.; Beth Coffman, B.A.; Emma Ford; Richard L. Foster, Ed.D.; Joseph Goldstein, Ph.D., Ll.B.; Paula Horowitz, B.A.; Mary Anne Kojan; Mary Lane, Ed.D.; Arthur Pearl, Ph.D.; Harvey Peskin, Ph.D.; Stephen Rauch, Ph.D.; Mildred Sabath, Ed.D.; and Robert Westfall, M.D.; as well as discussions and comments from the active participating audience are gratefully acknowledged. The Rosenberg Foundation of San Francisco and Mrs. Ruth Chance, former executive director, deserve our most sincere appreciation for their confidence, reflected in their supporting the symposium and making possible the publication of this volume.

Anna Maenchen, Ph.D.
Evelyn K. Oremland, M.S.W.
Jerome D. Oremland, M.D.

NOTES TO PREFACE

1. David Metcalf, Some Old and Some New Thoughts on Psychoanalysis as a Developmental Psychology, Sophia Mirviss Memorial Lecture, San Francisco, April 19, 1976.
2. Selma Fraiberg, *The Magic Years* (New York: Scribner, 1959), pp. 198-211.

✳ *Part I*

**The Developmental Approach
to Understanding Sex and
Gender**

✳ *Chapter One*

Sexual and Gender Development in the Context of the Family, School, and Society

Albert J. Solnit, M.D.*

Recognizing children's developmental needs and potentials can guide our efforts to help them to understand themselves as physical, mental, and sexual beings in the context of their families and the societies of which they are key members.

Born helpless, the human infant survives, matures, and develops because, ordinarily, an adult or a group of adults holds, nourishes, protects, guides, and stimulates him. Even before a child is born, he is a member of a societal institution, the family, since there is an adult associated with him without whom he could not survive. The family, here, is defined as at least one adult and one child, a basic social unit reflecting the mutual needs of adults and children. Efforts to question and put aside the old model of the family lead to the innovation of nuclear social units. Those innovations concerned with the needs of children and the values of privacy lead to the rediscovery of the family as we know it.

It is my assumption that both societal values and those that could be termed "health values" presume that sexual feelings and development are associated with affection, tenderness, and fidelity. When such attitudes involve a permanent commitment we are referring to a sense of family and community that share related societal traditions and values. Where erotic feelings and sexual development are associated with aggressive impulses and are devoid of affection and tenderness, we can expect that the understanding of sexuality and gender identity is likely to be limited and distorted.

A SIECUS report (September, 1974) by Dr. Robert C. Long states:

*Director, Child Study Center, Yale University.

3

The influence of the early familiar environment on sexual development and sexual and total health of adults cannot be overemphasized. The family, regardless of variations in its structure, is the preschool child's predominant influence. It is here the child gets his first impression of who he is and what is expected. It is within the family that most children first learn that they have a parent of one sex and a parent of another and that they are supposed to behave in the manner of one or the other. While these lessons are not learned in absolute terms, it is, nevertheless, through the family unit that the young child forms the first impression of masculinity, femininity, self, role value, and the value of the persons.

There is an infinite number of healthy ways to enable children and their families to sense that, when ready, they can question and understand the problems of sexual development and sexual differentiation. While various subcultures have different preferences for when, how, and what, human resiliency enables us to avoid formulas and to make our knowledge and methods available on the grounds preferred by those with differing life styles and with differing cultural and religious preferences.

In general it is realistic to assume that the child's biological equipment is normal and that there are no endocrine deficits or deviations. We cannot assess what is desirable educationally in connection with sexual development and gender expression without knowing the nature of the child's relationship to his parents and siblings, as well as the phase of his development. Thus, one cannot discuss the child's sexual and gender development without considering the child's general development, especially the identifications with parents and the powerful expectations of parents and their society.

The psychoanalytic view of individual psychosexual development serves as a useful frame of reference (see pp. 17-25 of this work). A major thesis is that each child's capacity for human relationship is a composite outcome of his biological endowment, his maturational unfolding capacities (biological timetable), and his developmental competencies as shaped by the social and behavioral expectations of his parents and other family members. Psychoanalytic drive theory, especially the sexual drive theory, has enabled us to have a developmental point of view about sexuality, gender identity, and the role of education as it is adapted to this developmental perspective. In 1905, Freud's three essays on the theory of sexuality forecast many of the biological findings of our present era in terms of what constitutes maleness and femaleness according to hormonal influences.[1] Further, this essay introduced Freud's view of bisexuality. The concept of bisexuality can be demonstrated by hormonal balance, as well as by

psychological attitudes and motivations, including the evidence of infantile sexuality. We are still sorting out what is more likely to be associated with maleness and what is more likely to be associated with femaleness in a given cultural and societal setting. This implies considerable overlapping. As a result we are accustomed to speaking of attitudes, motivations, and behaviors that are predominantly an expression of masculinity and those that are predominantly an expression of femininity.

Research such as that reported by Dr. Anneliese Korner (see pp. 11-16) indicates that there are clearcut normative sexual differences at birth between boys and girls; for example, in the areas of oral sensitivity and greater physical strength and vigor. The former has been found more frequently in girls and the latter in boys. Also, Dr. Korner's investigations and those of others clearly indicate that parents' expectations and behaviors differ from birth depending on the child's sex. Very likely this patterning of parental behavior is, to some extent, evoked by the neonatal behavior. For example, this research suggests that parents look at and talk more to baby girls and hold baby boys more closely.

Freud, in his contributions to the understanding of sexual development, spelled out certain aspects of the bisexuality and infantile sexuality of the human being. He modified his theoretical formulations in the light of advances in endocrine and biochemical studies. He had assumed these changes when he predicted that new knowledge would enable us to assign biochemical and endocrine definitions as well as psychological and behavioral characteristics to the differences between maleness and femaleness, as well as those descriptions that illuminated the bisexual or common characteristics.

These advances and refinements increase our awareness of the complexity of sexual development and gender expression and help us resist the urge toward oversimplified and stereotyped formulations. At the same time, we now have more tolerance and understanding of children's preferred ways of exploring, explaining, and phantasizing about their erotic feelings and wishes in a variety of cultural settings.

Parents and teachers are charged by our society with helping children to understand, cope, and have pleasure from their sexual selves as well as from their aggressive, thinking, imagining selves. Frequently, adults overlook the opportunity to let children know that the pleasurable aspects are desirable and can be characteristic of sexuality within a particular set of cultural expectations.

Preparation for sound sexual education begins with the assurance of a sound body and the affectionate, safe care of that body. Of singular importance in the first years is the continuing availability of

at least one adult who loves, protects, and guides the child into patterns of mastery, satisfaction, and a sense of self in the daily world. Ideally the adults will be comfortable and pleased with their own bodies, selves, and sexuality, proud of their own ethnic heritages, and at ease with their value preferences and religious inclinations. In this continuity of affectionate relationships, the child is able to define himself as separate and distinct from the parents and other significant children and adults who constitute the social human environment. Thus, the introduction into sexual awareness and definition is most promising when it takes place from the first in association with affection, continuity of attachments, and respect for the child's needs and tolerances.

Later, toward the end of the first year of life and beginning of the second, another principle of sound development can be exercised by enabling the child to be active in doing for himself what formerly had to be done for the immature child. The forerunner of this might be thumb sucking, where the child finds erotic oral pleasure while reducing tension and gaining a sense of pleasurable relaxation in his own body by his own intention. Toward the end of the first year and beginning of the second, the child begins to be able to feed himself, to touch various parts of the body, and to walk. This period also ushers in the dawning capacities to use mental and symbolic activities via memory and language. These mental and perceptual-expressive modalities can be useful and satisfying ways of exploring, learning, and gaining satisfaction. The child's self-starting resources are greatly increased, qualitatively and quantitatively.

Education about sexuality, then, has its best source in the close relationship to an adult. In the context of this continuing relationship, sexual education is most promising when the adult turns over to the child, as he is able, the care and pleasurable stimulation of the body in this early phase of development. Of course, the task is complicated, but not made impossible, when the child or those most responsible for his care have physical defects or disabilities.

There are important guidelines from psychoanalytic developmental theory and from Piaget's cognitive theory. For example, the maxim "If they are old enough to ask, they are old enough to know" must be tempered by our awareness that many questions do not come with question marks or that the content is not as important as the attitude that everyone can know when he is interested, ready, and able to understand a bit at a time. Ambiguity in sensitive doses may facilitate active learning. One need not and should not do it all for the child. Some things cannot be explained because they are not yet understandable to the developing child, until he or she is able to explore.

Children do best when they are active in behalf of their own knowledge. This active learning also facilitates a tolerance for preferred fantastic explanations, those idiosyncratic, personal, and private responses to fears, wishes, and uncertainties that allow for objective and subjective verities. Fantasies and fantastic explanations provide a bridge between the known and the unknown, and enable children to guess reassuringly before they can understand. Respect and admiration for the family myths and cultural legacies provide a historical cement for such learning. With this approach, respect and admiration for the preferences of diverse ethnic and cultural groups of our country can be nurtured.

Preparing and providing an environment in which the child can learn should be guided and tempered by our gradually increased understanding of how the psychosexual developmental tasks of the toddler (phallic, oedipal, latency, and pubertal phases) are synchronized or out of phase temporarily with the range of cognitive capacities described and classified by Piaget. These cognitive capacities can coexist profitably, with fantastic self-explanations based on infantile erotic experiences and associated mental activities of our children's earliest important experiences and impressions.

Logic and irrationality go hand in hand, so to speak. Adults, teachers, and parents can tolerate young children's irrational, infantile explanations, recognizing them as important pathways to significant early experiences that help build a sense of continuity and acceptance of self.

Tolerance and understanding of this aspect of mental development need not make less helpful and significant the rational, logical scientific mastery of our best working knowledge about sexual differentiation, sexual development and function, and sexual pleasure in all of the ethnic and societal settings that characterize our diverse cultural legacies. Adults often feel uncomfortable and threatened by these desirable connections with our infantile roots. These roots of infantile sexuality are part of a large reservoir of experience that serves as an unending source of human creativity, imagination, dreams, and problem-solving capacities. Such emotional learning and development are as essential to the human experience as are those capacities we characterize as cognitive, logical, and rational. In fact, it is the synthesis of these powerful capacities and experiences that constitutes the human dimension.

The new balance of self-regulatory ego capacities, self-critical super-ego functions, and instinctual drive demands enables school-age children to show their new functional capacities for use of language, logical thoughts, and memory that psychoanalysis characterizes as the latency (of the drives) period. These socializing and problem-

solving abilities are fostered by the school-age child's confidence that he or she can have private thoughts and impulses that are subject to intentional control.

However, there is nothing latent about the enjoyment of peer relationships and cognitive and physical skill mastery. School-age children also enjoy using their wits to utilize a toilet-sexual humor, implying their confidence and pleasure in the mastery of anal and urethral erotic impulses, and their playful curiosity about sex differences, pregnancy, and problems of human and terrestrial geography. They feel they are at a safe enough distance from the personal erotic impulses and phantasies that had been more dominant in the preoedipal and oedipal periods. Cognitively, they are now able to keep certain spatial arrangements in mind, to gain an early but incomplete understanding of the relationships between the inside and outside of the body, and to feel confident that they can keep secrets.

As adults, we have a great deal of difficulty explaining to latency children or to other adults how pregnancy takes place, what the delivery is like, and the details of sexual differences. After all, these "facts" are complicated, not easily yielding to a simple logical approach. Also, in our adult selves earlier explanations and theories persist and coexist with our more sophisticated knowledge. So, lest we think it is a simple matter, let us remember that medical students also find the study of the anatomy of sexual differentiation difficult even though they have scientific and social sanctions that foster such learning.

Sex education's focus on the inside-outside concept, that is, explaining to the child that conception and the baby have been done from "outside to inside" and then birth from the "inside to outside," demonstrates that a complex level of conceptualization is necessary, one that requires an advanced level of cognitive development. Thus, no matter what the setting, no matter what the ethnic, cultural, or language preferences, we recommend utilizing a level of explanation and of hearing that matches the child's level of cognitive and emotional development.

This is also the time to mention levels of stimulation. In some American households the enlightened or natural attitude toward sexuality in gender roles is often expressed dutifully, sometimes painfully, by using the "open-door" policy in bath and bedrooms and by encouraging pride in one's physical being by nudity. From the child's point of view, it may be useful to have these experiences if they are not too tense, uncomfortable, or stimulating. In some families such "privacy" is a matter-of-fact part of the life style,

ethnic preference, or economic and social reality. If there is little living space, for example if a family lives in one room, certain things become a matter of fact and necessity.

However, when it is done dutifully, out of an evangelical, intellectual conviction, what often is conveyed is excitement and conflict that are experienced by young children as more stimulation than they can cope with constructively. The discrepancy, for example, between the size of the child's body and the adult's, the adult genitals and the child's, is in itself a remarkable thing to understand and to come to grips with. For some children these "natural" experiences become upsetting confrontations with adults and with their own disturbing reactions. In these instances, excessive stimulation is experienced and can lead to inhibitions or regressive behavior.

Privacy, respect for boundaries, and the expectation that one will gradually be able to experience and learn is a useful and healthy way of knowing that sex can be and will be increasingly understandable and pleasurable. However, the "closed-door" policy, when it signifies shame and disapproval, can be associated with prohibition and conflict that can be crippling in its impact on sexual and intellectual development.

In the classroom teachers are expert in designing curricula that avoid the extremes of mechanistic drabness and excessive excitement and gratification. In curricula on family life and sexuality it is especially important to keep these avoidable extremes in mind in view of the earlier onset of puberty in our society. After all, puberty normatively upsets the balance between the various parts of the personality as sexuality matures somewhat ahead of the capacities for understanding and social skills. Thus, education should balance rather than exaggerate the imbalance that characterizes puberty.

The most important aim of education is to enable the child to feel that sexual differences, functions, and feelings can be thought about and understood in a way and at a time that is appropriate for each child. Content is less important than attitudinal influences. The desirable attitude is that sex is understandable eventually and that it is good to know about it. Further, it is expected that eventually each child will be able to know about it in his or her own preferred way. This implies that the curiosity and other developmental capacities of the child will provide guides for what is appropriate, just as the parents and the community will have a desirable and decisive influence on when, how, and what.

I favor working alliances between parents and teachers in family and sex education. I question putting a child in conflict by ignoring or minimizing the essential role of the parent in regard to planning a

curriculum on sex education. In fact, at the risk of sounding provocative, whether the child has a sex education curriculum in the school or not is less important than that parents should work with teachers and school administrators to plan and implement an agreed-upon curriculum. Parents and teachers may thus elaborate and refine their own understanding of family life and sexuality. This plan risks parental veto of such a curriculum, but it also can result in parents providing imaginative input into such a curriculum. The child will have a greater likelihood to feel that he is allowed and encouraged to know if time, energy, and skill are invested in parents and teachers working to find a way in which they can agree about what they are doing and wish to do as they attempt to help children learn about sexuality. This is especially true in order to demonstrate respect for and openness to subcultural preferences.

NOTE TO CHAPTER ONE

1. Sigmund Freud, Three Essays on the Theory of Sexuality, *Standard Edition* 7, 1905 (London: Hogarth Press, 1953), pp. 125-245.

Chapter Two

Sex Differences in Newborns

Anneliese F. Korner, Ph.D.*

Tentative evidence that behavioral sex differences exist in newborns supports psychoanalytic theory, particularly Erikson's theory of psychosexual development.[1]

As an investigator of newborns, I am in a rather strategic position to study behavioral sex differences that are relatively uncontaminated by sex-related, differential experience, which we know begins to exert an influence very soon after birth. A number of studies show that both mothers and fathers treat male and female babies differently, even while they are still at the hospital. Thus, behavioral sex differences during the first three days of life, when differing parental treatment would not as yet have left a great impact, can probably be considered as inborn more safely than at any other time during the life cycle.

Let me review what evidence we and other investigators have found on sex differences in newborns. Overall, the evidence is scant, which is, in part at least, a function of the fact that many investigators of neonates simply do not analyze their data for sex differences. Those who do often fail to find significant sex differences. The considerable overlap between males and females with regard to most behaviors further obscures what differences may exist. So it is very important that what evidence has been found about sex differences in newborns be considered tentative and subject to replication and further exploration. Notwithstanding such caution, it is striking that those studies which have pointed to sex differences in newborns have shown these only in certain target

*Adjunct Professor, Department of Psychiatry, Stanford University.

areas. It is the cumulative evidence of all these studies rather than the results of any single study that makes me think that innate sex differences actually do exist.

The female apparently emerges as more receptive to certain types of stimuli, and as orally more sensitized. At the same time, and this is important because of the female's reported greater passivity, the newborn female is in no way less active or expressive. There is also suggestive evidence that the male is endowed from birth with greater physical strength and muscular vigor. Let me briefly present the findings that support this summary statement.

A number of independent studies have shown that the female has greater tactile sensitivity and lower tactile thresholds.[2] In the visual modality, differences have been found only with respect to photic receptivity, as shown on EEG. The female's response to photic stimulation appears to be significantly faster than that of the male. Engel and his collaborators, who tested the mean photic latency of Oriental, Caucasian, and black neonates, found significantly shorter latencies of response in females in each of these races.[3] Female neonates also appear to be more responsive to sweet taste, the first of several examples that they are what I call "orally more sensitized." Nisbett and Gurwitz found that when females were given sweetened formula, they increased their milk consumption significantly more than did males.[4]

In one of our studies we took 32,000 feet of film of newborns, in time samples identical in length and in intervals since the last feeding for each child.[5] In one of our film analyses we found that in coordinating hand to mouth, female infants engaged in significantly more mouth-dominated approach behavior than did males. In attempting this coordination, males usually used the hand almost exclusively in seeking the mouth, whereas females more frequently approached the mouth to the hand, straining the head forward to accomplish this aim.

In several of our studies we investigated the sleep-wake cycles in newborns. In this context, we studied spontaneous behaviors in various sleep states. Peter Wolff, who was first to investigate these spontaneous behaviors systematically, postulated that since no known stimulus evokes these behaviors, they may represent the discharge of a neural energy potential, which occurs in inverse proportion to the degree of afferent input.[6] My own study set out to determine whether there were any sex differences in the reliance on certain spontaneous behaviors.[7] We found a sex-related trend which was, however, of only marginal statistical significance. We compared males and females by calculating the mean hourly rate of spontane-

ous startles, reflex smiles, and episodes of rhythmical mouthing in each of three sleep states, namely regular sleep, irregular sleep with and without REMs,[a] and drowse. In males, we also monitored the incidence of erections. In each state, the mean hourly rate of startles of males exceeded that of females. By contrast, females exceeded in reflex smiles and rhythmical mouthing in all of the states in which these behaviors occur. Since the overall rate of spontaneous discharge behaviors was almost identical for males and females when erections were excluded, it appears that females make up in smiles and reflex sucks what they lack in startles. If indeed these behaviors represent discharges of a neural energy potential, it appears that females tend to discharge this potential more frequently via the facial musculature, particularly the mouth region, whereas males tend to discharge it more frequently through total and vigorous body activations.

Females seem to exceed males in still another rhythmical oral behavior. Balint found that females during bottle feeding showed a rhythmical clonus of the tongue more frequently than did males.[8]

It is well known that statistically, males are, on the average, larger and heavier than females from birth on.[9] They also may be stronger, as suggested by Bell's research.[10] Bell found that when put in the prone position, males were able to lift their heads significantly higher than females.

The males' greater size and possibly greater strength does not imply, however, that males are more active than females. In many neonatal studies, including our own, no sex differences could be shown in the frequency or amplitude of the babies' motions.[11] Also, there were no significant sex differences in the activity-related oral behaviors such as the frequency of hand-mouth contact, or the efficiency or persistence of these behaviors.[12] Nutritive and non-nutritive sucking reflects no sex differences, probably because these are under the influence of the overriding and sex-unrelated biological function of hunger.[13] Furthermore, many different studies, including our own, have failed to show differences in expressive behavior such as the frequency or duration of crying.[14] And our soothing studies failed to show any sex differences in soothability.[15]

Perhaps it would be fruitful to view these neonatal differences as reflecting predispositions that feed into later sex differences and that are strongly influenced and elaborated by cultural pressures and differential experience accorded each sex. It is striking that for every one of the characteristics in which sex differences have been noted in newborns, there is evidence of continuity in later development of

---

[a]Rapid eye movements during sleep which in older children and adults is highly correlated with dreaming.

these same differences, either in direct or derivative form. Some of these differences have been greatly emphasized in psychoanalytic theory; others have not.

One sex difference that shows this continuity into later life but that has not been of primary concern to psychoanalysis is the greater cutaneous sensitivity of the female neonate, which finds its counterpart in the adult female. Studies using evoked potential in response to electro-cutaneous stimulation have shown shorter latencies and higher amplitudes of response in the adult female than in the male in both normal and psychiatric populations.[16] Similarly, adult females showed shorter latencies and greater amplitudes of response to photic stimulation than males, just as newborn females do.[17]

The sex differences in newborns that are of direct relevance to psychoanalytic theory are those dealing with the greater oral sensitization of the female. Erikson, in particular, stressed that in progressing through the ontogenetic stages of psychosexual development, the oral-incorporative mode colors the female's development much more than the male's, beginning in infancy and going right through to the final stages of genitality.[18] Thus, the female's development, both normal and pathological, seems to be characterized by a more frequent residual from the oral phase of development. Perhaps the female's greater oral sensitization as reflected in her behavior shortly after birth constitutes a predisposition that feeds into her later development, finding expression in a number of characteristics in which females are reported to predominate. For example, the female newborn's greater responsivity to sweet taste finds a correlary in the greater taste sensitivity and taste discrimination that has been found in adult females.[19] It is also supported by the animal literature, which shows that female rats consume more glucose and saccharin solutions than males.[20] Female children, from age one on, are both more frequent and more persistent thumbsuckers than males, as suggested by several large-scale studies.[21] While on the whole the incidence of psychiatric, developmental disturbances in the male far exceed those of the female, particularly in the learning disorders, the speech pathologies, autism, etc., eating disorders and other difficulties connected with the function of the mouth are much more common in females than in males. For example, the incidence of anorexia nervosa is from 10-1 to 20-1 in favor of females.[22] Also, in those obesity studies which compare the sexes, consistently higher prevalence of obesity has been reported for women.[23] Furthermore, once women take up smoking, they seem to be less likely to give it up than men, at least according to a recent HEW report. More derivatively, in psychopathology, oral fixations

and regressions are more common in females than in males.[24] A good case in point is hysteria, a syndrome that in itself primarily affects women, in which oral fixations have been described as an important underlying feature.[25]

The male newborn's greater strength or muscular endowment may foreshadow much of his later development, which is characterized by superior physical strengths and behaviors reflecting physical prowess often considered "phallic."

The question still remains, What could possibly account for the sex differences at birth which, in direct or derivative form, seem to persist through much of later development? Aside from possible genetic determinants, the most plausible explanation must lie in hormonal influences that play a major role in sexual differentiation *in utero.* To become male, the undifferentiated fetus must first develop testes, which seems to occur under genetic influences. The fetal testes must secrete, first, a duct-organizing substance and, second, androgens for the embryo to become male. The continued secretion of androgens from the testes is essential for maleness to develop both in the anatomical and the functional sense. Speculating from the animal literature, I wonder whether the prenatally circulating androgens of the male may not act to suppress the male's perioral responsiveness and skin sensitivity. The prenatally circulating androgens certainly could explain the male's greater strength.

NOTES TO CHAPTER TWO

1. Erik H. Erikson, The Theory of Infantile Sexuality, in *Childhood and Society* (New York: Norton, 1950), 44-92.

2. R.Q. Bell and N. Costello, Three Tests for Sex Differences in Tactile Sensitivity in the Newborn, *Biologia Neonatorum* 7, 1964, 335-347; P.H. Wolff, The Natural History of Crying and Other Vocalizations in Early Infancy, in *Determinants of Infant Behavior* 3, ed. by B.M. Foss (London: Methuen, 1969), 113-138.

3. R. Engel, D. Crowell, and S. Nishijima, Visual and Auditory Response Latencies in Neonates, in *Felicitation Volume in Honour of C.C. DeSilva* (Ceylon: Kularatne and Co., Ltd., 1968).

4. R.E. Nisbett and S.B. Gurwitz, Weight, Sex and the Eating Behavior of Human Newborns, *J. Comp. Physiol. Psychol.* 73, 1970, 245-253.

5. A.F. Korner, Sex Differences in Newborns with Special Reference to Differences in the Organization of Oral Behavior, *Journal of Child Psychology and Psychiatry* 14, 1973, 19-29.

6. Peter H. Wolff, The Causes, Controls and Organization of Behavior in the Neonate, *Psychological Issues* 5(1), Monograph 17, 1966.

7. A.F. Korner, Neonatal Startles, Smiles, Erections and Reflex Sucks as Related to State, Sex and Individuality, *Child Development* 40, 1969, 1039-1053.

8. M. Balint, Individual Differences of Behavior in Early Infancy and an Objective Way of Recording Them, *J. Genet. Psychol.* 73, 1948, 57-117.

9. J.E. Garai and A. Scheinfeld, Sex Differences in Mental and Behavioral Traits, *Genet. Psychol. Monogr.* 77, 1968, 169-299.

10. R.Q. Bell and J.F. Darling, The Prone Head Reaction in the Human Neonate: Relation with Sex and Tactile Sensitivity, *Child Development* 36, 1965, 943-949.

11. A.F. Korner, Individual Differences at Birth: Implications for Early Experience and Later Development, *Am. J. Orthopsychiat.* 41, 1971, 608-619.

12. A.F. Korner and H.C. Kraemer, Individual Differences in Spontaneous Oral Behavior, in *Third Symposium on Oral Sensation and Perception: The Mouth of the Infant*, ed. by J.F. Bosma (Springfield: Charles C. Thomas, 1972).

13. J. Dubignon, D. Campbell, M. Curtis, and M.W. Partington, The Relation between Laboratory Measures of Sucking, Food Intake, and Perinatal Factors during the Newborn Period, *Child Development* 40, 1969, 1107-1120; W.H. Bridger, Ethological Concepts and Human Development, *Rec. Adv. Biolog. Psychiat.* 4, 1962, 95-107.

14. V.C. Fisichelli and S. Karelitz, The Cry Latencies of Normal Infants and Those with Brain Damage, *J. Pediat.* 62, 1963, 724-734; A.F. Korner and E.B. Thoman, Visual Alertness in Neonates as Evoked by Maternal Care, *J. Experiment. Child Psychol.* 10, 1970, 67-78.

15. A.F. Korner and E.B. Thoman, The Relative Efficacy of Contact and Vestibular-Proprioceptive Stimulation in Soothing Neonates, *Child Development* 43, 1972, 443-453.

16. C. Shagass and M. Schwartz, Age, Personality and Somatosensory Cerebral Evoked Responses, *Science* 148, 1965a, 1359-1361, Somatosensory Cerebral Evoked Responses in Psychotic Depression, *Br. J. Psychiat.* 112, 1966, 799-807.

17. C. Shagass and M. Schwartz, Visual Cerebral Evoked Response Characteristics in a Psychiatric Population, *Am. J. Psychiat.* 121, 1965b, 979-987.

18. Erikson, pp. 44-92.

19. H.C. Soltan and S.E. Bracken, The Relation of Sex to Taste Reactions, *J. Heredity* 49, 1958, 280-284.

20. E.S. Valenstein, J.W. Kakolewski, and V.C. Cox, Sex Differences in Taste Preferences for Glucose and Saccharin Solutions, *Science* 156, 1967, 942-943; G.N. Wade and I. Zucker, Hormonal and Developmental Influence on Rat Saccharin Preferences, *J. Comp. Physiol. Psychol.* 69, 1969a, 291-300; Wade and Zucker, Taste Preferences of Female Rats: Modification by Neonatal Hormones, Food Deprivation and Prior Experience, *Physiol. and Behav.* 4, 1969b, 935-943.

21. M.P. Honzig and J.P. McKee, The Sex Difference in Thumbsucking, *J. Pediat.* 61, 1962, 726-732.

22. A. Stunkard, Anorexia Nervosa, in *The Science and Practice of Clinical Medicine*, ed. by J.P. Sanford (New York: Grune and Stratton, 1972).

23. A. Stunkard and J. Hirsch, Obesity, in *ibid.*

24. O. Fenichel, *The Psychoanalytic Theory of Neurosis* (New York: Norton, 1945).

25. J. Marmor, Orality in the Hysterical Personality, *J. Am. Psychoanal. Assoc.* 1, 1953, 656-671.

Chapter Three

The "Givens"—The Psychoanalytic Schema

Calvin F. Settlage, M.D.*

Although the psychoanalytic theory of human sexual development constitutes the oldest systematic theory extant, it is in fact just over seventy years old, having been set forth in 1905 with the publication of Freud's *Three Essays on the Theory of Sexuality.*[1] The sections of the essays on the sexual theories of children and on the pregenital organization of the libido—the oral and anal psychosexual stages—were added still later, in 1915.[2] Psychoanalytic theory is thus also a young theory, and one that has undergone continued revision and elaboration. In addition to the mentioned additions to the essays, later revisions were made by Freud. Advances in biochemistry caused him, for example, to rewrite in 1920 the section on the chemical basis of sexuality; and, at the very time of the publication of the *Three Essays*, Freud was in the process of abandoning his earlier theory that infantile sexuality was stirred up by adult stimulation or seduction in favor of his newer perception "that sexual impulses operated normally in the youngest children without need for outside sexual stimulation."[3]

During the past decade, revisions and extensions of psychoanalytic theory have been formulated on the basis of data from direct observational studies of child development during the first three years of life carried out by psychoanalysts. Thus, the building of psychoanalytic theory concerning normal psychological development rests today not only upon the long-standing retrospective and reconstructed view from the psychoanalytic situation, but upon the

*Chief, Child Psychiatry, Mt. Zion Medical Center; Faculty, San Francisco Psychoanalytic Institute.

current and prospective view from the direct observational situation.

The following is my understanding in schematic form of the psychoanalytic theory of sexual and gender development as it has been revised and elaborated to the present time.

My review of the stages of development is facilitated by Stoller's helpful distinction between *sex* and *gender*.[4] According to his definition, *sex* refers to male or female and has a biological connotation. To determine the sex of the individual, one must assess the chromosomes, the external genitalia, the internal genitalia, the gonads (ovaries or testes), the hormonal status, the secondary sex characteristics, and, in the light of recent research, possibly central nervous subsystems concerned with the regulation of sexual behavior.[5]

Gender refers to masculine or feminine and has a psychological or cultural connotation; gender is learned. The individual's sense of gender can be independent of his or her biologically determined sex. The sense of gender begins with the awareness that one belongs to one or the other sex. The individual's *gender role* refers to overt behaviors that establish one's gender in the eyes of others.

The individual's *sense* of maleness or femaleness, as distinguished from the biological fact of being male or female, precedes the development of the more definitive and complex sense of being masculine or feminine, of being manly or womanly. Core gender identity—the sense of maleness or femaleness—derives from three factors: the anatomy and physiology of the genitalia; the attitude of the parents, siblings, and peers toward the child's biological sex and gender role; and an innate biological tendency which, depending upon its strength, can more or less modify or resist the attitudinal or environmental forces. Generally, as Stoller's studies of transsexualism have demonstrated, one becomes a member of that sex to which one has been assigned by the familial-cultural environment, regardless of the state of the biological determinants.

THE STAGES OF SEXUAL AND GENDER DEVELOPMENT

Psychoanalytic theory holds that human personality is shaped by both biological endowment and the influence of environment and experience. The term *maturation* refers in psychoanalysis to the individual potentials provided by heredity and biology, such as temperament, intelligence, and sex, and to the innate biologically predetermined timetable for the unfolding of changes due to growth, such as the onset of locomotion, language development, cognitive or

intellectual development generally, and the advent of puberty. The term *development* is used to encompass those aspects of psychic or psychological development which result from the experience of the biologically maturing individual in interaction with the forces of his unique physical, familial, and sociocultural environment. Thus, the shifts from one stage to the next in the progression through the oral, anal, phallic-oedipal, latency, and adolescent stages of psychosexual development delineated by Freud are determined by nervous-system maturation and changes in hormonal balance. In the cognitive realm, the emergence of the capacity for fantasy prior to that of reason and thought is similarly determined, the highest level of abstract thought resulting, according to Piaget,[6] from the hormonal and central nervous system changes of puberty.

On the developmental side, the sense of core identity, the sense of self, body-image formation, gender identity, and the capacity for object or human relationships are all learned or experientially determined. In psychoanalytic terms, this means that the bulk of human personality structure—of ego and superego—results from the internalization, through identification, of experience in interaction with others. That the human offspring is endowed more with potentials than with inherited, fully predetermined psychic structure and patterns of behavior accounts on the one hand for man's great adaptive capacity and on the other for his vulnerability to emotional and mental disorders. In other words, interaction of biologically provided potentials with environmental influences can eventuate in either normal or pathological development.[7]

Turning now to the developmental schema of sexual and gender development, I will attempt to integrate Freud's psychosexual stages and the more recently delineated phases of separation-individuation formulated by Mahler.[8] I wish to stress that sexual and gender development as conceptualized by these psychoanalytic theoretical frameworks is, however, an integral part of total personality development.

The outcome of development as manifest in the adult demonstrates that the fullest attainment of sexual and gender identity and sexual functioning occurs in conjunction with the fullest attainment of the capacity for human relationship.

The Preverbal or Precognitive Stage
(0 to about 8 or 9 months of age)
Observational studies, such as those of Korner,[9] have shown that there are biologically determined individual differences in behavior patterns among neonates, and that some of these are sex-linked.

They have also shown that mothering behavior toward the infant can differ depending upon the sex of the infant. It has been observed, for example, that mothers tend to vocalize more with their female than with their male offspring.

The importance of the "assignment of sex" by the environment, which occurs when the child is an infant, is demonstrated by its pervasive influence in two differing circumstances: (1) the development of a gender identity that is the opposite of the anatomically clearly defined sex of the child; and (2) the development of a gender identity appropriate to the child's *apparent* sex as defined by external genitalia, when the true sex as defined by internal genitalia, gonads, and reproductive organs is the opposite of the apparent sex.[10] Sexual and gender development begin, then, in this earliest period of life when the child has yet to develop the capacity for discernment of himself as a separate entity from his mother, let alone as an individual of a given sex, and when he is also incapable of conscious memory or symbolic representation in language and lacks the capacity for cognitive understanding. The determinant factors during this period are the biological "givens": the initial "assignment of sex" by the environment and the formation in the child of engrams or primitive memory traces of the sex-linked nurturing experiences resulting from the assignment of sex.

The Preoedipal or Early Phallic Stage
(8 or 9 months to about 36 months of age)

Observational studies of normal development and data from the psychoanalytic treatment of young (particularly preoedipal age) children indicate that the child's *sense* of being male or female begins during this stage.[11] These studies have shown that there is, in this stage, an early nonconflictual phase of gender development which overlaps with a later conflictual phase. The nonconflictual beginning of gender formation is influenced not only by the previously mentioned environmental attitudes, but by the child's developing awareness of those biologically determined physiological, anatomical, and behavioral characteristics which are uniquely male or female. This awareness stems largely from the child's experience with his or her own body, from the sensory receptions and motor activities that differ in the two sexes because of the different sex organs and the different skeleto-muscular systems.[12]

The conflictual aspects of gender formation in this stage (disciplinary) has its origin in the child's perception of implied or actual threats of loss in the relationship with the primary love object, the mother, such threats being inherent in the developmental process of

separation-individuation, as formulated by Mahler. This process begins at about 5 or 6 months of age, with the infant's emergence from the dual unity of the mother-infant social symbiosis, and reaches a plateau at about 36 months of age, with the attainment of libidinal or emotional object constancy and a first or basic level of psychological independence. It is conceived to have four sequential subphases:[a] (1) a subphase of *differentiation* (5 to 10 months) of the self from the mother marked at about 8 or 9 months of age by a transient separation anxiety; (2) a subphase concerned with the practicing (10-15 months) of emerging primary motor and cognitive skills in the interest of beginning autonomy; (3) a subphase of *rapprochement* (14 to 22 months) with the mother characterized by a need for reassurance in the face of the intensified separation anxiety stimulated by the child's now acute awareness of his state of dependency and relative helplessness; and (4) a subphase of *attainment of libidinal object constancy* (22 to 36 months) in which a firm sense of the dependability and continuing availability of the mother, even in the face of brief separations from her and mutual anger in the relationship with her is sustained by stable, inner, mental images of the mother.

The threats of object loss and of loss of love and approval associated with separation-individuation and reflected by separation anxiety are transformed into a concern about loss of body parts which is closely linked to castration anxiety.[13] In this transformation, which is evoked by the toilet training and other disciplinary experiences of the rapprochement subphase, the separation conflict merges initially with a conflict over bowel movement and loss of the stool, the stool being experienced as having been a part of the body. With the discovery of the genital, anatomical distinction between the sexes—the obvious presence of the penis in one sex and its absence in the other—the child's concern about loss and the now present capability to fantasize that the absence of the penis in the female is the result of loss, combine to cause castration fear or anxiety.

This conflict-determined castration anxiety, which predates the castration anxiety of the phallic stage associated with the child's rivalry with the parent of the opposite sex in the oedipal conflict, calls for revision of Freud's original formulation. Freud held, in essence, that the psychological processes eventuating in gender formation are initiated in the phallic oedipal phase.[14] The fact that gender formation is initiated during the preoedipal period and has both a nonconflictual and a nonoedipal conflictual beginning has

---

[a]The age spans for the subphases vary in length and in age of onset and offset in different infants, and the subphases are not discrete but overlapping.

significance for both sexes, but particularly for the female. Thus, female gender formation is not, as was thought by Freud, initiated by penis envy, and the female's move toward female gender does not represent a shift away from an earlier, essentially male gender identity. However, this important revision in theory does not eliminate penis envy as a factor in female psychological development. Rather, the role of penis envy in individual female development varies from minor to major importance, depending largely upon the adequacy or inadequacy of development during the separation-individuation phase. Although an observable developmental phenomenon, penis envy is now thought to be a normally resolvable conflict and not necessarily a persistent unconscious issue in the older girl or the adult woman.[15]

The Phallic-Oedipal Stage (3 to about 5 or 6 years of age)

As it is now formulated, the child's move to the phallic stage associated with the oedipal relationship is based not only on the biological maturational shift from the anal to the genital psychosexual level, but on the attainment of the described initial level of independence represented by intrapsychic object constancy. It is in this stage that gender formation begins to acquire meaning in terms of sexualized interest in and attraction to the opposite sex. The child's biologically stimulated increased preoccupation with the genitals and curiosity about their intended functions in sexual relationships are played out in the relationships with the parents, mostly in fantasy.

The boy finds his relationship with his mother, the primary love object of his earlier childhood, to be now complicated by genital sexual or erotized feelings. He seeks at first to incorporate these new feelings into the relationship with his mother, but experiences increasing discomfort because of awareness that he has thus become a rival with his father, whom he also loves and needs. Under normal circumstances, the boy, pushed by the self-conceived threat of castration for coveting his mother as well as by the unreality of his oedipal wishes, resolves his oedipal conflict. He does so by relinquishing his mother as a sexual object in favor of a still more independent, tender relationship with her, and by identification with his father in the masculine role of a male who will thenceforth direct his sexual urges and feelings increasingly outside of the family.

The girl, out of awareness of her femaleness and her early gender formation, as they may or may not have been significantly influenced by disappointment with the mother for not having provided

her with a penis, shifts her sexualized love feelings away from her mother to her father. She too seeks at first to incorporate and manage her sexual feelings in the relationship with her father, but with increasing discomfort because of the resulting rivalry with her mother, whom she also continues to love and need. Under the threat of loss of her mother's love for coveting her father and out of awareness of the unreality of her oedipal wishes, the girl resolves her oedipal conflict by relinquishing her father as a sexual object and by strengthening her feminine role through identification with her mother while directing her sexual strivings outside the family. In both the girl and the boy, this further separation-individuation leads then to new nonfamilial relationships, including sexual relationships. In relation to the educational focus of this volume, it is significant that the resolution of the oedipal complex has coincided, historically, with society's prescription for the child to begin his education outside the family in the school, at least in the prenursery-school era.

The Latency Stage (5 or 6 to 10 or 11 years of age)

The original impression that sexuality receded and was latent, rather than overt, in this stage has long since been corrected. Sexual curiosity, feelings, and explorations are observably present. The latency stage can, however, be characterized as a period of concentrated development and consolidation of ego skills and functions, including socialization capacities, and of integration within the personality of the superego or value system which was crystallized out as a psychic structure with the resolution of the oedipal conflict. Given this characterization, latency becomes a period of relatively diminished sexual conflict and of preparation for the advent of the intense sexual conflicts to be evoked by puberty and adolescence.

The child's move into the sphere of influence of the school's broader culture results in gender formation being influenced not only by the continuing attitudes of the parents, siblings, and extended family, but by the much enlarged experience with peers and by the culturally institutionalized definitions of the sexes and their gender roles as these are communicated by teachers and other adults. Characteristically, the peers of one sex tend to cling together as a way of both defining and protecting their developing but not yet stable sense of gender identity.

The Adolescent Stage

The thrust of puberty brings a striking spurt in general physical growth, striking maturational changes in sexual physiology and

anatomy, and a surge in sexual and aggressive urges and feelings. The adolescent becomes, thus, acutely aware of the impending attainment of adult physical, sexual, and intellectual capacities, and of the expectation—indeed, the necessity—that he relinquish his childhood psychological dependency in preparation for a definitive move toward independence from the family. In the psychological processes of adolescence, separation and castration conflicts and anxieties and the sexual and gender identity issues of the earlier developmental stages are revived and relived along with the related superego attitudes toward sexual behavior. These important developmental issues can therefore be in some measure reworked, but now in the context of gaining familiarity with and mastery over one's adult-level sexual urges, feelings, and capacities. As Blos formulated,[16] there takes place, ideally, a further intrapsychic relinquishment of ties to the inner representations of the parents of early childhood and a reintegration that results in a second individuation as the adolescent moves toward the attainment of an initial level of adult sexual capacity and adult gender identity.

The Post-Adolescent or Adult Stages

Having outlined the theory of sexual and gender development of children from birth to adulthood, I wish to focus attention on ourselves, the former children now adults, who work with children in our professional capacities.

Human psychological development and, therefore, the development of gender identity continues throughout the life cycle. The assumption of adult responsibilities leads to further emotional maturity and further definition of masculinity and femininity or manliness and womanliness as influenced by culturally prescribed role definitions. Gender identity is refined and affirmed in courtship, in dating, and in marriage or its equivalent. The issues of gender identity are vicariously relived, reworked, and reaffirmed in the parenting of one's own developing children. When their children proceed, for example, through the adolescent stage, the firmness of the gender identity of the parents is threatened, tested, and sometimes favorably realigned. A part of this parental experience which also tests and affirms gender identity is the necessity of relinquishing the mothering or fathering role. Gender issues are similarly reexperienced, tested, and affirmed in the grandparenting role, and in the often identity-threatening move into retirement, including, finally, the preparation for the relinquishment of life.

NOTES TO CHAPTER THREE

1. Sigmund Freud, Three Essays on the Theory of Sexuality, *Standard Edition*, 7, 1905 (London: Hogarth Press, 1953), 125-245.

2. See Editor's Note, *ibid.*, p. 126.

3. *Ibid.*, p. 128.

4. Robert J. Stoller, *Sex and Gender* (New York: Science House, 1968).

5. *Ibid*, pp. 5-6.

6. Jean Piaget and Bärbel Inhelder, *The Growth of Logical Thinking From Childhood to Adolescence* (New York: Basic Books, 1958).

7. Calvin F. Settlage, Danger Signals in the Separation-Individuation Process: The Observations and Formulations of Margaret S. Mahler, *The Infant at Risk*, ed. by D. Bergsma (New York: Stratton Intercontinental Medical Books Corp., 1974).

8. Margaret S. Mahler, *On Human Symbiosis and the Vicissitudes of Individuation* 1 (New York: International Universities Press, 1968); *The Psychological Birth of the Human Infant: Symbiosis and Individuation* (New York: International Universities Press, 1975).

9. A.F. Korner, Neonatal Startles, Smiles, Erections, and Reflex Sucks as Related to State, Sex and Individuality, *Child Development* 40, 1969, 1039-1053.

10. Stoller, 1968.

11. V.L. Clower, The Development of the Child's Sense of his Sexual Identity, *J. Am. Psychoanal. Assoc.* 18, 1970, 165-176; Eleanor Galenson and Herman Roiphe, The Impact of Early Sexual Discovery on Mood, Defensive Organization, and Symbolization, *Psychoanal. Study of the Child* 26, 1972, 195-216; Mahler, *Psychological Birth of the Human Infant*; Herman Roiphe, On an Early Genital Phase: With an Addendum on Genesis, *Psychoanal. Study of the Child* 23, 1968, 348-365; Calvin F. Settlage, On the Libidinal Aspect of Early Psychic Development and the Genesis of Infantile Neurosis, in *Separation-Individuation: Essays in Honor of Margaret S. Mahler*, ed. by J.B. McDevitt and Calvin F. Settlage (New York: International Universities Press, 1971), 131-154.

12. Phyllis Greenacre, Early Physical Determinants in the Development of the Sense of Identity, *J. Amer. Psychoanal. Assoc.* 6, 1958, 612-627.

13. Settlage.

14. Freud, 1905.

15. Calvin F. Settlage, Introduction to the Panel on the Psychology of Women: Late Adolescence and Early Adulthood, *J. Am. Psychoanal. Assoc.* 24, 1976, 631-645.

16. Peter Blos, The Second Individuation Process of Adolescence, *Psychoanalytic Study of the Child* 22, 1967, 162-186.

Chapter Four

The "Givens" from a Different Point of View: Lessons from Intersexuality for a Theory of Gender Identity

John Money, Ph.D.*

A person is unable, in view of the rearing traditions of our society, to develop a personal identity without its being differentiated as either masculine or feminine. Personal identity is always gender dimorphic, at least to some degree. It is extremely difficult for a human being to live in a state of indeterminate gender identity. In fact, in my experience with well over two hundred cases of people born with ambiguous-looking genitalia that remained ambiguous in appearance during childhood or later, there have been only two of whom it might be said that their gender identity was indeterminate. It is easier for a person to swing on a pendulum, as it were, from masculine to feminine than to remain indeterminate at the midpoint. In fact, such a swing is characteristic of the person with a diagnosis of transvestite/transsexual.

Gender identity is not preordained from the beginning of life. Along the developmental pathway on which an individual personality becomes gender stereotyped there are several bifurcations. At any one of these bifurcations, nature or nurture may switch from male to female. In animals, these switching effects can be demonstrated by means of planned and intentional intervention. In human beings, one learns not from planned laboratory experiments, but from unplanned experiments of nature, namely those involving intersexuality or hermaphroditism.

It is possible, for example, for an environmental intervention of unknown origin to deprive a fertilized egg cell of one of its sex

*Professor of Medical Psychology and Associate Professor of Pediatrics, The Johns Hopkins University.

chromosomes. Provided the surviving sex chromosome is X, the cell is able to survive and grow. Thus it is possible for the Y chromosome to be lost without destroying the cell's viability. The embryo that nature would otherwise have programmed to differentiate as a 46,XY chromosomal male thenceforth is programmed to differentiate as a 45,X chromosomal female. The 45,X female is said to have Turner's syndrome, a condition marked by various possible birth defects, the chief of which is agenesis or dysgenesis of the gonads. Turner's syndrome has been recorded in one of a pair of monozygotic twins. Here is manifest the paradoxical phenomenon of identical twins, one with a penis and one with a vulva, surely a remarkable instance of how an early prenatal environmental intervention of unknown origin can so affect cellular development as to completely reprogram the sexual development of the embryo and fetus.

Loss of the Y chromosome leads to female sexual differentiation on the basis of what may be called the *Adam principle*. According to the Adam principle, nature has decreed that the sexually undifferentiated early embryo will, irrespective of its genetic sex, differentiate as a female unless something is added. The something added, to simplify only slightly, is the male sex hormone. This male hormone is supplied by the testis which itself, under instructions from the Y chromosome, differentiated from the neutral or ambisexual gonadal tissues. Alteration of the prenatal hormonal environment, timed to synchronize with the appropriate critical period, may prevent or arrest masculine differentiation. That is to say, events in the prenatal environment can prevent or arrest masculine differentiation, so that the *Eve principle*, the reverse of the Adam principle, takes over. Thus, the 45,X condition leads to feminine differentiation. Experimental embryonic castration, surgical, chemical, or by irradiation, of animals leads also to subsequent feminine differentiation, as does chemical suppression of fetal testicular androgen production. The latter is achieved pharmacologically by means of injecting the pregnant mother animal with antiandrogen.

Pharmacologic intervention can be used to demonstrate also the other side of the Adam principle, namely masculinization of the genetic female. If a pregnant monkey is injected with male hormone when she is carrying a female fetus, the daughter's external genitals (in this case not the internal organs) will differentiate as male.

Prenatal nonmasculinization of the external genitals of the sex-chromosomal male and masculinization of the sex-chromosomal female both occur spontaneously in human beings. Both are possible because the embryonic undifferentiated state of the external organs is the same for each sex. In the case of the chromosomal male, the

condition of nonmasculinization is known as the testicular-feminizing or androgen-insensitivity syndrome. In the case of the chromosomal female, the condition of masculinization is usually the adrenogenital syndrome, in which the excess of androgen is supplied by the fetus's own adrenocortical glands. Female hermaphroditic masculinization has also been known to occur as a result of a now outmoded hormonal therapy of the mother to prevent miscarriage.

The Adam principle in fetal life applies not only to the differentiation of the external sexual anatomy, but also to certain sex-differential pathways in the central nervous system. In animals, the neuroanatomical evidence has been empirically demonstrated. In human beings, the neuroanatomical evidence is inferential. The behavioral evidence in human beings is that prenatal androgenization of the sex-chromosomal female produces a disposition toward tomboyism. Not aggression, but dominance assertion is characteristic of tomboyism; it does not necessarily entail fighting. Rehearsal of parentalism in doll play is subordinate to athletic energy expenditure. Tomboyism is compatible with a feminine differentiation of gender identity, adding as it were a special hue; it does not necessarily include romantic and erotic lesbianism. There is no word for the opposite of tomboyism in insufficiency of the Adam principle in sex-chromosomal males. Also, there is not the same quantity of available human clinical evidence as in tomboyism, though there is substantial experimental evidence that feminine sexual behavior results from hormonal nonmasculinization or submasculinization in the rat.[1]

To review, early in embryonic life and up to about six weeks, there are no sex organs to make either a male or a female. There is only a small protuberance of tissue that is going to grow out to become either a clitoris or a penis, and there is an opening that is going to stay open in a female or cover over in a male. It is going to be covered over by the two strips of skin that wrap around to become the foreskin and the tubular covering of the penis, or else stay separated as the hood of the clitoris and the labia minora on either side. The final covering over is going to be done by the outside swellings which, if the embryo is going to be a male, join themselves together to make the sac or carrying bag of the scrotum, and, if it is going to be a female, stay open.

By interfering at about the halfway point, one can prevent the covering over in the male, or make too much covering over in the female. This may happen if the prenatal hormones are out of balance, which sometimes happens owing to a genetic condition of the fetus itself or because the mother might have a hormone-producing tumor during the pregnancy or when, as formerly happened,

mothers were given a new kind of pregnancy hormone to prevent a threatened miscarriage.

As an example of the wide variation, a baby that is a genetic male with two testicles in the abdomen or descended into the labial swellings may have a vagina. This is usually a hereditary condition in which the fetus is unable to use the male sex hormones its testes produced prenatally. Nature proceeds to try to make a female, and one has a genetic male baby with the X and Y chromosomes in place, and two testicles growing internally. The balance of the program is in the female direction and the baby is born looking like a female.

Testicles can make enough female hormone to make a feminine kind of body shape provided the male hormone which the testicles make can't be used. This is very helpful if one is reared a woman, but very distressing if one is reared a man. In such a situation a person may be totally feminine without a trace of tomboyism, even though genetically a male.

The counterpart can also exist in that all women make some male hormone. An example is a baby born with a penis. It may not be realized until some years later that the baby is a genetic female with two ovaries, a uterus, and two fallopian tubes. By this time the child differentiates his gender identity as a boy. He is ruggedly and strongly a little boy in all of his behavior. Rational medical treatment involves allowing the patient to keep his external organs and removing the internal ones. He is able to grow up as a perfectly adequate male and have a family by donor insemination. Should such a child have been forced to change to live as a girl and to undergo surgery to have his external organs removed so that he could look like a girl, technically he could have had a pregnancy and carried it. In actuality he would not have done so, for he could not be sexually attracted to an impregnating male, only to the members of the sex he would recognize as the opposite of his own—that is, to girls.

Tomboy girls who have had a prenatal overflood of the Adam principle have good athletic abilities and they love putting them to use. They like body contact sports and they release a lot of energy in body movement. It is always directed behavior. They are known as tomboys by their family and friends and themselves, and they are proud of it. They don't like doll play, nor do they like rehearsing parental behavior in play. They like boys' toys which give them a chance for vigorous play. They like plain clothes and cannot be bothered with fussy frills. They always are keen on developing a nondomestic career. They are not aggressive, fighting, and belligerent. Erotically, they do not turn to lesbianism as a general rule, though they may have bisexual fantasies. They are slow in reaching

the romantic stage, but eventually they reach it; and they all seem to combine a nondomestic career with marriage and the domestic career of raising one or two children.

Tomboy girl or nontomboy, macho boy or otherwise, all human beings at puberty and subsequently produce some of the three sex steroids, namely, progestin, androgen, and estrogen. Nature elaborates one from the other, in that order. The difference between the sexes, hormonally, is in the ratio of the three hormones, not in whether they are present or absent.

POSTNATAL DIFFERENTIATION OF GENDER IDENTITY/ROLE

Incursions of nurture on nature during prenatal sexual differentiation leave their mark by changing nature itself; that is to say, they bring about a change in the constitution of the body and its functioning. Moreover, such change is in the literal sense innate, because the individual is born with it. So, in one's everyday way of thinking, prenatal environmental effects seem somehow scarcely to be environmental at all, as compared with postnatal environmental effects. Nonetheless, it is true that sex differences programmed to take place after birth become incorporated into the body quite as firmly and indelibly as do those that take place before birth. Differentiation of gender identity/role is here included: dimorphism of behavior and imagery as masculine or feminine becomes programmed into the central nervous system as firmly as if it were genetically determined, though, in fact, it is a product of early social interaction. It is analogous to native language, insofar as it is a product of early social interaction without which it cannot develop.

There are no clinical cases better suited to demonstrate the importance of early postnatal experience in the formation of gender identity/role than matched pairs of hermaphrodites. These pairs are matched in that they are concordant for diagnosis and prenatal history, but discordant for sex of assignment and postnatal history.

In my clinical work, I know of several pairs of XY chromosomal males, born with undescended testes and with an incompletely differentiated phallus. One of each pair was considered a boy at birth, assigned as a male, and given appropriate rehabilitative surgical and pubertal-hormonal therapy. The other, considered to be a girl, was assigned as a female and surgically and hormonally rehabilitated accordingly. The girl in each case has differentiated a feminine gender identity/role and is not remarkably different from other young women of her age, romantic and erotic life included. The

contrary applies to the boy, who has married as a man with a man's professional or vocational career.

The lesson to be learned from hermaphroditic matched pairs is also paralleled in a pair of identical twins, one of whom lost the penis in a circumcision accident.[2] This twin was reassigned as a girl and now, in late childhood, has a gender identity/role dimorphically different from that of her twin brother.

There are two principles according to which the differentiation of gender identity/role takes place postnatally in infancy and childhood. One is the principle of identification, the other the principle of complementation. Of these two, identification is generally discussed, whereas complementation is less well recognized. Usually, it is said that a child identifies with the parent, or another person of the same sex, copying and imitating that person's customary expressions and behavior.

A daughter who identifies with her mother inevitably, in interaction with her father or other male substitute, complements her feminine behavioral schema to his masculine schema, and he to hers, reciprocally. This reciprocity or complementarity between parent and opposite-sexed child first became freely evident to me in discussing parental behavior with those parents of ambiguously sexed children who were required to negotiate a sex reassignment of their child at or after eighteen months of age. Under such a circumstance, it is clearly evident that the infant's newly reassigned sex completely redefines the behavior of each parent toward the infant, and eventually the behavior of the infant to each parent respectively. In other words, there is an interchange of roles: the parent who had the role of identification model becomes the one with the role of complementation model, and vice versa.

One actual example is that of a father who would never have danced with his infant to whom he once related as a son. After the infant's sex reassignment, he was overtly drawn to teach her to dance with him as a daughter, complementing his masculine behavior with her mother-identified feminine behavior.

IRREDUCIBLE DIFFERENCES

My experience with the total range of intersex variations leads me to the conclusion that the only irreducible sex differences are that women menstruate, gestate, and lactate, and men impregnate. These differences are hormone regulated and are, therefore, associated with other hormone-regulated dimorphic traits, particularly those associated with height, physique, and strength. However, these traits are

not sex specific, but are distributed with considerable overlap between the sexes.

Behavioral traits, including aggression and parentalism, are not sexually dimorphic in the absolute sense as is conventionally assumed. However, the threshold for their elicitation and the effective evoking stimuli may be sexually dimorphic, or at least variably distributed between the sexes. Threshold is here the key concept. Thresholds notwithstanding, most sexually dimorphic behavior as we know it is the product of cultural history and not of some eternal verity programmed by noncultural biology.

As a people we have a long history of maximizing sex differences in behavior rather than minimizing them. This is an anachronistic policy that doubtlessly made good sense in neolithic times and later, but does not serve us well today.

You cannot easily change your own gender identity once it is formed, but, as a regulator of the lives of young infants, you can change the input of what is shaped into them.

NOTES TO CHAPTER FOUR

1. F. Neumann and W. Elgee, Permanent Changes in Gonadal Function and Sexual Behavior as a Result of Early Feminization of Male Rats by Treatment with an Antiandrogenic Steroid, *Endokrinologie* 50, 1966, 209-224; I.L. Ward, Prenatal Stress Feminizes and Demasculinizes the Behavior of Males, *Science* 175, 1972, 82-84.

2. John Money, Ablatio Penis: Normal Male Infant Sex-Reassigned as a Girl, *Archives of Sexual Behavior* 4, 1974, 65-71.

✳ *Chapter Five*

Lessons from Normative
Development:
A Response

Albert J. Solnit, M.D.*

There are two basic issues to be considered in responding to Dr. Money's extraordinary information and experience (see pp. 27-33). There is sexual development *per se*, which is primarily, though by no means exclusively, a biological issue; and there is sexual behavior that we call gender, a primarily cultural and psychological issue, though not exclusively so.

Where nature has not been ambiguous sexually, that is, where the external sexual structures and essential physiological and hormonal balance are considered normative according to present-day understanding, we are then allowed to face perspectives in sexual development and gender identification that are more subtle than the examples from which Dr. Money draws his important conclusions.

It is true on the whole that in the late nineteenth and early twentieth centuries there were widespread assumptions that normal behaviors and health characteristics could best be understood by the study of those who were severely deviant; i.e., by studying pathology. It is true that we learned a great deal from such cases and from direct experimental research, as that of Spemann in embryology. These studies have given us such central concepts as those of organizers of phase-specific functions and structures, and other penetrating insights.

We are now confronted with the need to understand early evidence of deviation by a more sophisticated and direct understanding of *healthy development* and its variations. In fact, we now are facing the danger that studies of the deviant that are not

*Director, Child Study Center, Yale University.

corrected or balanced by studies of the healthy or normative will exchange one stereotype for another.

Many facets of maleness and femaleness are in the range of healthy development. Our daily challenge is to understand and tolerate the uniqueness of each child as we assist each to understand, find, and accept himself or herself as a unique person and as a boy or girl and a future man or woman.

The biological characteristics and capacities, including the morphology of the primary and secondary sexual organs, the balance of hormones, and the complicated physiology of sex, are not a sufficient basis on which to make long-term predictions about sexual preferences and behavior according to our present knowledge of gender identity and sexual development. Biological potentials and capacities are significantly influenced by the powerful expectations of the parents and the social, cultural matrix in which families are formed and developed.

This complex mixture and resultant of biological, psychological, and social forces can be reassuring, for it limits and modifies constructively our tendency to be absolute in our expectations and tolerances. Perhaps this limitation of our knowledge is a constructive curb on our tendency to act as though we were omniscient and omnipotent. For example, without this curb we may be tempted to suggest that we can, by our use of hormones, plastic surgery, and powerful expectations, decide, regardless of the child's endowment, whether the child will be a boy/man or a girl/woman. If we avoid this temptation, we are better able to embark on constructing a balanced, multifaceted formulation about how to understand sexual and gender development of the human being, taking advantage of studies of the many configurations that we classify as normative or healthy maleness and femaleness.

As has been indicated, each human being is bisexual with a predominance of maleness or femaleness. It would seem that there are those who are vulnerable to psychosocial expectations, and there are those who are resistant to them. In other words, there are boys, raised in situations in which the expectation is that they should be feminine and female, who are able to resist this and assert their maleness, often with appropriate neurotic conflicts. There are also those boys, more vulnerable to this expectation, who end up with a very profound wish, from the time they can remember, of wanting to be girls. The same can be said about girls.

Also there are children in whom biological tendencies run in the same directions and are consistent and harmonious with the psychosexual and psychosocial expectations of their parents and their

society; and there are those in whom biological vulnerabilities are further weakened or run counter to the psychosexual expectations of their parents and their society. Therefore, I speculate that there is a range of vulnerabilities and resistances to psychosocial expectations that are based on biological variations within the range of normal.

Thus we can agree that given a normative biological and intrauterine experience, the parental and societal expectations are powerful. Perhaps these expectations can even have physiological impact influencing hormonal levels. There are studies that suggest that moods and motivations can, indeed, influence the level of hormonal discharge.[1] In addition to the stunning examples Dr. Money has presented we are in need of careful studies of early individual differences, and the understanding of phase-specific development.

We must be cautious in the lessons we draw from observations of the severely deviant as we attempt to establish a basis for understanding normal and deviant sexual and gender development.

NOTE TO CHAPTER FIVE

1. G.F. Powell, J.A. Brasel, and R.M. Blizzard, Emotional Deprivation and Growth Retardation Simulating Idiopathic Hypopituitarism, *New England Journal of Medicine* 276, 1967, 1271, 1279.

Chapter Six

Sexual and Gender Development in the Nursery School Years

Morris Peltz, M.D.*

It is my intention (1) to illustrate the ways gender identity influences play and social interactions in nursery-school-age youngsters; (2) to reciprocally show how such typical play sequences, both individually and in groups, enhance gender identity; (3) to discuss the role of sex education in the nursery-school-age child; and finally, (4) to discuss some sex-education practices that, in my view, can lead to harmful consequences.

I would like to propose first that we consider the terms *social image* and *social role* to connote the collective view held by social groups regarding behaviors as being masculine or feminine or neutral. These three definitions then, sexual identity, gender identity, and social image and role, cover the spectrum from the purely biological through the more purely social. At the one extreme, sexual identity, there is virtually no flexibility; whereas at the other end of the spectrum, social image and role, there is extreme variability, determined by time and place and culture. Gender identity falls within these poles and emerges out of the continual interactions between what is innate and what is experienced.

To begin with, massive developmental steps have already been taken by the three-year-old as he or she enters school. I can only list a few adapted from developmental lines proposed by Anna Freud.[1]

1. From the biological unity that existed between mother and infant, the three-year-old's emotional life has become very vivid and intense. Characteristically the three-year-old is extremely possessive

*Director of Training, Children's Hospital, San Francisco; Faculty, San Francisco Psychoanalytic Institute.

of the parent of the opposite sex and jealous and rivalrous with the parent of the same sex. The child does have vivid sexual fantasies which are frequently accompanied by genital masturbation. The love and jealousy may simultaneously be enacted with both younger and older siblings.

2. From being nursed at the breast or bottle, by schedule or on demand, the three-year-old has by now progressed from an early belief in which mother and food were equated. Now, if there are irrational attitudes about eating, these may be determined by largely unconscious infantile sexual theories.

3. From an initial phase where the child has complete freedom to wet and soil, most three-year-olds are in the process of, or have already mastered, their excretory functions. Though accidents are not uncommon, the three-year-old will often react with shame if such an accident occurs. The three-year-old experiences shame because he fears teasing from peers and because the mother's role in teaching bowel and bladder control has become internalized. The three-year-old experiences the need for sphincter regulation as an inner demand.

4. From the neonatal insensate state of being at one with the universe (mother), the child entering nursery school has developed a complex intellect. He is mastering the unique human acquisition of language which, in the three-year-old, is used for both emotive and symbolizing functions. The three-year-old has developed discrete inner mental representations of mother and father and siblings, such that normally the mental image of these loved ones can be preserved even when they are not physically present. The young child in nursery school has reached the point where he can evoke the beloved image of mother or father in times of need or distress and can feel comforted by these inner images. The three-year-old also has a discrete inner representation of himself as a person, a unique individual. At the center of this mental representation is his gender identity—the sense that "I am a boy" or "I am a girl."

What is the developmental path the child has traveled to arrive at this inner conviction?

Very early in life, biological forces are at work creating the differences which in this instance lead to male and female sexual identity at birth. Those physiological forces which operate to produce anatomical differentiation at birth also seem operative in behavioral differences between neonatal girls and boys. My hypothesis is that a sense of gender identity evolves out of sexual identity and does so by the end of the second year.

We assume the neonate has no mental image of himself as an

individual, let alone a gendered individual. Consciousness of the sense of self gradually emerges from the mother-infant dyad.

By the beginning of the second year, what formerly had been understood between mother and child purely by nonverbal means successively yields to the addition of verbal modalities of communication, which are employed by both mother and child. From the birth of the child parents vary greatly in attitudes and behaviors, crucially determined by the infant's sexual identity. Certainly in most instances by the time the baby has reached his first birthday, "baby" is clearly and distinctly a "he" or "she" for the parents. Whereas formerly the child's sense of his bodily self stemmed primarily from endogenous sources (sensations emanating from the genitals), now a dawning sense of gender receives verbal and non-verbal confirmation from parents.

Research by Galenson and Roiphe[2] conducted in naturalistic settings suggests that at the end of the second year there is a phase of primary genital arousal. By primary genital arousal these investigators mean a specific stage in the development of genital awareness in which the external genitalia becomes more sharply focused as body parts for the child. These researchers advance the view that this stage of primal genital arousal occurs as the result of the increased attention focused on urinary and anal sphincters as toilet training is undertaken. As these muscles are specifically manipulated there is a spread of excitation to the genitals which subsequently serves to enhance their mental representation. I believe it is just this primary genital phase and how it interacts with parental reactions which becomes the two-year organizer for gender identity.

Let's look at some observations of interactions of nursery-school children to see how these ideas help us understand their behavior. I will briefly portray a pair of siblings, Betty and her brother Sam, two years older. My descriptions will focus especially on these youngsters' free play, their social interchanges, and their use of dressing and costuming as means of mastering not only their social roles and images, but of mastering their gender identities.

Sam entered nursery school at age three. He was a bright, alert, confident youngster. After some initial shyness, he was eager to join in play with other boys. He loved running and chasing and playing on the jungle gym. The playground and its equipment became the focus of his play and friendships, which usually included two or three other boys. Whereas early in the third year he had become somewhat fearful of slides, as if for the first time becoming distinctly cognizant of their height, his former interest and excitement in slides returned. He loved to propel his body through space in actual play. He further

elaborated "flying" in fantasy. Sam became captivated with Superman. He contrived a variety of Superman costumes from odds and ends at home and at school. The most important element of the costume was the cape. It seemed for Sam that the cape was the necessary magical element needed for flying. He would run through the school yard and ask that his spectators assure him that his cape was billowing up behind him. At home he would leap from the tops of pieces of furniture, and would become especially delighted if mother assured him that his cape flew up high. At the same time Sam asked father for a kite and briefly developed a love of kite flying.

At home Sam initiated a special and regularly enacted costume game. It centered primarily on Daddy's daily departure for work. As Daddy would leave each morning, Sam would get one of his father's old jackets and a pair of his shoes or boots and, with great ceremony and with a lunch pail in hand, would prepare to leave for the office.

In his second year at nursery school, Sam was an old hand and full of confidence. He resumed his friendships of the year before, and his play and social life once again had the backdrop of the playground equipment. The Superman fantasy had receded, but interest in costumes continued. At school Sam, as the other boys, was ambivalently invited by the girls to join in their dollhouse play. Sam enjoyed playing the postman or robber, and a billed cap was sufficient for his impersonation. Sam looked forward to Hallowe'en and couldn't decide whether to be a pirate or a cowboy. But much of Sam's former interest in costume play was now displaced onto a doll, the then popular GI Joe. Now Sam, in his play with peers, dramatized many adventures with his doll, primarily but not exclusively dictated by the costumes available for it. This doll play was in sharp competition with his interest in cars, an interest avidly shared with his cohorts.

Betty was two years, nine months old in the spring when she entered nursery school. Sam was to continue in the school for the next three months. Sam oriented Betty to the social and physical structure of the school and initially protected her. As she became familiar with the surroundings and the children, Betty detached herself from Sam and began singling out a child her age, a boy or girl, with whom to engage in parallel play. Around the time of her third birthday, and for much of the year that followed, Betty's play changed. Her language skills had taken a great stride. She became articulate and expressive. She became more interested in friends as cohorts with whom to play. She expressed to them and elicited from them opinions on a variety of subjects. She talked about her dolls, what they were like, if they were happy or unhappy. She mothered

these dolls and was interested in their eating and toilet habits. Her interest in clothes, always lively, now became exaggerated. She would don layers of clothes at home and at school. Her nursery-school teacher reported that one day Betty dressed in the following costume, on top of her school clothes: a long billowy white nightgown with long full sleeves, a red velvet bolero trimmed in gold, a yellow terry-cloth jacket which she attached by tying the sleeves at her waist to make a full-length skirt, gold high-heeled pumps, a light green beret with a pine cone stuck in the top (this for her wig), and a black felt cloche on her arm as a purse. When encumbered in play by this elaborate costume, Betty simply removed as many items as necessary and later redressed.

Nearing her fourth birthday Betty's interest in clothes continued, but the content changed. She no longer layered her clothes, but instead became preoccupied with what she was going to wear. There was usually great discussion at home about her costume, with many moments of indecision. Once dressed, she might change her mind and dress again in a different outfit.

Betty's social relations were changing now. She played with four or five girls who were more or less a steady group. They played house, dressed up, mothered dolls, took them for walks. Boys would sometimes join in as fathers, postmen, burglars. Often the girls would assume the male roles if no boys were interested. The girls did not dress as boys, however. The younger girls were sometimes called upon to be the babies. Betty and her friends also used playground equipment with enthusiasm, did art work, and joined in running and chasing games with the boys. Dress-up play continued as a staple of their daily activities.

Betty's interest in sexual differences between boys and girls became more prominent after her fourth birthday. She sometimes peaked in on the boys in the large group bathroom at school. She was modest when using the bathroom herself, but not to the point of refusing to use the toilet at school. At home she knew she could best tease her brother by saying she had seen his penis. His fury would bring forth a gale of giggles from Betty. She developed a verbal confusion between breasts and hips. She would watch her mother putting on her brassière and say, "When I grow up I'll have great big hips like you," and stick her chest out in an exaggerated manner. In spite of many corrections, Betty persisted in this lexical confusion for some months.

I propose that Sam and Betty illustrate one of many variants in the developmental path. In their behavior we can see a progression toward gender identity and knowledge of social image and social role.

Sam's vivid interest in Superman certainly has its social-cultural roots. In middle-class America, manly strength, right over wrong, are values early conveyed to youngsters. Sam viewed his father as the Superman he was in competition with, and with whom he had to join forces. If he could fly he might even best his father. Sam's play was endorsed and enjoyed by his parents. They selected his toys according to his interests and admired his "machismo." With his peers Sam played out cultural values already learned.

The automobile figures prominently in the United States, and boys learn early the cultural value of fast cars. What I want to emphasize is that children's personalities are not a tabula rasa that can be simply impressed in a given image. Children's biological and maturational givens are continually interacting with the social forces impinging on their lives. Sam's more discrete awareness of his penis, with its erections and deflations, were projected onto the Superman flying fantasies. Erections are not always within the young child's control, but his play is. And in his play Sam was constantly mastering not only his social role but also his specific gender identity, a phallic organization that had at its nucleus a penis capable of tumescence and detumescence.

For Betty, the task of consolidating her feminine phallic stage of gender identity followed a different line of development. The influence of Betty's culture, both at home and at school, is obvious. I am proposing that Betty's interest in clothes, however, was not determined by social forces alone. Most current investigators are in agreement that children are quite capable of observing sexual differences by the end of the second year. Betty saw her brother's penis, and knew she didn't have one. She saw her mother's "breast-hips." She was assured by her parents that she would develop these structures later on. But one week, let alone ten years, seemed like forever—or never—for a child of three. Betty had to master her anatomic phallic organization differently from her brother. There is evidence that young girls have some awareness of their vaginas, but that awareness is not sharply focused, and, for a variety of reasons, becomes rapidly repressed. Though Betty received vivid genital sensations (her mother had observed her masturbating on several occasions), her visible organs did not compare to her brother's. I take as evidence of Betty's envy her frequent teasing of her brother about his penis. My thesis is that Betty mastered her phallic organization and her temporary disappointments (no penis, no breasts, no hips) by in part displacing the focus of her attention from her genitals to the surface of her body, the surface she could adorn and embellish ad infinitum. Betty's costume play was related to two developmental

concerns: (1) in terms of social mastery, "I'm a great big beautiful mommy dressed up in all my finery," and (2) in the service of gender identity, "I'm a girl whose surface adornments conceal what is not yet developed, but what promises to come."

Sam and Betty, however, were not only idly concerned with mastering their own gender identities as I have outlined above. This brother and sister, as all nursery-school-age children, were vitally concerned with gender identity opposite to their own. Betty's curiosity about her brother's penis and her attempts to watch the boys urinating in the school bathroom are but muted expressions of an intense sexual curiosity which all children have. Their sexual curiosity is sharp and intense, not only by virtue of their own intense sexual feelings, but also because of their more complexly organized cognitive abilities. They have developed, certainly by the fourth year, the capacity to conceptualize that girls belong to the class *female* and boys to the class *male*, as mommies belong to the class *woman* and daddies to the class *man*. (Complete operational intelligence with capacity for reversibility is not achieved until several years later.) This cognitive achievement enables them to pursue their quest for sexual information with greater clarity.

Mutual exploration and undressing games, though frequently frowned on by parents, are but the logical extensions of these youngsters' specific quests for information to aid further consolidation of their sexual identities. The frequently encountered "doctor" game played by children of these years serves the purpose of not only mastering the many traumas experienced at the hands of doctors, but also serves to master, through structured play sequences, these children's pursuit of sexual information and stimulation. This mutual looking and showing behavior is normative and enhances the child's ability to understand and master the fact of sexual differences.

If knowing the difference between boy and girl, mommy and daddy, is perhaps a first sexual question, certainly the second sexual question must be: What does daddy do with his penis, what does mommy do with her vagina? Children develop all manner of fantasy about these questions. Their fantasies are based on their prior experiences and information. Children master the information supplied to them in various ways. However, though we see that children are able to master sexual information supplied in simple, straightforward language, nonetheless, *oftentimes they will embellish and distort this information according to their own needs and wishes.*

Where babies come from and how they're made are of course the other questions for which children yearn to have answers. Quests for

such information are heightened if mother should happen to be pregnant during these nursery-school years.

The consensus of most child analysts is that children be given answers *to the questions they ask*. They need these answers in simple, understandable language, *dosed* according to their needs. The good-enough average parent can sense when the child has heard enough at a given moment, and will postpone further information until the child is ready for it. The child senses parental attitudes toward revealing sexual information. Children have very alert intuitions to parental inhibitions, and they are attuned to the opposite of parental inhibitions, heightened parental need to convey sexual information in detail.

Of all the ages, the nursery-school age is the best, I believe, to begin the child's sexual education. Beyond five and six, a very normative modesty develops in both boys and girls, and they frequently shy away from requesting the sexual information they may wish to have. By the time adolescence is reached, parents are the least appropriate purveyors of sexual information to their children.

In summary, with regard to methods of sexual education for a young child, I believe that (1) dosage is important and (2) the method by which the information is conveyed is important. Words, drawings, pictures are all useful tools for explaining to the child what he needs to know.

I have talked with many parents who have gone beyond these simple measures. Most of these parents wished to spare their children the false modesty and sexual conflicts that they experience and experienced. To achieve these ends these parents and children bathe together and see each other in toileting activities. Though this may be a point of controversy, in my experience it is potentially traumatic for a child to see adults nude.[a] It is traumatic in the sense

---

[a]Three definitive opinions regarding parental nudity developed in the symposium. In addition to Dr. Peltz's view, as indicated, Dr. Richard Green felt that an important indicator for the child in terms of establishing the core-morphologic component of sexual identity, "I am male/I am female," is the opportunity at a very young age to know the anatomic difference between males and females. This may be through observing parental nudity within the home. That does not mean constant nudity, but a comfortable, unpretentious occasional opportunity for the child to see male and female anatomic insignia.

One thing which is immutable, irrespective of changing culture definitions of "masculinity" and "femininity," is genital insignia. It really does not matter whether Daddy cooks and Mommy works. The important thing in terms of preventing sexual identity conflict is to be aware of and accept one's basic coremorphologic identity. Transsexualism is the classic example of nonacceptance; transsexualism is a difficult life road to travel.

This early cognitive labeling can take place as the child makes a comparison between his or her own body configuration and that of the two most significant

that it may be overwhelmingly stimulating, a combination of being exciting and frightening, and this can lead to a variety of symptomatic behaviors.

Let me illustrate with a single clinical example. Marc was five years, three months old when his parents asked for psychiatric consultation. Marc was encountering severe problems in school in his reading readiness program. Not only was he reversing left to right, but he would also turn his book upside down in his attempts to decipher the written words. An extremely ambitious youngster, Marc was often reduced to tears in the classroom. His parents reluctantly acknowledged that Marc had other emotional symptoms: he was extremely fearful of dogs, was excessively frightened of seeing blood (Marc's father was a surgeon!), and was enuretic.

In our initial meeting Marc, an extremely handsome but shy and frightened youngster, gradually permitted himself to play freely in the office. He was most fascinated by the toy firehouse, and spent a delightful moment pretending to be the fireman squirting out the fire. In this initial encounter I told Marc that his mother had told me that sometimes he squirted his bed at night. Unabashed, Marc answered, "Yes," and further, "I do something else too. I like to hold my book upside down and read it. I know I'm holding it upside down. But I like to do it anyway."

In the early phase of the psychotherapy, Marc repeated several play sequences. He was not only the big fireman, putting out fires, he was also the doctor who would cut off fingers, unafraid of the torrents of red blood. In contrast to this imaginative play, Marc would engage in a series of stereotypic activities always evoked by the same stimulus. Whenever he saw a hole, he had to fill it. The holes drilled in the firetruck for windows were filled in with marbles; zeroes, sixes, and nines on the calendar pad were ritually colored in.

Psychological tests of Marc suggested, "a mixed neurosis, with both hysterical and obsessive-compulsive features . . . Central to the patient's conflicts appear to be severe castration anxieties, often

adults in the environment. In this way, household nudity may aid in establishing the first component of sexual identity.

Striking a balance between these views, Dr. Albert Solnit stated that in certain families, in certain cultures and certain socioeconomic settings, children do see their parents and others naked. If the atmosphere is one of matter-of-factness and one in which a great deal of erotic stimulation is not conveyed, there is no evidence that that can't be handled quite well. Sometimes lack of privacy can't be avoided, even though it may not be a preference of the parents. However, intellectual middle-class people who practice nudity as a matter of duty to help their children overcome inhibitions and who aren't comfortable with it often convey the tension, the conflict, and the erotic arousal which makes it hard for children.

manifested by a preoccupation with limbs and bodily appendages. These conflicts relate to a conflictual over attention of looking and knowing. There is also evidence of a need not to know. There is no evidence of organic impairment." Educational testing showed that Marc "has strong cognitive ability, good receptive and expressive skills and the ability to concentrate for long periods of times on tasks."

Marc's parents were well intentioned, with essentially loving attitudes toward him. He was never physically threatened, and only spanked when he had driven his mother to the point of exhaustion because of his fearfulness and/or stubbornness. Marc's parents told me they didn't want him to be ashamed of his body or to have incorrect impressions of a woman's body. No precautions were taken at home, and Marc frequently saw his mother and two-years-older sister nude. A family custom had been initiated some years before in which Marc bathed weekly with his father, and sister with mother.

From both Marc's play and the psychological testing, it is suggested that Marc had "seen too much," was too excited by what he had seen, and needed not to see in situations that evoked too much excitement and anxiety. Apparently looking had become closely associated with his excited but dreaded examination of his mother's and sister's bodies. Looking had also become associated with his envious, attacking attitudes toward Father's body. His efforts at reading had been invaded by these psychological conflicts. Marc's other symptoms could also be understood within this matrix.

Dr. Martinson, in this volume and in his monograph *Infant and Child Sexuality*,[3] cites experience that there is no demonstrated proof of untoward consequences resulting from a child being ex-- posed to the nudity of parents or other adults. This is an issue on which we are in obvious disagreement; however, we are in complete agreement when he notes that children need to be protected from sexual molestation by adults.

In summary, I have advanced evidence that the nursery school years, ages three through five, are the prime years for sexually educating our youngsters, educating them according to their stage of readiness, without unduly stimulating them and without making them unduly anxious or guilty.

NOTES TO CHAPTER SIX

1. Anna Freud , The Concept of Developmental Lines, *Psychoanalytic Study of the Child* 18, 1963, 245-265.

2. Herman Roiphe, On an Early Genital Phase: with an Addendum on

Genesis, *Psychoanalytic Study of the Child* 23, 1968, 348-365; Eleanor Galenson and Herman Roiphe, The Impact of Early Sexual Discovery on Mood, Defensive Organization and Symbolization, *Psychoanalytic Study of the Child* 26, 1971, 195-216.

3. Floyd M. Martinson, *Infant and Child Sexuality: A Sociological Perspective* (St. Peter, Minnesota: The Book Mark, 1973). See also this volume, pp. 79, 81.

Chapter Seven

Sexual and Gender Development in the Latency Years

Morris Peltz, M.D.*

The second five years of life was denoted by Freud as the latency phase of development.[1] The psychological requirement for entry into this developmental stage is stated to be the giving up of the infantile incestuous wishes, the resolution of the infantile oedipus complex. A new psychological structure, the super-ego, is integrated, which stands guard over forbidden sexual and aggressive derivative impulses and affects. Yet all observers of school-age youngsters agree that sexual fantasies and behaviors do not suddenly or completely disappear from the child's life.

It must follow that whatever sexual fantasies these youngsters permit themselves, their fantasies and behaviors are anchored in a gendered view of the self. This intrapsychic image, deeply experienced and perhaps never explicitly conscious, may be schematized: "I am a boy with a penis, with testicles enclosed in a scrotal sac, from which I experience exciting, exhilarating, if not forbidden, sensations. I experience these sensations both when I masturbate and when I think about specific persons." "I am a girl with a clitoris and a less accessible vagina, from which I experience exciting and exhilarating, if not forbidden, sensations. I experience these sensations both when I masturbate and when I think of specific persons."

As has been previously noted, a gendered image of the self emerges sometime during the second year of life.[2] This self-image has a continuous line of development but achieves a new stability from the critical identifications employed in resolving the oedipus complex.

*Director of Training, Children's Hospital, San Francisco; Faculty, San Francisco Psychoanalytic Institute.

Paralleling this psychological development, and in my view facilitating it, is the cognitive development that occurs in early latency: the progressive consolidation of what Piaget has defined as operational intelligence.[3] Now the child is able to organize his knowledge of classes and subclasses and to reverse that mental operation. That is, he can know that Daddy and plumber belong to the same class, as men, and he can distinguish that not all daddies are plumbers, nor are all plumbers daddies. This progress to operational intelligence further enables the latency-age child to shift the center of his emotional universe from mother, father, and siblings to the many new, interesting, and exciting persons he encounters as he enters school.

Manifestly, the latency-aged child has achieved relatively stable intrapsychic gendered images of the self and other (objects). It is my thesis that this developmental task has not yet reached its terminus. Indeed, during latency, there is an ongoing structuring and stabilizing of gendered images. These images are, however, buffeted by internally perceived challenges in these second five years of life. The child actively, though largely unconsciously, reacts to these threats by engaging in behaviors, fantasies, and interpersonal relationships that serve the developmental, defensive, and adaptive functions of replicating and integrating gendered self and object images. That the array of observable behaviors in these children is so commonplace and ordinary may be the reason that their function in the service of stabilizing gendered self and object images has been overlooked.

Since Bornstein's classic paper,[4] latency has been viewed as occurring in two phases. In the first phase, ages five-and-one-half to eight, the child is threatened not only by genital but by regressive pregenital impulses. His or her superego is a new, harsh, and brittle structure. There are strong masturbatory temptations and strongly perceived prohibitions against these impulses. The second phase of latency, from ages eight to ten, is characterized by greater flexibility in ego and superego functioning and less dramatic evidence of conflict.

Examining latency along the developmental axis of gender images, I would like to describe two stages: first, the stage of *gender vigilance*, coinciding with Bornstein's first phase; and second, the stage of *gender role exploration*, coinciding with Bornstein's second phase. By gender vigilance I mean the constant and ever watchful attitude the boys and girls have of themselves as boys and girls, the external manifestation of which is the ever present male and female chauvinism so typical of five-and-a-half to eight year olds. By gender role exploration I mean the progressive relaxation of the former continuously guarded attitude toward one's own gender and a

simultaneous playful experimentation in behavior and fantasy toward the opposite gender. Typical expressions of the gender role exploration are the sexual jokes, both anal and genital, of the eight-year-old and the renewed, oftentimes disguised and distorted, interest in the opposite gender.

THE STATE OF GENDER VIGILANCE

Very typically, as the child enters kindergarten (which coincides roughly with the onset of latency) play and games which boys and girls had enjoyed jointly cease abruptly. Playing house together, for example, is no longer tolerable for either the boy or the girl. Public displays of interest in a child of the opposite sex are shunned, not only because of peer pressure but because of intrapsychic forces. During these years often the only legacy of mutually shared games is the running and chasing games of former years. Nevertheless, these running and chasing games are engaged in along sharply demarcated lines cleaved according to gender. The boys chase the girls or the girls chase the boys. Though derivatives of sexual impulses motivate these games, the child's consciousness of sexual excitement is muted. This attenuation stems not only from defensive activity but is probably due to the increasing fusion of derivatives of sexual drives with aggressive drives. These chasing games are but one of the many ways in which the early-latency child progressively masters not only his instinctual life but his expanding universe. The universe I am describing includes school, with its intellectual challenges and tasks, and school with the demands for relationships with cohorts and teachers.

Central to the refinement of interpersonal relationships is the progressive stabilizing of self and object images. The early-latency child asks, "How fast am I?" "How strong am I?" "How smart am I?" Boys make these comparisons with other boys as they conceive of themselves belonging to the class of *boy*. They also continuously, but at a distance, make these comparisons with girls, both individually and as a class. This mental activity is identical for girls. *Gender rivalry* of this age group is but another aspect of gender vigilance, the imperatively perceived need to distinguish one's gendered self from the other.

Why is "sexism" so intense in this era? What psychological functions and mechanisms are employed to serve this end?

As noted before, with entry into latency, the boy and the girl have largely relinquished incestuous attachments to mother and father. Both the boy and the girl employ identifications with the parent of

the same sex to help ward off and master these incestuous feelings. But surrendering sexual love for the parent of the opposite sex does not preclude the child's continued love for that parent. An emotional tie is maintained. This love is largely detached from its sexual aim. In a like fashion, a desexualized love continues as a bond with the parent of the same sex. The legacy of these sexualized love relationships with parents of the oedipal era is found now in the new identifications grouping in superego organization. It is these identifications which are responsible for the sense of well-being and comfort one experiences when one has lived according to his or her percepts; the pride one experiences in having made the correct moral choice.[5] The identifications the boy and girl make with their parents' unconscious superegos give the sense of power to the child's unconscious conscience.

It seems apparent to me that boys and girls during latency continuously identify with aspects of the content parental images. Those aspects selected will be congruent with the child's ego interests. These identifications add complexity and richness to the continuing development of self-images. For example, it is commonplace in the biographies of composers and musicians that mother was the first teacher. Women in competitive skiing have first snowplowed the mountain in the tracks of Father. I suggest it is the ego-function of gender vigilance which scrutinizes the content of cross-gendered images. This watchful activity of the ego specifically excludes for identification sexual images of opposite-gendered parent, images that would evoke too intense castration anxiety in boys or too intense penis-envy in girls. It is gender vigilance that permits Mother to shape the young composer's life without compromising his gendered view of himself. It is gender vigilance that enables the girl to cherish her hope of an Olympic victory according to Father's dream while at the same time retaining her view of herself as feminine.

The defensive processes that aid the ego in gender vigilance are largely projective-introjective mechanisms. What is perceived as feminine in boys is cast out, preferably to be hurled on one's worst enemy: "You fag," "You sissy." What is regarded as masculine is taken in and "metabolized" to increase the structure and stability of a gendered image of the self. The same process takes place in girls. These projective-introjective mechanisms here in the service of gender development are supported by an array of behaviors engaged in by boys and girls. In the "good enough family" the child is encouraged to align himself with the parent of the same sex, who is intrapsychically perceived as being like him or being like her. I believe that in one-parent families, the child "creates" in fantasy or

reality the parent surrogate he or she needs to complete this developmental task.

It is commonplace for both boys and girls to develop passionate friendships with each other again along lines of gender cleavage. It is my impression that these early intense friendships are the prelude to what reappears for both boys and girls in preadolescence. But in early latency these relationships, which are essentially love relationships, rarely involve sexual intimacy. The companion who is loved is overvalued, idealized, and jealously possessed. These relationships are manifestly not homosexual or narcissistic, descriptive terms used for aberrant object choice in adolescents and adults. Rather, gender sameness is a requirement, because it serves the human need for a peer love relationship during these years of gender vigilance. This view, I believe, coincides with Sandler's notion of the "safety principle" of the ego.[6] Sandler suggests that the ego actively scans the environment via perceptual-integrative processes to ensure a relatively stable state of ego safety. During the years of gender vigilance, boys and girls can then engage in intimate, close-up, same-gendered relationships while at the same time, but at a safe distance via perceptual processes, pursuing interests in cross-gendered relationships. Thus, the boy and the girl scanning identifications with cross-gendered parents (or their surrogates) seek in interpersonal relationships objects that sustain and objects that differentiate gender sameness and gender differentness. The "sexism" of these years is but the external manifestation of those complex mental processes that establish firmly structured images of maleness and femaleness.

THE STAGE OF GENDER ROLE EXPLORATION

At approximately age eight, notable shifts in functioning of boys and girls are clearly observable. These children are clearly less symptomatic. Nightmares have largely subsided. Often boys who have been enuretic now achieve mastery of this symptom. Although playmates are still selected according to gender, the imperative need for a best friend seems to diminish. Rather, both boys and girls are more aware of peer groups, and their efforts are directed at securing some position within that social hierarchy. Complex competitive games, involving the participation of several children, are planned and executed. Boys will collect in groups to plan "war games" which may take hours to complete and encompass an entire neighborhood. Institutional sanctions lend support, as for example Little Leagues and scouting organizations. Peer groups and status within them are of

equal importance to girls. Though the manifest content of girls' play varies from that of boys, it serves the same psychological function. Secure in a gendered view of the self, intragender competition partially replaces competition between the genders.

There is, normatively in these years, a great lust and exuberance for doing and learning. Energies formerly needed for vigilant intrapsychic gender image integrations can now be freed for sublimations and explorations. Self-confident and sustained by more permissive and flexible superegos, boys and girls permit themselves to engage in zestful sexual fantasies. These fantasies are seldom represented in sexual behavior. In cars and buses boys and girls boastfully tell their dirty jokes, sometimes to the embarrassment, more often to the pleasure, of their cross-gendered listeners. Although members of the opposite gender are still publicly shunned, a boy might privately talk about a girl whom he admires, even likes. The girl between eight and ten will talk about the cute boy at school, though never speak to him in the classroom. This progressive exploration of the perimeters of gender role with the renewal of sexual fantasies accounts, I believe, for what are often the two stormiest years between cross-gendered siblings of this age. Sexual fantasies of parents usually remain sharply repressed, but not so of siblings. One can observe, in brother and sister, sharp alternations of behavior between moments of great, tender, almost sensuous love and moments of equally intense hatred. These alternations are the result of reaction formations summoned up when the threat of incest evokes too much anxiety. "I hate her. She bugs the hell out of me" and "I can't stand that brother of mine. I wish he were dead" are but the verbal rejoinders that support defensive operations. It is this flexibility to shift emotional gears that enables the latency-age boy and girl to play out in experience and fantasy emotional and specifically sexual interest in the opposite gender for short periods of time. It is from this position of relative strength that children enter the stormier phase of prepuberty.

Because the psychological activity that I have just described seems to be carried out in such a "silent" fashion, and because the behaviors noted are so mundane, I would now like to briefly describe two latency-aged children, both with conflicted gendered self-images. In these clinical vignettes, I hope to illustrate the usefulness of the concepts gender vigilance and gender role exploration as ego functions that promote normal development.

A LATENCY BOY

Bucky, age seven, was in grave difficulties when his parents first consulted me. Not only did Bucky have that ominous trio of symp-

toms—enuresis, fire-setting, and cruelty to animals—but he was impulsive and destructive in the classroom. He was about to be asked to leave his school. Bucky had just cause for his chronic, enraged, impulsive-driven behavior. He had been adopted to preserve an already deteriorating marriage. His adoptive mother, rather than being buoyed up by having an infant to care for, became more depressed and withdrawn as her new child began making demands of her. Father, devoted to Bucky, could only partly fill in for Mother. There were two trial separations between Bucky's parents before they were ultimately divorced when Bucky was five. When Bucky began his psychotherapy at age seven, he was a ruggedly handsome masculine boy, eager for love and affection. He was also guilty because of his fury and ashamed of his neediness and periodic loss of control. He struggled mightily with two percepts of himself. The more conscious and certainly the more acceptable was his image of himself as a lusty boy ready to play and fight with cohorts; ready to scoff publicly at girls, though privately admitting to me that he counted them among his friends. A second, less conscious image readily emerged in the transference; a very threatening image because of the intense passive aims associated with it. Bucky's fighting helped ward off his longing to be passively loved by his now frequently absent father. The hypermasculinity also warded off his unconscious identification with the mother, who was so often lost to him because of her depressions.

Gender vigilance enabled Bucky to defensively ward off this second threatening image. *Gender role exploration* enabled Bucky to experiment in fantasy that he was the sexually active giant he imagined his father to be. (These latter fantasies were also employed in mastering the sexual overstimulation Bucky experienced at the day care center where he spent several hours each day after school.) For example, early in the therapy Bucky not only drew Superman and Batman, superheroes whom he admired, but he drew graphic captioned illustrations of sexual intercourse. In one picture a nude woman is shown receiving the gigantic penis of a little boy who is standing to her side. The lady is quoted as saying, "I don't fart because of that man." The boy, who is really just an appendage of his penis and testicles, is shouting, "Oh, get lost." But off in the distance on the other side of the picture is a man saying "Let's fuck, lady. After him." The adult man is also connected with the woman, not by his penis but by a vortex of lines extending from his mouth to her vulva. The second picture, very similar in content, shows in the foreground a young boy with an enormous Afro hairdo not only urinating but directing a stream of curliques at a woman's entroitus. The woman is receding in the background. An adult man stands at the side looking on.

These drawings vividly illustrate Bucky's gendered image of himself as a boy on his way to becoming the sexually potent man. Yet Bucky was not truly threatened by his passivity and homosexual love for his father until some eighteen months after treatment had begun. The threat to Bucky's masculinity occurred under the following circumstances. Father, who had been in psychotherapy, married Jean, a mature, loving woman who, notwithstanding Bucky's difficult, often provocative behavior, loved Bucky, set limits for him, and physically cared for him on weekends. Realistically, Father now believed he could provide a better and more nurturing home for Bucky than Bucky's mother could. Confident, Father initiated a legal suit for Bucky's custody and won a temporary court order which permitted Bucky to live with Father and Jean.

Bucky couldn't have been happier. He warmed even more to his stepmother. He discussed many issues with her, foremost among which were why, how, and when she took her birth control pills. Bucky clearly knew that he wanted no interlopers in his newfound Garden of Eden. In his psychotherapy hours Bucky was casual about his interest in his stepmother's sexual behavior. What was uppermost in his mind was his desperate need to believe Father would be awarded custody. It seemed like endless weeks of waiting for Bucky before Mother suddenly capitulated and custody was awarded to Father. I saw Bucky on that day. It was not only that Bucky had never been more blissful, but he had a new, expanded capacity for performing tasks that I had never before witnessed. After announcing the news, with deeply felt joy, Bucky proceeded to build out of Tinker toys—a most frustrating play item—an extremely complicated windmill. He was absorbed in this activity for the whole hour, and I could only think to myself that Bucky was making the wind machine that had blown away all his troubles.

Two days later Bucky was in quite an altered state. He came to the office sobbing and protesting as if his heart had been broken. Lying on the couch he screamed, "They shouldn't do it. It's nasty. How could they do it?" It took a great deal of consoling and empathizing before Bucky could reveal that what was most painful was the feeling of being excluded by both his stepmother and father from their intimacy. In succeeding hours Bucky experienced in the transference his rage, sexual longing, and his guilt. Hours would begin innocuously enough. But very soon Bucky was throwing furniture around the room. The attacks became more personalized. He would grab for my necktie and grab for my genitals, forcing me to physically restrain him. He demanded that I give him the stapler so that he could staple his finger. Repeatedly I interpreted to Bucky his

fury at me for not giving him what he wanted. He wanted to play sexual games with me.

In succeeding weeks, Bucky worked through this theme in many derivative forms. Later, in a more controlled version, these same wishes appeared in the microsphere of play. In one hour, with his own toy car brought from home, he, directly upon entering the office, went to the play cabinets to get a tow truck. He hooked the tow truck to his car and pulled it along the floor. He then announced triumphantly, as he unhooked them, "No more fucking around, see. No more farting and fucking around." Later, including a toy firehouse in his play, Bucky carefully arranged the bedroom and bathroom for the sleeping firemen. Then, transformed into a monster from outer space, Bucky destroyed the firehouse and its sleeping occupants. Bucky's continuing furious sexual jealousy regressively revived intense negative oedipal homosexual love.

In another session, having brought several male dolls, characters from *Star Trek*, Scotty, one of the characters, was trying to shove his shoe up Captain Kirk's rectum. With mounting sexual excitement, the locus of the play was shifted to the macrosphere, and Bucky again attempted to tug at my necktie and provoke me into over-powering him. At the same time Bucky enacted his identification with Mother, a sexualized identification, which evoked extreme castration anxiety.

In another hour from this same era, Bucky began ruminating about what gift he wanted for his birthday, even though that event was months away. He asked for a Leggo game from me. Now, pretending he was the greedy pig he perceived himself to be, he imitated Porky Pig signing off with his stuttering, "Well, that's all folks." Next Bucky looked down at his pants and noticed the bulge. "That's my wiener. Let's cut it off with a scissors." He laughed uproariously, the uproar betraying his anxiety.

The assault to Bucky's masculinity was overdetermined but at this time came largely from his extreme jealousy. Once safely anchored in a new family, with a loving father and stepmother, Bucky could neither tolerate the idea of Father sexually loving someone other than Bucky, nor could he bear the idea of his new, beloved stepmother sexually loving a man other than himself. In the transfer-ence, Bucky enacted the two roles alternately. He was the man sexually loving the woman; and he was the woman being sexually loved by a man. It was this latter wish, of course, which reanimated earlier self-images within Bucky, self-images that threatened a gen-dered view of himself as a boy belonging to the class of men. My thesis is that in spite of attacks on Bucky's gendered image of himself

as a boy, prior development with its nuclear identifications, an ongoing vigilant ego activity spared Bucky greater manifest psychopathology.

A LATENCY GIRL

Another child, a girl, entered latency with an already compromised gendered view of herself. At five-and-one-half, Rose was an irritable, grumpy child who was known at home as "the prison matron" not only because of occasional cruel attacks on her two-years-younger sister and playmates, but because of her domineering, controlling attitude. At school, in spite of superior intelligence, Rose was not responsive to her teacher, remaining instead distant and aloof. Her teacher reported that Rose seemed to spend most of her time daydreaming and seemed especially preoccupied with sexual fantasies. The figures Rose drew were always endowed with both a penis and breasts. At home, Rose played out these bisexual fantasies on her own body. Ever since age three, whenever the opportunity arose, Rose would steal underpants from Tom, a two-years-older neighbor, and stuff them into her own underpants. When permitted, she would endow herself with more than ample breasts by stuffing her halter-type undershirts with tissue or small articles of clothing. Mother also despaired over Rose's sometimes deliberate, sometimes mindless smearing. Unless carefully watched, Rose would smear a whole bottle of lotion over her body, extrude the entire contents of a tube of toothpaste across the bathroom mirror, or web an entire room with scotch tape.

Historically, Rose suffered multiple early traumas. Collateral information suggested that Mother had been moderately depressed during Rose's first year. When Rose was six months old, Mother began babysitting for other children, presumably to supplement the family income. Tom, then two years old, was the first of these children. Instructions were given to Rose's mother that Tom be toilet trained by allowing him to remain nude in order to assure him of unencumbered access to the toilet. Rose and Tom also swam nude in the backyard pool. By the time Rose was three, her fascination with and envy of Tom's penis were clearly apparent. It was at that age that Rose began to simulate the bulge she viewed in Tom's genital area.

A succession of infants and toddlers followed Tom into Rose's home to be cared for by Rose's mother. The clearest manifestation of Rose's envy of these children centered in her interest in the boys' penises. Mother described: "Rose always seemed to glory in looking

at the boys' penises. She would rush to the bathroom to watch them urinate, then laugh and say, 'Yuk.' " Her envious, sadistic impulses were turned against herself and other girls. Beginning in her fourth year, scissors were to be a most carefully guarded item in the house. On several occasions Rose cut her own bangs almost to the forehead. Her parents were more furious and horrified when Rose butchered the long blond curls of a two-year-old girl being cared for in the household.

Rose's fourth year was also marked by health problems, which undoubtedly interfered with normative body image schematization. During the first half of this year Rose's hearing became progressively compromised because of repeated ear infections. The increasing deafness initially escaped Mother's attention; she attributed Rose's unresponsive behavior to her usual negativism. When Mother observed that Rose did not respond to sudden loud noises, Rose was examined by her pediatrician. A minor surgical procedure fully restored Rose's hearing. Rose herself remembered in psychotherapy that at about three-and-one-half she contracted pinworms. (This report was later confirmed by Mother.) Not only did the nightly migration of these worms produce extreme periatal itching, but a part of the prescribed medical treatment required Mother to swab Rose's rectal area at night, further increasing this anal stimulation.

Toward the end of Rose's fourth year, Mother found her almost unbearable. Not only was she often angry, sullen, and cruel, but if not carefully watched, Rose would smear herself with makeup and lotions. She would often get into the disposable diapers, both clean and soiled, which mother used in caring for day-care infants. Rose would pin these diapers on herself and her dolls. The hope that school would remedy Rose's problem was dashed by the parent-teacher conference at the end of the kindergarten year.

As Rose entered latency there was no question that she perceived herself as truly feminine. She loved to have her hair combed in a variety of styles. She was attentive to her clothes. Indeed, though she had but few, she did have friendships with other girls; and she loved to tease and chase the boys. Consciously Rose viewed herself as a girl, proud and arrogant—disdainful and contemptuous of boys. There is also no doubt that her intrapsychic gendered image was defective. There was an imperative need to deny in word and deed those defects she perceived in herself. Her defensive denials were aimed at warding off her sadistic rage toward Mother, her severe castration anxiety, and her intense penis envy. Her extreme ambivalence toward Mother sharply compromised her ability to identify with her. Cross-gendered identifications with Father were based on

images of Father as a passive aggressor rather than with Father as the protector. During treatment Rose confided that she learned teasing from Daddy, who would sit on the toilet to urinate in order, he claimed, to avoid Rose's eager interest in his penis.

Rose's imperative wish for a penis, breasts, and baby could not be relinquished, because these wishes had become deeply linked with a compromised gendered self-image. Yet under the aegis of gender vigilance, Rose arrived at a compromise employing the synthetic function of the ego. Her defective gendered image was magically repaired by endowing herself in fantasy with breasts and penis.

To illustrate some aspects of the integrative processes of gender image formation during early latency, processes usually "silent," I'll describe· a brief segment from the end of the first year of Rose's psychotherapy. In Rose, because of her special psychopathology and because of the psychotherapeutic processes, these integrative tasks were audible and articulated.

The first six months of Rose's therapy were largely dominated by a mother transference in which Rose vividly experienced her anal rage against her mother. Her frequent epithet to me, "Hey, stupid," was not only a derisive catcall but represented her attempt at projecting feelings of being stupid and defective. Weeks before Christmas she forlornly named the gift she wished to receive from me: Baby Alice, the mechanical doll that eats and drinks, urinates and defecates. Several months later, when Rose learned that a friend of her mother's was to have twins, Rose's envy knew no bounds. In her next hour, defensively ebullient, she began stuffing wads of tissue into her underpants. With hands on hips which were thrust forward, she paraded in front of me, blissfully satisfied with her paper pregnancy. I interpreted that she could pretend to be pregnant, maybe even with twins, so she wouldn't have to feel so jealous and incomplete about her body. Angrily she responded by spraying jets of water at me from a nearby plant sprayer. I told Rose that when she could no longer pretend she was pregnant, she had to pretend she was somebody else—a girl with a big squirter, the kind of squirter she knew that Tom had.

Several hours later, more aware of her positive feelings for me, she announced, as we were playing a game of war, that she liked hearts, because hearts stood for love. Blushingly, she confessed she loved Davey of *The Monkeys* and Steven, a boy in her class, whom of course she had never spoken to. As we continued to play our card game, I suggested, "When I take your heart cards, it must mean I'm taking your love. And when you take my heart cards, it must mean you're taking my love." Rose now confessed that in the week before she had stolen an orange marker pen from the office. She had used

this pen to write me messages of "I love you" and "I hate you." I interpreted to Rose that loving me and feeling loved by me didn't seem to be enough. She had to take something from me, my marking pen, to make her feel complete.

In this early phase of her psychotherapy, Rose continued to need to believe in the magic of the illusory breast-penis-baby. Yet, resolution of her vengeful hatred of Mother permitted her greater closeness and identification with her. Additionally, in rediscovering her intense love of her father via me, Rose could now identify with specifically nongendered aspects of me. For example, she could now talk about her feelings and reflect about them instead of exclusively dramatizing them in impulsive behavior and play. Though much work lay ahead, Rose was beginning to make the changes in self-representations which would permit her a view of herself as anatomically intact, secure in her gender.

CONCLUSION

I have attempted to illustrate that although gender identity is a stable structure before latency, there is an ongoing, largely silent gender development during the second five years of life. I have described this development as occurring sequentially in two stages: the stage of *gender vigilance* and the stage of *gender role exploration*. I have denoted that these stages are characterized by similarly named ego functions. Gender vigilance filters the continuing ongoing identifications with Mother and Father during the more turbulent first two years of latency, specifically excluding sexualized identifications that evoke anxiety. Gender role exploration permits playful anticipation and fantasy of one's gender vis-à-vis the opposite gender, setting the stage for prepuberty. Behavioral manifestations of these stages are influenced by environmental cues and expectations that may modify their form. The essential issue is the developmental need: securing stable intrapsychic gendered images of the self and other objects. Clinical material has been presented to illustrate that these structures, as all new structures, are vulnerable and will regress in the face of specific trauma.

NOTES TO CHAPTER SEVEN

1. Sigmund Freud, Three Essays on the Theory of Sexuality, *Standard Edition*, 7 (London: Hogarth Press, 1953), 125-245.

2. Margaret Mahler, Fred Pine, and Anni Bergman, *The Psychological Birth of the Human Infant* (New York: Basic Books, 1975); Morris Peltz; this volume, p. 41.

3. Hans Furth, *Piaget and Knowledge* (Englewood Cliffs, New Jersey: Prentice-Hall, 1969).

4. Berta Bornstein, On Latency, *Psychoanalytic Study of the Child* 6, 1951, 279-285.

5. Roy Schafer, The Loving and Beloved Superego in Freud's Structural Theory, *Psychoanalytic Study of The Child* 15, 1960, 163-188.

6. Joseph Sandler, The Background of Safety, *Int. Journal of Psychoanalysis* 41, 1960, 352-356.

Chapter Eight

The Early Pubertal Student

George C. Kaplan, M.D.*

The stage of psychological development as the child nears puberty is referred to as *preadolescence*. Changes in a child's behavior associated with preadolescence occur before any signs of obvious physical changes. Whereas puberty may be described in terms of the appearance of secondary sexual characteristics, the psychological situation, preadolescence, is more difficult to pinpoint. For our purposes we may select an approximate age grouping of nine to thirteen, allowing for physical, psychological, and socially significant variations. There are striking differences between children in their latency and preadolescent phases of development.

Crises and opportunities are presented by the challenge of new phases in normal development. Responses to these challenges are both defensive and adaptive. The outcome of any new phase of development has relation to how prior stages of growth and development were resolved. A satisfactory latency results in significant achievements in ego development that help the child tolerate the disruption of that phase. Some of these achievements are: the difference between fantasy and reality is established; socialization at school and with friends allows distancing from the parents, affording the opportunity to achieve relative independence; the increasing confidence of the growing child in the use of his more mature and coordinated body contributes to the sense of mastery; and defenses are established to support repression. All contribute to relative comfort from the continuing pressure of the potentially disruptive, aggressive, and sexual drive derivatives.

*Faculty, San Francisco Psychoanalytic Institute.

Although differences between boys' and girls' behavior at school are present during latency, these are minimal when one considers what happens at preadolescence. The increased sexual and aggressive energy disrupting latency results in a regression that can serve or impede normal development. With preadolescence we see a regression to the pregenital stage of development. There is increased evidence of derivatives from oral, anal, and phallic stages of psychosexual development. This does not imply total regression nor imply pathology. The significant achievements in ego development during latency are not dissolved; I refer particularly to the ability to tolerate regression without fear of disintegration. The capacity of the ego to integrate is not permanently affected. The normal child does not lose the capacity to distinguish reality from fantasy, although one sees recurrence at this age of magical thinking and the increased use of projection and denial.

The typical preadolescent conflict is based on castration anxiety in relation not to the oedipal figures, but to the preoedipal, sometimes referred to as "phallic" mother.[a] Resolution of the bisexual identification is required. Defenses ward off the unconscious tendency to identify with the "phallic" mother.

The boy builds forts and forms clubs excluding disruption by girls, except the few tomboys. The tomboy escapes the condemnation and ridicule the boys heap upon her more feminine girlfriends. The male child's concern for his genitals, their size and safety, is increased by the observation of more rapid development of girls his age, particularly their height and breast development. He is concerned about the nonspecific, uncontrollable erections he experiences. Motility is diffusely increased. Dirty language is profuse, often focusing on anal activities. Sadistic acts surprise parents and teachers. He seems unconcerned about the well-being of others. At school and at home he may become increasingly sloppy and games are played more aggressively. It is more difficult for him to be still and attentive. Exhibitionistic behavior helps ward off fear of uncontrollability, helplessness, and passivity. In his fantasy life he must renounce wishes for baby, breast, and passive sexual aims, all that's revived in relation to the early mother and early negative oedipal situation.

The situation is different with girls. The question of the pregenital

---

[a]A phantasy image of the mother derived from the preoedipal stages of psychosexual development, emerging from a predominantly dyadic relationship with the mother who is imagined to be all-powerful, capable of being all-giving and all-depriving. Much of this imagery and the fears associated with it results from the projection of the child's aggressive impulses.

regression has led to varying opinions in the literature. Deutsch descriptively states that the girl turns more readily towards the male.[1] Blos understands this move toward males as defensive against the regressive pull toward the preoedipal mother.[2] The relationship with the mother is intense and more threatening than for boys. The mother often is seen as active and aggressive. Responses may include identification with this image, contributing to tomboyishness or other active, aggressive behavior.

If the girl moves toward boys, it is often in an aggressive manner. She may appear confident, even "cocky." She insists upon equality with the boys, demands to participate in their activities, at which she may, because of her physical development, excel. This conflicts with the boys' demands for exclusivity. Her increased abilities, greater stature, and need to distance herself from her mother may contribute to prolonging her sexual role confusion. Acceptance of this is not reflected in conscious gender doubt, but in fantasied possibilities of role changes. A nine-year-old discussing her friend's newborn brother asked, "Does he have a penis *yet?*"

A twelve-year-old bitterly protested the separation of boys and girls in her private school. She envied the boys' activities and freedoms, insisting that there were no differences between the boys and herself. Belatedly and mournfully she noted only the absence of a penis, which "wasn't her fault." She daydreamed of being a boy and of having a boy sexually interested in her. She pictured sexual relations as aggressive acts to which she wished and would be forced to submit, as well as in which she would be the active initiator. Her feelings of helpless submission were quickly balanced by those of aggressive sadistic behavior.

The problem of relinquishing the female child's dependence upon her mother is often helped by turning outside the family to a special friend, who may be a peer or older. The special friend is idealized and imitated without the anxiety that would be present if the preadolescent considered herself to be similar to mother.

I would like to place special emphasis on an aspect of body concern with which adolescents struggle. It is during these years that awareness and anticipation of body changes heighten. Much depends upon earlier experiences, especially in relation to the caretaking mother (or father if he substituted). We have first the reality of what the parents look like. The child wonders and hopes that he will be stronger or taller, helping him to ward off feelings of passivity. But he does assume that in many ways he will resemble his parents.

The male child is particularly concerned about his height and strength. He has only recently achieved sufficient control of his body

to participate successfully at sports requiring great coordination. He may now find that his friends have grown and he hasn't. In an attempt to appear big, he brags, uses words that reveal his concerns from all levels of early development, and talks of sex even though he does not understand the process. He is concerned for his body and his future.

The uncontrollable, nonspecific erections heighten his increasing preoccupation with his genitals and their function. The testicles grow rapidly during these years and begin to become sensitive to pain, increasing his awareness of their vulnerability. His wishes and fears for his genitals are often played out in games of "self-castration." He may limp or otherwise pretend injury. He may experiment with his body by hiding his genitals and/or squeezing his nipples. During these years he is usually informed by a peer that his own parents have sexual relations, which he desperately tries to deny.

The female child has similar concerns. She too notes the disparate growth of her friends. She waits impatiently for her breasts to develop and often rushes prematurely to get her first brassière. If she defensively becomes a tomboy, she may try to hide her development behind sloppy skirts or large sweaters. She may gain much weight as a defense against sexuality and as an expression of her oral greed. She begins to talk about boys and sex, with little understanding of the process. She knows that she can someday have babies but isn't sure if she wants any. Massive confusion about her body and its functions continues. Evidence has accumulated that early vaginal awareness and masturbation are not unusual.

Her friends may begin to menstruate and she may or may not know anything about that mysterious process. As a powerful confirmation of femaleness, it may be looked forward to or despised. She may exaggerate complaints of the injustices done to her. If she resists turning toward men, she may emphasize the stupidity of her male teachers, branding them as ineffective, that is, impotent. She may treat her female teachers as she does her mother. Any exercise of control by the teacher would then be resisted with fervor. She may find relative safety in a strong protective male teacher or select a younger, more "liberal" female teacher to idealize as a protection against the regressive pull toward her own mother.

With both boys and girls in sixth to eighth grades we see the tendency toward establishing a more stable structure, the ego ideal. A teacher may perfectly fill this role.

Few children of this age doubt their gender. Blos states: "Children know whether they are boys or girls . . . there is no doubt about that in their minds . . . but there exists a set of ideas and imageries that do

not correspond with the facts as the child knows them." It is a problem of sexual identity that concerns the preadolescent. An example may illustrate my point. Although the circumstances to be described may not be frequent ones, we will likely be able to empathize with this girl's dilemma.

AN EARLY PUBERTAL GIRL

Bea presented no problems to her parents, teachers, or her few friends during her latency years and so was described as a normal child; nonetheless, she had fewer friendships than others. She had been a serious student in her latency, achieving outstanding marks at school.

Bea's history does not contribute toward understanding her complaints of isolation, loneliness, and tearful sadness. She felt "different" from the others, a self-description that was not clear until she was able to reveal her fantasies. Masturbation was frequent, repetitive, and clearly remembered from age four or five. Stimulation was promoted by thigh pressure. She fantasied "lovemaking" as a man and a woman touching and/or rubbing against each other. She was distressed and confused by what she felt during her vaginal explorations. There was "something inside but near the outside," an extra "piece sticking" from her genitals. She could not understand what it was but knew that she was different from her girlfriends. She feared humiliation if this difference should be discovered. This was despite her conscious recognition that "this piece" really did not protrude. Her fantasies included ideas that she was defective, and that she had caused the problem by masturbation.

During preadolescence she feared she was hermaphroditic. She thought of the advantages of being self-sufficient with both a penis and a vagina, but at no time was there any doubt as to her gender. She knew she was female.

Later in preadolescence she was able to question her pediatrician and was told of an anatomical anomaly, an "extra piece of skin from the vaginal fold that usually causes no difficulty." She was not greatly reassured by the offer of surgical removal.

During her adolescence her concern that she was different increased. She now worried about other protrusions that cannot be hidden, her breasts. Her self-images included being pretty and desirable as well as defective and ugly. Exhibitionistic wishes were inhibited, resulting in her beginning not to perform well. Inhibition led to decreased effectiveness at competitive sports and further loss of confidence in her body adequacy.

Bea idealized one older girl, who became her confidant and without whom she believed she could not function. She also admired a particular teacher during her early adolescence and chose to reveal to her the extent of her anxiety and wish for help, which led to her referral for treatment.

AN EARLY PUBERTAL BOY

A different problem was posed by a preadolescent boy. Thirteen-year-old Dennis was considered effeminate by his father. He enjoyed his close relationship with his mother and minimized his continuous difficulty with his male peers. At school he was unmercifully teased with such pejoratives as "fag." This was encouraged by his behavior, which included dressing differently from the other boys, carrying lunch pails more usually selected by girls, and associating with girls. His relating to his teachers was an extension of how he experienced his parents. The female teachers were seen as potentially protective and accepting; the male teachers, in contrast, were not understanding, critical, unfair and distant. Dennis was exquisitely sensitive to the moods of adults, especially his mother, and eventually his therapist. He often referred to himself as being like his mother. His words mimicked hers, and it took several months before he was able to separate his opinions from his mother's. His identification was mixed, but he was more accepting of his mother's attitudes and interests, whereas his father was portrayed as ineffectual, uneducated, and unsupportive. A "silent" (unconscious) conspiracy existed in which his mother, grandmother, and the patient demeaned his father.

Although Dennis was convinced that women had a more important role in family life, and although he presented himself as possessing many so-called "feminine" traits, he was in no doubt that he was a male. His fantasies dealt with much confusion as to what kind of a man he wanted to, or could, be. He considered his father and many of the boys at school as vulgar. He castigated them for their use of foul language, which he denied using despite complaints that he had cursed a male teacher. When material relating to sexual curiosity and masturbation occurred in psychotherapy, he wondered with angry astonishment how the therapist could think he was "one of those kinds of boys." It was necessary at first for him to insist he was above that "sort of thing." His body anxiety became clear as he imagined what he would look like when he grew up. He worried that he had been told that he looked exactly like his father. This was disturbing as he recalled pictures of his father as a late teenager. With

much concern he used the displacement to describe his fears. He imagined himself as his father was—white-skinned, pale, frail, thin, and very young-looking when compared to other men in the pictures—a most unmanly description. It was relatively simple for Dennis to learn that he was concerned with his unknowable future. This allowed him to explore many derivatives of his body anxiety. He described many physical complaints, reflecting an exaggerated concern with his body. Encouraged by his mother's overprotectiveness he withdrew further from his peers, refusing to participate in athletic competition. It was easier for him to contemplate the distant future, old age, questions of death and reincarnation, than his more immediate future and the anticipated conflicts of becoming a teenager.

When his attempts to repress and deny sexual interest failed, he would use other techniques to deal with derivatives of his sexual drive. These included suppression, externalization, projection, and intellectualization, demonstrating the wide range of his ego's ability to respond to anxiety. Aggressivity was also a problem. Although he was able to experience affects of anger and rage, and was conscious of wishes to retaliate against his tormentors, including peers, parents, therapist, and teachers, his behavior was generally passive. He was the victim who dared not fight lest he be severely punished by authorities. He dared not venture into new experiences, as the world was viewed as dangerous and hostile. These fears were not only projections of his extreme anger, but also an identification with an attitude of his mother.

Dennis's hobby was magic. His intense curiosity was directed toward understanding and performing tricks. The ego mechanism of "identification with the aggressor" was prominent in his becoming the magician who could cut people in pieces and put them back together. Castration anxiety was relieved both by becoming the castrator as well as insisting upon magical restoration. His role alternated between that of the active magician who relished describing his tricks to his therapist, and the passive victim who wished to be hypnotized by his therapist.

The problems that Dennis experienced are not unusual. His referral was due to the intensity of his preoccupations and his inability to adequately resolve his phase-appropriate conflicts. As his development was impeded, therapy was recommended.

His need for therapy was in large part the result of much earlier experiences in which he had inadequate role models. His school experiences were crucial, as it seems likely that without the increasing turmoil with his peers, and the frequent recommendations of his teachers, Dennis would not have received therapeutic help.

My description of the neurotic youngsters highlights the typical fantasies of preadolescence, revealing concerns about what kind of a man or woman, or what bisexual mixture, one may be, despite a definite sense of gender. There are concerns about masturbation and associated fantasies including ideas of damage and defectiveness. There are issues of shame, humiliation, aggression, guilt, and sadomasochistic sexual fantasies. There are concerns about one's future body configuration and confusion of body image. There are admixtures of interest in penises and breasts and defenses against such interests. There are concerns about active and passive sexual aim and how this is expressed in being masculine or feminine.

NOTES TO CHAPTER EIGHT

1. Helene Deutsch, *Psychology of Women* 1 (New York: Grune and Stratton, 1944).
2. Peter Blos, *The Young Adolescent* (New York: Free Press, 1970).

Chapter Nine

Eroticism in Childhood:
A Sociological Perspective

Floyd M. Martinson, Ph.D.*

We are grateful to Freud for his pioneering insights into infant and child sexuality, recognizing that his conclusions were based on psychoanalytic investigations and that these need to be amplified by studies in other disciplines, including sociology.

A social theory of psychosexual development would hold that the individual begins life with a biological capacity for sexual maturity and a psychosexual plasticity capable of developing along a variety of lines dependent upon the definition of social roles in his particular culture and community as well as upon his unique learning, especially during the formative period of life.[1] Such a truly psychosexual theory of development seems consistent with the empirical data.

Gentle, as opposed to violent, tactile stimulation is innately pleasurable in humans. In fact, the capacity to react reflexively to tactile stimulation is present prenatally, by about the eighth week of gestation.[2] Fetal movement is necessary to the development of bones and joints, but the fetus apparently moves as well for the sensual reason of making itself more comfortable in the uterus. The fetus is responsive to pressure and touch. Tickling the scalp and stroking the palm, for instance, elicit reactions. In fact, the areas from which cutaneous reflex can be obtained are very generalized in the fetus.[3] The fetus may also be experienced in autostimulation before birth. It is not uncommon to detect the fetus sucking its thumb, fingers, or toes. Hence habituation and perhaps even some sensate learning takes

---

*Professor of Sociology; Gustavus Adolphus College, St. Peter, Minn.

73

place before birth. So even before birth, the human infant begins to develop a system of tensional outlets.

This capacity for pleasant response to tactile stimulation continues throughout life. Given a favorable social climate in which to grow, there is no reason to posit anything but a straight-line developmental continuity in response to tactile stimulation from infancy to maturity. This is not to deny that we must not be led into "a too simple and excessively linear notion of development."[4] In a significant study of personality development of individuals over a period of years from childhood to early adulthood, Kagan and Moss[5] found that many of the behaviors exhibited by the child aged six to ten years of age, and a few aged three to six, were moderately good predictors of theoretically related behaviors during early childhood. Kagan and Moss interpret these findings to signify strong support for the popular notion that aspects of adult personality begin to take form during early childhood. We must hasten to add, however, that the degree of continuity of these response classes was intimately dependent upon its congruence with traditional standards for sex-role characteristics. When childhood behavior conflicts with sex-role standards, the relevant motive is more likely to find expression in theoretically consistent substitute behaviors that are socially more acceptable.

Since all normal persons are capable of responding to stimulation, it is not capacity that is problematical, but experience. Will the society grant newborns the privilege and provide the opportunities for continuous pleasurable stimulation? This cannot be assumed. Societies differ markedly, human beings are malleable in this regard, and sociocultural influences can interpret and modify biological influences.[6] Feeding, bathing, oiling, powdering, and transporting the infant give innumerable opportunities for closeness and stimulation in infancy. Perhaps no more than about one-third of American mothers nurse their babies, however, and one-fourth of these nurse for less than one month.[7]

So far we have been careful to restrict our definition of sexual stimulation to reflexive responses to tactile stimulation. But there comes a time of sexual awakening, a time when the individual not only becomes a person with self-awareness but also becomes eroticized, that is, becomes a person both personally aware of sensate satisfaction and motivated to seek again the experience or to expand and enhance the experience.

This sexual awakening is of several kinds, depending upon the object, and is of variable emergence depending in part, perhaps, on innate capacity of the given individual and in part on experience. Autoerotic awakening takes place when the person is aware of the

capacity to tactilely stimulate self and when one has the volition to stimulate self. This is a major difference between genital play and masturbation.[8] Masturbation is more organized and volitional. Hence, random genital play is more characteristic of infancy, and masturbation is more characteristic of childhood. The second kind of sexual awakening, heteroerotic,[9] is sociosexual in nature. That is, rather than being stimulated by oneself, one is sexually stimulated by the touch, sight, or the thought of another person.

There may be no clear line between reflexive and erotic autoeroticism, however. Infants in the first year of life are not generally capable of the direct volitional behavior required for the masturbatory act, yet Kinsey records data on six infants under one year who were observed to masturbate.[10] It is not clear from Kinsey's data whether he is making the same distinction between genital play and masturbation that Spitz makes. Some adults can recall their autoerotic awakening even though it occurred at three years of age or younger. (All cases are from the author's files unless otherwise indicated.)

> The first time I can recall having a sexually pleasing sensation was when I was around three or four. I remember feeling very proud of what I had learned [how to masturbate] and the strange sensation it aroused.

Many at older ages will recall this autoerotic awakening.

> I [a boy] first masturbated at the age of seven, as far as I can remember. I had no idea of what I was doing or what it meant, but the feeling was terrific. In view of the fact that masturbation was so enjoyable, it served to make time pass rapidly. Therefore, before the crushing boredom of a second grade classroom would grip me, I would swing my legs under my desk in a fashion which would end in an orgasm. I knew not what I was doing, but I may have embarrassed a few teachers.

> I was first told about masturbation in a movie theater by one of my friends who said, "Man, I don't know how, but I was just rubbing and all of a sudden this great thing happened to me." It was considered the "great, new fad."

Spitz concluded from a small sample study of children in their first eighteen months of life that autoerotic activity, in the form of genital play, is an indicator of whether or not an infant is having adequate affectional encounters with others. The infant with adequate encounters is the infant who will engage in genital play.

As already pointed out, heteroerotic awakening involves the

consciousness that others play a part in the satisfying stimulation. Kinsey found that among three-year-olds, handling of their own genitals, cuddling, touching, and kissing others were common. Among four-year-olds there was kissing, some homosexual and heterosexual play, mild masturbation, cuddling with family members, touching, and tickling. On occasion a boy as young as five or six will experience an erection merely at the sight of or thought about a pretty girl. A six-year-old boy told his father: "When I see a pretty girl my penis gets so hard!"

A young man recalled

> having erections when I was seven or eight years old. All I really noticed about them was that they occurred when I thought about a young girl I felt romantically inclined toward. Also, they made it very difficult to roll over in bed. I never knew the purpose of the arousal, but I was aroused.

In the following description a five-year-old girl experienced this sexual satisfaction from looking at the picture of a nude boy.

> Whenever my girlfriends and I would look at books while playing, I would always choose the book *Little Black Sambo*. The picture I would refer to is that of the tiger chasing Sambo around the tree as he is melting into butter. The tiger has previously taken all of Sambo's clothes. The sight of the nude little boy's rear end is what excited me. . . . I would stare at the picture for quite some time getting a funny feeling the whole time . . . my body would tingle all over and my stomach would seem to have butterflies inside of it. I loved this new feeling and wanted to experience it over and over again.

Another girl reported a sexual "awakening" in an encounter with an older girl.

> When I was about seven years old, my eleven-year-old neighbor girlfriend and I would get together and play games which involved fondling and exploring each other's body . . a game that we played was referred to as "upper" and "lower" and this would include choosing one of the words and the other person would stimulate that portion of the body for about ten to fifteen minutes. This we did anywhere since it did not involve taking off our clothes, just placing the hand inside the clothing. By sexual contacts I had a release to strange feelings inside me and got much physical satisfaction when arms were holding me.

Overt sexual dreams have been described in childhood.

> Wild and confused dreams made me feel funny—just as if I had to urinate. The dreams included boys and girls kissing, and the funny feeling I got was

both distressing and exciting. I had no idea as to what the dreams meant, but I definitely realized that they pertained to sex."

Parent-child and brother-sister incestuous relationships can also be the source of sexual realization.

My brother is a year older than I am. We were very fond of each other. When I was in seventh grade we got very sexually involved. He told me all about sexual intercourse. Every day after school we would go to his room and talk and fondle one another.

The following description is a good example of how an "innocent" physical encounter for a preadolescent boy ushered in a whole new attitude toward girls.

My awakening came one day when my girl cousin, four years older than I, and I were wrestling on the couch. She was in control and I soon found myself underneath her and was ready to privately acknowledge defeat. Suddenly she started showering kisses on my face. I protested with shouting and vows that I wasn't going to stand for this situation any longer. She calmly said to be quiet or our parents would hear. This continued for about five or ten minutes and I found my aversions to being kissed gradually declining. We kissed with mutual consent perhaps five or six times with each kiss lasting about ten seconds. During the remainder of her visit I avoided her. I would have liked to go back to the couch and her, but I was afraid to do it. I guess I wasn't sure if I had done something wrong or not. I realized from that time on that I could never interact with a girl by treating her as a boy again. Mysteriously, I began to feel differently when I was around females than when I was near males. It was the first sexual encounter in which I was consciously aware of being a participant and having sexual feelings.

A distinct characteristic of the traditional American culture is its lack of permissiveness regarding sexual experiences in infancy and childhood. For example, Sears et al., tabulating mothers' reported evaluations of their reactions to sex play among children and the severity of the pressures brought to bear on children found that only 2 percent rated themselves as "entirely permissive."[11] However, an additional 14 percent reported that they had made no attempt to stop sex play when they encountered it. Sex is seldom treated as a strong and healthy force in the positive development of personality in the United States,[12] and only on occasion does a young person remember having received good grounding in sex from his parents during the childhood years.

The first time I remember my mother explaining anything to me I was no more than four or five years old, possibly right before or after my first

brother was born. The details are very vague now, but I do remember her talking about the egg from the mother and the sperm from the father and that there was a place in Mommy's body where Daddy's penis fitted into place and that was how the sperm and egg came together. Throughout my childhood all the body parts including the sexual organs and all the body functions were never referred to by substitute "baby talk" names.

When the child is old enough to clearly remember encounters with the mother regarding child sex play, the mother is frequently remembered for her negative injunctions, often coupled with unambiguous instructions: "That's terrible; don't let me ever catch you doing that again!" College students recalling their relationships with their mothers can recall such instances with striking frequency. The emotional overreaction of the mother is often a cause of wonderment and embarrassment to the child. On the other hand, children remember fondly cases in which the parent reacted calmly and with dignity. The following case is a case in point.

We stood rooted to the spot as she took in the scene, her surprise showing in her red face. Then she calmly told Johnny to put his pants back on and for both of us to come down for dessert. She seemed pleasant enough, but I felt very guilty and couldn't look at either her or my cousin the rest of the evening. Later that evening, after the guests had left, my mother came into the room and shut the door. I was afraid to face her, but she turned out to be very understanding, telling me that boys and girls were different, which of course I knew, and that adults and children alike tend to explore new things. Looking back, her approach to the subject seems especially good, in that she left me with the feeling that my cousin was not a naughty boy to be avoided, but simply someone who was curious about other people, which is a basic human trait. She also said that where we live it isn't proper to run around "bare naked."

Despite fairly careful surveillance by parents, children do find occasions for sexual encounters, albeit furtive and sporadic, and often accidental in nature. The following cases are not atypical.

My neighborhood environment has always been quite permissive which enabled me [a boy] the time and freedom to become the finest five-year-old doctor in my neighborhood. I clearly remember associating my penile erections with examination of the next door girl's anatomy.

I [a girl] encountered a sexual experience that was confusing at kindergarten age ... some afternoons we would meet and lock ourselves in a bedroom and take our pants off. We took turns lying on the bed and putting pennies, marbles, etc. between our labia. The other two liked to

pretend they were boys and used a pencil for a penis. As the ritual became old hat, it passed out of existence. I enjoyed the sexual manipulation, for it was stimulating.

In older childhood or preadolescence, exposure occasionally occurs as does touching and fondling, kissing, dancing, "making out" at parties in the home, and occasionally mutual masturbation and even attempts at coitus.

One day my cousin [boy, age twelve] whom I admired more than anyone in the whole world, and I [girl, age nine] were playing on the bed when everyone else was out. In the course of our play we began to explore each other's body and to manipulate each other's genitals. This made us both a little uneasy, so we quit after a while and went into the living room. Then one day we found ourselves playing in the basement on the bed. He asked me if I had ever been "fucked" before. I said no. Then he said that it was really important that every boy be able to say that he had "fucked" a girl and would it be all right to "fuck" me.

Though parental repression of child sexuality is a general pattern in the United States, there are at least a few communities of parents who openly accept sexual acts involving both parents and children. The following cases are from research conducted by Larry and Joanne Constantine.[13]

John and his co-spouse Mary [group married] were enjoying sexual intercourse when his nineteen-month-old daughter wandered into the room. She hadn't seen this before, and her father, realizing she might be upset, first started to panic and cover Mary with a pillow (all that was convenient). Then he realized how silly that was and just relaxed, smiling and talking calmly with his daughter. She wasn't a bit bothered and, in fact, wandered out of the room as casually as she had entered.

Dianna (age two-and-one-half): "Daddy, would you kiss my clitoris?" Casually, he responds, "Sure," bends over and gives her a light smack.
Dianna: "No, do it long like you do it to Mommy." The father reports he thought briefly about it and decided there was no harm in it. Dianna enjoyed it and later asked for a repeat performance.

Research I have been conducting, along with observations on childhood in Sweden, raises the question whether, *other things being satisfactory*, children are adversely affected by exposure to early sexual encounters, which often are cited as being traumatic (see pages 46-48).

Prescott and McKay have hypothesized that human societies

characterized by enrichment or impoverishment of the stimulation that comes from touch during the formative years of development might initiate predominantly peaceful or violent adult behavior.[14] In an ingenious, though at best partial, test of the hypothesis, these researchers examined published data on forty-nine societies. It was assumed that high physical intimate affection would be predictive of permissive and tolerant sexual behavior in adulthood and that low physical intimate affection would be predictive of punitive and repressive sexual behavior in adulthood. The data, however, did not indicate a significant relationship between early infant affection and later permissive sexuality.

Prescott and McKay returned to the data and asked if it could be possible that deprivation of affection imposed during the early formative years (denial of the right to premarital intercourse, for example) contributes to high adult violence despite the presence of high infant affection. An examination of seven societies that did not provide a high level of infant affection and yet had a record of low adult violence revealed that they were characterized by freely permitted premarital sexual behavior. Prescott and McKay suggest that the effect of early affectional deprivation is compensated for by adolescent affectional permissiveness.

According to Prescott and McKay, premarital sexual relations may constitute an effective prophylactic against later destructive and violent interpersonal behavior. With both early (infant) and later (adolescent) ages, when permissiveness or the lack of it were considered together, it was possible to accurately predict adult interpersonal behavior in forty-seven of the forty-nine societies studied. Prescott and McKay conclude that these data offer compelling validation for the effects of affectional enrichment or deprivation on human behavior and indicate that a two-stage developmental theory of affectional stimulation, the first in infancy and the second in adolescence, is necessary to accurately account for the development and expression of peaceful or destructively violent interpersonal behavior in adulthood.

Prescott has also hypothesized that it is reasonable to assume that affectional deprivation can have neurobiological consequences that are produced by the absence of physical touching.[15] Neurostructural, neurochemical, and neuroelectrical measurements document abnormal development and functions of the sensory system resulting from sensory deprivation during formative periods, at least in rats. Studies of rats have shown significant increase in cell numbers in the cerebellum of handled against nonhandled rats. Human infants deprived of touch—holding, caressing, fondling—exhibit more than

their share of violent-aggressive behavior and social-emotional disorders in later years as well.[16]

To return to my central question, more and more authorities on child development are accepting intimate and even sexual encounters as a normal and perhaps conducive part of the maturational process.[17] Frustration or the withholding of positive reinforcement of infancy needs including sexual activity may result in an increase rather than a decrease in the motivation to satisfy such needs.[18] From this view it is the repressive rather than the permissive parents who contribute most to the high level of personal interest in sex and the high sexual-erotic content of our culture.

There is extensive research evidence demonstrating that responsible behavior can be readily elicited if appropriate models are provided. If a child is exposed to a variety of models, he may select one as a primary source for his behavior patterns, but he rarely confines his imitation to only one model. Children can *learn* to discriminate the circumstances under which various kinds of affectional and sexual behavior are responsible and appropriate. The elements of secrecy, repression, anxiety, and isolated negative encounters with adults create sociosexual attitudes, as do positive experiences. Whatever pattern of sexual life has developed early in childhood, it is regulative and difficult to change in later life.

In conclusion, I should like to ask: Should we be less permissive so as to avoid eroticizing the child at too early an age? My investigations and my view of the existing cross-cultural studies encourage me to opt for more rather than less affectional-intimate encounters even at the risk of early eroticization of the child, a view that is at variance with the psychoanalytic position as I understand it. I suspect, other things being in balance, that the rewards of affectional intimacy outweigh the dangers of early eroticization. The normal child can accept and live with his eroticism.

NOTES TO CHAPTER NINE

1. Daniel G. Brown and David B. Lynn, Human Sexual Development: An Outline of Components and Concepts, *Journal of Marriage and The Family* 28, May, 1966, 155-162.

2. A.W. Liley, The Foetus as a Personality, *Australian and New Zealand Journal of Psychiatry* 6, 1972, 99-105.

3. Orthello R. Langworthy, Development of Behavior Patterns and Myelinization of the Nervous System in the Human Fetus and Infant, *Contributions to Embryology* 24, September, 1933, 1-57.

4. Personal correspondence with John H. Gagnon, 18 February 1974.

5. Jerome Kagan and Howard A. Moss, *Birth to Maturity* (New York: Wiley, 1962).

6. William Simon and John Gagnon, Psychosexual Development, *Transaction* 6, March, 1969, 9-17.

7. Prenatal-Postnatal Health Needs and Medical Care of Children, United States, Washington, D.C.: U.S. Dept. of Health, Education and Welfare, April, 1973.

8. René A. Spitz, Autoerotism: Some Empirical Findings and Hypotheses on Three of its Manifestations in the First Year of Life. *Psychoanalytic Study of the Child* 3-4, 1949, 85-120.

9. Alfred C. Kinsey, Wardell B. Pomeroy, and Clyde E. Martin, *Sexual Behavior in the Human Male* (Philadelphia: Saunders, 1948).

10. Alfred C. Kinsey, et al., *Sexual Behavior in the Human Female* (Philadelphia: Saunders, 1953).

11. Robert R. Sears, Eleanor E. Maccoby, and Harry Levin, *Patterns of Child Rearing* (Evanston, Ill.: Row, Peterson, 1957).

12. Margaret A. Ribble, *The Personality of the Young Child: An Introduction for Puzzled Parents* (New York: Columbia University Press, 1955).

13. From unpublished case materials provided by Larry Constantine, personal correspondence.

14. James W. Prescott and Cathy McKay, Human Affection, Violence and Sexuality: A Developmental and Cross-Cultural Perspective for Cross-Cultural Research, Philadelphia, February, 1973.

15. James W. Prescott, Developmental Neuropsychophysics, National Institute of United Health and Human Development, 1972.

16. James W. Prescott, A Developmental Neural-Behavioral Theory of Socialization, American Psychological Association Symposium, September 8, 1970.

17. Marshall Katzman, Early Sexual Trauma, *Sexual Behavior*, February, 1972, 13-17.

18. Albert Bandura and Richard H. Walters, *Social Learning and Personality Development* (New York: Holt, Rinehart and Winston, 1963).

Chapter Ten

Children's Development: Social Sex-Role and the Hetero-Homosexual Orientation

John P. DeCecco, Ph.D.* and
Michael G. Shively[†]

This chapter has a dual purpose: to describe the psycho-social conflicts that arise as children develop sexual identities, and to show how adult caretakers can help children resolve these conflicts in ways that integrate different expressions of social sex-role and sexual orientation. First we will define the components of sexual identity, describe their development, and describe the conflicts that inevitably arise among the components.

Sexual identity has four components: (1) biological sex, (2) gender identity, (3) social sex-role, and (4) sexual orientation. *Biological sex* is defined by chromosomal configuration and sex organs of the child. *Gender identity* refers to the child's basic conviction of being male or female. This conviction is not necessarily contingent upon the child's biological sex. *Social sex-role* refers to cultural stereotypes of masculinity and femininity. *Sexual orientation* refers to the individual's physical and affectional preference for other individuals.

This paper is primarily concerned with the last two components, social sex-role and sexual orientation. Social sex-role can be viewed as two independent continua of masculinity and femininity (Figure 10-1). Qualitatively children can be described as masculine, feminine,

*Professor of Psychology, San Francisco State University, and Director, Center for Homosexual Education, Evaluation and Research, †Co-investigator, Civil Liberties for Homosexuals Project, and Research Associate, Center for Homosexual Education, Evaluation and Research, San Francisco State University. We wish to thank Dr. Fred Minnigerode and Marcy Adelman for their helpful critiques and suggestions. The research to which we refer (DeCecco, et al.) is part of the project entitled, "Civil Liberties for Homosexual Men and Women," Grant No. 1-RO-1-MH-26740-01-SP, funded by NIMH.

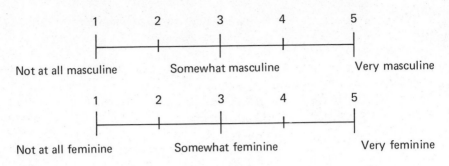

Figure 10-1.   Masculinity/Femininity Continua

or both masculine and feminine. Quantitatively, children can be described as having masculinity and femininity ranging from very much to very little. Individuals who are equally masculine and feminine have been described as psychologically androgynous.[1]

Sexual orientation can be viewed in two ways: as physical preference and as affectional preference. Physical preference refers to an individual's preference for male or female sexual partners. Affectional preference refers to an individual's emotional preference for male or female affectional partners.

Physical preference can be viewed as two independent continua of heterosexuality and homosexuality (Figure 10-2). For each individual there is one continuum for heterosexuality and another for homosexuality. Qualitatively, individuals can be seen as heterosexual, homosexual, or both. Quantitatively, individuals can be seen as having heterosexuality and homosexuality ranging from very much to very little.

Affectional preference, in similar fashion, can be viewed as two

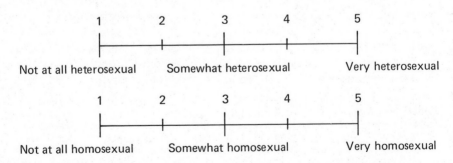

Figure 10-2.   Physical Preference, Heterosexuality/Homosexuality Continua.

independent continua of heterosexuality and homosexuality (Figure 10-3). Figure 10-3 shows the two continua and the relationship of one continuum to the other.

The distinction between physical and affectional preference is useful for two reasons. First, it can be used to conceptualize the great variety of ways in which sexual orientation is expressed. Second, it emphasizes that homosexuality and heterosexuality are not limited to physical expression and are not mutually exclusive.

Previous research on homosexuality has been based on a less analytic view of sexual orientation.[2] These investigations conceive of sexual orientation as bipolar (Figure 10-4). In this conception an individual expresses one sexual orientation at the expense of the other. Furthermore, they do not conceive of the two dimensions of sexual orientation, physical and affectional, as varying independently.

The bipolar conception of sexual orientation defines bisexuality as consisting of equal physical preference for both men and women.

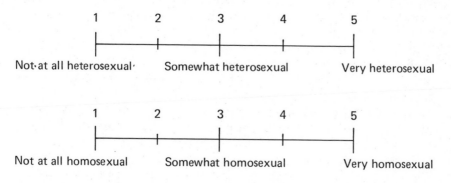

Figure 10-3. Affectional Preference, Heterosexuality/Homosexuality Continua.

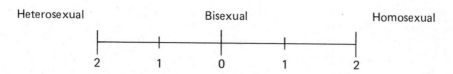

Figure 10-4. Bipolar Model of Sexual Orientation.

Our conception of sexual orientation provides many ways to operationalize bisexuality. In our research we are finding men and women who are physically attracted to one biological sex but are affectionally attracted to another.[3]

The developmental sequences of the components of sexual identity appear to overlap in time. Biological sex develops first and is determined at conception. Gender identity presumably occurs between one-and-one-half and four years of age.[4] Social sex-role and sexual orientation are believed to develop between the ages of three and seven years.[5]

While there are general patterns of development, considerable individual variation is observed. First, children vary in innate biological capacities. For example, they vary in the capacity to react to environmental stimulation. Some children react more positively than others to being held and touched by parents. Second, children vary in rate of development. Third, children vary in the vicissitudes of development they experience. Development combines both genetic capacity and individual experience. Conflicts inevitably arise because there is never a perfect match between capacity and experience.

With the four basic components we can generate six possible combinations of psychosocial conflicts that arise in developing a sexual identity. There are conflicts involving biological sex. There can be conflict between biological sex and gender identity. A biological-male child may develop the conviction that he is female. There can be conflict between biological sex and social sex-role. A biological-male child may act in ways considered feminine. There can be conflict between biological sex and sexual orientation. A biological female may physically prefer female sexual partners.

Gender identity can involve conflicts over issues other than biological sex. Conflicts can occur between gender identity and social sex-role. A male child may be seen as masculine even though he may see himself, perhaps secretly, as female. There can be conflict between gender identity and sexual orientation. A male child who believes that physical relations with another male make him female may experience this conflict when he fantasizes sexual experience with that male.

Conflicts can occur between social sex-role and sexual orientation. These conflicts arise when an individual who appears stereotypically masculine or feminine has a physical and affectional homosexual orientation. The popular belief, sometimes reflected in clinical literature, is that homosexual men do not appear masculine and that homosexual women do not appear feminine. The gay liberation movement has provided an opportunity for masculine men and

feminine women to publicly disclose their homosexuality. These disclosures have increased awareness that social sex-role and sexual orientation are distinct variables. Bieber confuses these variables when he assumes that homosexuality in men is necessarily expressed at the expense of masculinity. In our current research we have obtained evidence that very masculine men and very feminine women can be exclusively homosexual.[6]

The psychosocial conflicts that arise as children develop sexual identities have been described. We will now examine how adult caretakers can influence how children deal with these conflicts. They may impose on the child the norms for social sex-role and sexual orientation, or they may act as arbitrators.

Adult caretakers can act as arbitrators in conflicts between the child and social institutions. As arbitrators the adults occupy authority positions over both parties and hand down decisions binding on both parties. In our conception of arbitration, both parties may obtain gains and suffer losses. In the interest of social institutions, the child cannot be allowed to express every impulse experienced. In the interest of the child, social institutions cannot be allowed to entirely block the development of the child's individuality. The adult caretaker, as arbitrator, should balance the interests and set appropriate limits for both parties.

By imposing social norms adult caretakers may force the development of sexual identity without regard for the child's capacity or experience. This forcing may result in the development of some aspects of each component at the expense of other aspects. Some aspects may be overdeveloped while others are neglected. While none of the aspects of sexual identity is ultimately given up, what is underdeveloped may find expression in ways that are neither personally satisfying for the child nor socially useful.

Consider this example: the hypermasculine heterosexual adolescent boy may have been the child who, under the pressure of imposed norms, may fail to develop his femininity and homosexuality and force all personal expression into a rigid masculinity and heterosexuality. For this child the possible psychological costs may be the inability to express femininity as nurturance toward women and children and homosexuality as affection toward men. There are also identifiable costs to homosexuals and heterosexuals as groups.

First we will consider possible effects on homosexuals. The male homosexual subculture is characterized by heavy emphases on physical sexual activity and exaggerated expressions of masculinity and femininity. The emphasis on physical sexuality may result from the failure to develop their heterosexuality and the affectional aspect

of their homosexuality. The exaggerated expressions of either masculinity or femininity may curtail development of one aspect of social
sex-role and the integration of their femininity and masculinity.

There are possible costs in imposing standards of sexual identity
for heterosexuals. Heterosexuals as a group, are characterized by the
double standard of sexual behavior and the stereotyped expressions
of masculinity and femininity. The double standard allows men
expression of their physical sexuality in ways denied to women, such
as having many partners, frequent contact, and extramarital relations. Physical sexuality in women is either ignored or condoned
solely for childbearing. The preservation of the double standard may
be the result of the early neglect of their homosexuality. Heterosexuality which is limited to physical expression isolates heterosexual
men from other men, heterosexual women from other women, and
both groups from homosexuals.

Men forcing their femininity into masculine expression or women
forcing their masculinity into feminine expression result in the
preservation of social sex-role stereotypes. The forcing results in a
variety of blocks to the development and use of talents. In our
research on conflicts of homosexual and heterosexual couples we
found that men believed their conflicts were over issues of power,
and women believed their conflicts were over issues of dependency.[7]
Power is associated with socialized masculinity and dependency with
socialized femininity. To the extent that most adult caretakers
exhibit only these stereotypes, they provide children rigid models to
imitate.

By using arbitration, adult caretakers provide children the opportunity to develop all aspects of their sexual identities. The integration of these components, it is proposed, allows the child to become
a more resourceful and autonomous adult, more able to adapt to a
variety of social situations. Bem found that psychologically androgynous individuals are more generally adaptive to different situations.
We are also proposing that individuals who express heterosexuality
and homosexuality would be generally adaptive.

A girl who is physically and affectionally homosexual, for example, can integrate her homosexuality, heterosexuality, masculinity, and femininity in a variety of ways. Her homosexuality may be
physically and affectionally expressed in sexual and emotional
relationships with girls; her heterosexuality may be affectionally
expressed in close work and social relationships with boys. Her
masculinity may be expressed in assertiveness; her femininity may be
expressed with boys and girls at school and at home.

Since the women's liberation movement has enabled women to

participate in activities and groups formerly reserved exclusively for men, men are participating in activities and groups that were reserved exclusively for women. Just as the women's movement is changing traditional stereotypes of masculinity and femininity, the gay liberation movement has begun to change the stereotypes of sexual orientation. Homosexuality in boys and girls is still sacrificed so that children will conform to heterosexual social norms. New policies on homosexuality, however, are being enunciated by governments at all levels, by churches, and by professional organizations concerned with the welfare of children and adults.[8] These policies are now broadening social norms to include homosexuality. Clinical programs that attempt to modify feminine behavior in boys and masculine behavior in girls have been criticized.[9] Adult caretakers can now allow children to develop sexual identities that more fully integrate children's own expressions of masculinity, femininity, heterosexuality, and homosexuality. Instructional materials for children are beginning to have fewer sex-role stereotypes. Few schools, however, have attempted to modify the old social norms for sexual orientation.[10]

We have shown that adult caretakers do influence the development of children's sexual identities. By acting only as social agents, they may prevent children from developing aspects of sexual identity that are not acceptable to heterosexual institutions. By acting as arbitrators they can balance the interests of children with the interests of institutions.

NOTES TO CHAPTER TEN

1. S.L. Bem, The Measurement of Psychological Androgyny, *Journal of Consulting and Clinical Psychology* 42, 1974, 155-162.

2. E.g., A.C. Kinsey, et al., *Sexual Behavior in the Human Male* and *Sexual Behavior in the Human Female* (Philadelphia: Saunders, 1948, 1953); I. Bieber, et al., *Homosexuality—A Psychoanalytic Study of Male Homosexuals* (New York: Basic Books, 1962); I. Bieber, A Discussion of "Homosexuality: The Ethical Challenge," *J. of Consult. and Clin. Psych.* 44(2), 1976, 163-166.

3. Michael Shively, *Sexual Orientation Survey*, San Francisco State University, unpublished, 1976.

4. Richard Green, *Sexual Identity Conflict in Children and Adults* (New York: Basic Books, 1974); John Money and A. Ehrhardt, *Man and Woman, Boy and Girl* (Baltimore: Johns Hopkins, 1972).

5. Eleanor Maccoby, and C. Jacklin, *The Development of Sex Differences* (Stanford: Stanford University Press, 1974); Sigmund Freud, *Beyond the Pleasure Principle* (London: Hogarth Press, 1922); Sigmund Freud, Three Contributions to the Theory of Sex, in *The Basic Writings of Sigmund Freud*, ed., trans., by A.A. Brill (New York: Modern Library, 1938); Peter Blos, *On Adolescence: A Psychoanalytic Interpretation* (New York: Free Press, 1962).

✳ *Part II*

**Psychological Disturbances,
Family Disruptions, and
Alternative Styles—Their
Effects on Sexual and
Gender Development of
Young Children**

Chapter Eleven

Sexual Disturbances and Their Early Detection: The Role of the Educator

Philip M. Spielman, M.D.*

Early detection of sexual disturbances depends on an understanding of sexual behavior, feelings, and fantasies in childhood. Compared with the many studies of preschool or adolescent youngsters, there is a dearth of behavioral descriptions of normal and deviant sexual behavior in the school-age child (ages five to eleven). One likely explanation for this is the relative quiescence of sexuality in this "latency" period. While clinicians have long noted excessive sexual behavior and concerns in disturbed latency-age children, the variety of overt and covert expressions of sexuality in normal school-age children has been the subject of more recent studies.[1] An issue of special interest in this age group is the progressively earlier onset of puberty in girls, sometimes as early as nine or ten.

AN OVERVIEW OF OUR CURRENT UNDERSTANDING OF CHILDHOOD SEXUALITY

Though the existence of childhood sexuality is by now well established, it is useful to remember that it was an insight won against great resistance. We may still encounter this resistance in adults who insist that children have no such feelings and are in fact "innocent." When Freud's theories of childhood sexuality were mentioned at a meeting seventy years ago, a physician cried out that this was not a matter for a scientific convention but rather a matter for the police.

Erikson described the relatively invariant sequence of sociosexual

*Faculty, San Francisco Psychoanalytic Institute

development, proceeding through the now well-known psychoanalytic libidinal phases: oral, anal, phallic, oedipal, latency, prepuberty, and puberty.[2] It is against such a timetable, including the phase-specific manifestations of each libidinal phase, that we may judge the normality or deviance of sexual behavior. In addition to the clearer recognition that diminished sexuality during the school-age period does not mean an absence of sexual expression (we are just becoming familiar with the normal range of sexuality in this period), there are other considerations of importance in evaluating such children. These include the arrest of development so that latency is never really achieved and sexuality never brought under control for some children; the appreciation that there is a normal phase of early latency during which sexuality, though diminished, is still quite active (with typical latency not achieved until ages eight-and-a-half to nine); the occurrence of normally expectable regressions to earlier modes of sexual expression, particularly with stress; and finally, recognition that sexual disturbances may manifest themselves in nonsexual areas such as learning disorders and, conversely, that nonsexual disturbances may appear in sexual forms, as when a depressed, lonely, or frightened child resorts to or finds a sexual outlet for his distress. Sexual disturbances may be merely one striking aspect of a more serious personality disorder.

Studies of very young children and of serious adult sexual disturbances, particularly the perversions, demonstrate that sexual awareness, sexual conflict, and the formation of gender identity occur much earlier than we had thought, for example, before the phallic or oedipal phases, sometimes as early as the second year of life.[3] Also we have a much greater understanding of how the development of sexuality and gender identity is linked to subtle disturbances in the parent-child relationship. While the relationship to the mother remains paramount in early development, the study of the significance of fathers is coming into its own.[4] Among the implications of these findings for the school-age child are the possibilities for fairly well-established gender identity disturbances and sexual conflicts at this age, and the appreciation that manifest sexual disorders may really be but a facet of a more deeply set disturbance in the basic relationship between parent and child.

FACTORS DETERMINING THE EMERGENCE OF SEXUALITY IN THE SCHOOL SETTING

The child's past development may be reflected in the persistence of old sexual and gender disturbances, never resolved. Developmental

phase-specific behavior, including the normal expectable sexual behavior of the latency-age child, may also reveal the more overt expression of sexual feelings and anxieties of the early latency period. These may appear again as the child enters prepuberty. I have already noted the earlier onset of puberty in girls; the resulting unevenness in sexual development between girls may make for special behavior problems.

Cultural styles that prohibit or sanction certain forms of sexual expression are crucial to understanding how the child behaves at school. Acute stress within the home and family may precipitate brief periods of increased sexual interests and conflict. Such situations include illness in a child or parent, a death in the family, pregnancy, a new sibling, divorce, overstimulation (particularly when a child is unnecessarily exposed to nudity, parental intercourse, or sleeping with a parent), or when a child of divorced parents is preparing to stay with a separated parent over the weekend.

Group dynamic factors, including school experiences that are directly or indirectly stimulating to the child, must also be considered. Directly stimulating experiences may be the management of bathroom trips, the lack of safety in bathrooms, punishment procedures (particularly those that imply or effect physical punishment), teacher pregnancies, and the nature and degree of allowable physical contact between children and between children and adults. Indirectly stimulating behaviors include those that had no direct sexual meaning as such, but may be experienced by the child as sexual or may arouse sexual concerns. For example, fears of competition and injury in games and lack of appropriate adult supervision and protection may so compromise the child's inner feeling of safety as to force him to withdraw or regress to more childish modes of functioning. This may show up in silliness and various attempts to arouse others in a sexual way, as by poking or exhibiting buttocks and genitals, for example. It has also seemed to me that sexual excitement increases before weekends or vacations, possibly because of the stressful meaning of these periods to many children or because of the letdown in routine that typically occurs at such times.

DETECTION AND INTERVENTION

The acceptance by school personnel of the value and importance of evaluating sexual behavior in the school setting is of paramount importance. Problems arise when teachers can't acknowledge such behaviors, either for internal reasons or because they believe that the school administration would prefer that sexuality be ignored.

A variety of skills must be developed to evaluate the significance of the sexual behavior or problems in order that management be appropriate. For example, developmental phase-specific behaviors should either be tolerated or gently discouraged when they interfere with educational activities. Group dynamic factors contributing to excessive and disruptive sexual behavior may be dealt with by modifying school procedures. Problems arising from acute disturbances within the family or problems that represent long-standing sexual or personality disorders require consultation with the parents.

An essential aspect of the necessary skills is the development of an ability to consult with parents about a child's behavior. We all know how easily parental anxiety and guilt may be aroused by such consultations, yet it is only with effective interviewing techniques that the educator's job of detection can be moved to the next level of securing help for the child.

NOTES TO CHAPTER ELEVEN

1. C. Sarnoff, *Latency* (New York: Jason Aronson, 1976).

2. Erik Erikson, *Childhood and Society* (New York: Norton, 1950).

3. Herman Roiphe, On an Early Genital Phase, *Psychoanalytic Study of the Child* 23, 1968, 348-365; Richard Green, *Sexual Identity Conflict in Children and Adults* (New York: Basic Books, 1974); John Money and A.A. Ehrhardt, *Man and Woman, Boy and Girl* (Baltimore and London: Johns Hopkins, 1972); Robert Stoller, *Sex and Gender* (New York: Science House, 1968).

4. Ernest Abelin, The Role of the Father in the Separation-Individuation Process, in *Separation-Individuation, Essays in Honor of Margaret S. Mahler*, ed. by J.B. McDevitt and Calvin F. Settlage (New York: International Universities Press, 1971), 229-252.

Chapter Twelve

Atypical Sexual Identity:
The "Feminine" Boy
and the "Masculine" Girl

Richard Green, M.D.*

Three components of sexual identity reflect sequential developmental events. First is core-morphologic identity: "I am male" or "I am female." This primitive self-labeling probably occurs during the first year or two of life. Second is gender-role behavior, what our culture currently defines as "masculinity" and "femininity." These behaviors begin to manifest at around two or three years of age and are emphasized and more behaviorally dimorphic at five and six. Third is sexual partner preference, attraction to males, females, or both. This typically manifests itself during the teenage years, though earlier precursors may be evident.

With respect to sexual identity of children during grade-school years, there are parameters by which boys and girls of this age group, five through eleven, reveal their identity. It is seen in dress, peer-group companionship, toy preference, game and activity preference, and roles taken in fantasy play, such as when playing "house" or "mother-father" games. These are the behaviors by which our culture discriminates boys from girls.

Our research has focused on children who prefer the dress, toys, activities, and companionship of the other sex, who role-play as persons of the other sex, and who state their wish to be members of the other sex. They are contrasted with children whose development follows more typical sex-typed patterns. The children and their parents experience extensive research/clinical evaluation and are engaged in a longitudinal study.[1]

*Professor, Departments of Psychiatry, and Behavioral Science and Psychology, State University of New York at Stony Brook, Stony Brook, New York

These are the children we feel are more likely to show an atypical sexual identity during adulthood. However, we must keep in mind that the behaviors fall on a continuum and there are degrees of overlap on all parameters of gender-role behavior. Typical same-sex children differ from each other. Their behaviors fall along a spectrum. The points comprise a bell-shaped curve and there is considerable cross-sex overlap. Thus, for clinical evaluation, we must observe the intensity and duration of several behaviors to determine the degree of atypicality.

The boys in our sample began their cross-dressing, in three-fourths of the cases, by the fourth birthday. Female-type doll play also began during this period. Some boys, when feminine materials were not directly available, improvised costumes.

The cross-dressing in most of the children studied is at home, rather than in school. The concerns about "cross-dressing" emanate from neighbors or parents, not teachers. The same is true with respect to doll play. However, in school, roles selected in fantasy games such as "house" or "mother-father" offer significant clues if the role chosen is consistently that of the other sex.

Most clinically referred atypical children are male. In a clinical setting, one rarely sees "tomboys" sent for counseling concerns in the way that "sissies" are sent. The pejorative nature of the term "sissy" reveals how the culture regards feminine behavior in the male. The "tomboy" label is not pejorative, does not elicit peer-group rejection, does not usually elicit conflict in the child, and does not usually elicit parental concern. There is more support for considering "tomboyism" a "normal passing stage" than for "sissiness." Although there are more "tomboys" than "sissies," far fewer adult women request sex-change operations,[2] and the reported incidence of female homosexuality is about half that of the male.[3] However, a few "tomboys," at this time not clinically distinguishable, do not outgrow "tomboyism," but endure with an atypical sexual identity. When Saghir and Robins[4] studied fifty female homosexuals, they found that two-thirds reported being "tomboys" during their preadolescent years, and half remained "tomboys" into teenage. In their group of heterosexual women, none of the "tomboys" remained "tomboyish" into teenage. More recently, we have begun a longitudinal study of "tomboys." They are not clinically referred, but are paid volunteers.

The social and behavior problem one witnesses as the feminine boy progresses through grade school is the development of feminine gestures and mannerisms. This continues to set that child apart, results in greater peer-group teasing, ostracism, and labeling, and

drives him into a position of peer-group alienation.[a] This is destructive to self-image and causes significant social hardship at home and in school, perhaps resulting in academic underachievement.

An additional source of conflict for the feminine boy during school time may be locker-room/shower/physical-education class anxiety. There are children who experience considerable anxiety and embarrassment in taking showers with same-sex peers. This may be true for both males and females and is possibly related to concerns about same-sex arousal. Although arousal may be a more visible phenomenon for the male, it does not cause any less anxiety for the young adolescent female who finds herself aroused by females.

The peer group of the sexually atypical child is of the other sex. A provocative question is why a heterosocial peer group during the latency years typically leads to homosexual partner preference during adulthood, and a homosocial peer group during latency years to a later heterosexual partner preference.

Does research support the position that feminine behavior in grade-school males is correlated with later atypical sexual identity? A study of eighty-nine adult male homosexuals found that two-thirds described a female peer group during latency years, were called "sissy," and showed "girl-like behavior," including the wearing of women's clothes during childhood.[5] In a study of five hundred adult cross-dressers, half reported commencing cross-dressing prior to the teen years.[6] Most transsexuals report a lifelong pattern of cross-sex identity.[7] Thus, overlap exists for the childhood behaviors of the adult who is transsexual, transvestic, or homosexual.

Our culture and our educational system do not provide those children emerging with a same-sex partner preference much useful information. How are they to know that they are not the only persons in the universe with such an experience? Tragically, some emerge with a "freak" identity: "What's wrong with me? What's happening to me?"

Adolescents who continue with an extensively atypical identity, to the point of emerging as transsexuals, pose another school problem. They may refuse to attend high-school class unless allowed to enroll in the opposite sex role. This elicits major conflict within the family.

---

[a]It should be noted that the new greater social tolerance for less sex-stereotyped behaviors may be useful to some in this group. This is especially true for boys whose behavior has traditionally been stigmatized because they are not rough-and-tumble, aggressive boys. Traditionally these boys were ostracized and labeled by the male peer group as not fitting into the male sexual stereotype demanded, and perhaps pushed along a track of social deviancy. Often needlessly subjected to painful unhappiness, these children may be helped by the current change in culture which calls for more tolerance for a wider range of behaviors.

It is an exercise in education, both for parents and school authorities, to convince all parties involved that perhaps on a trial basis, the best course for this teenager is to do just what is requested: let the person live in the role in which he or she desires. Let the person find out whether it works. Doing the *reversible* before the *irreversible* can meet with success and avoid tragedy. It can also permit the continuation of formal education. Some teenagers return and say, "I was wrong"; others continue as transsexuals and do well.[8]

Another school sex "problem" often brought up by teachers is masturbation. I suggest that the *absence* of masturbation may be indicative of abnormality. When one inspects the data on nonhuman primates and human infants, masturbation is ubiquitous.

In a consideration of sexual disturbances during adulthood, I count two as being of greatest concern. One is the person with sexual dysfunction; the other is the sexual offender. Sexual dysfunctions are erectile failure and too-early ejaculation in the male, and dyspareunia and nonorgasmia in the female. Sexual offenders are rapists and pedophiliacs.

People who are sexually dysfunctional or who are sex offenders typically reveal that they came from the strictest sexual backgrounds, with little sexual permissiveness and little factual information about sexuality.[9] Teachers, parents, children, and the peer group share a responsibility to provide and obtain factual information, permit sexual expression to manifest as a natural human function, and to promote sexual health. This cannot occur in an atmosphere that labels masturbation a sin or sickness, and trains persons to experience guilt in association with a natural behavioral expression.

NOTES TO CHAPTER TWELVE

1. Richard Green, *Sexual Identity Conflict in Children and Adults* (New York: Basic Books; London: Gerald Duckworth, 1974); One-Hundred Ten Feminine and Masculine Boys: Behavioral Contrasts and Demographic Similarities, *Archives of Sexual Behavior* 5, 1976, 425-446.

2. Harry Benjamin, *The Transsexual Phenomenon* (New York: Julian Press, 1966).

3. A. Kinsey, W. Pomeroy, and C. Martin, *Sexual Behavior in the Human Male*, 1948; *Sexual Behavior in the Human Female*, 1953 (Philadelphia: Saunders).

4. Marcel Saghir and Eli Robins, *Male and Female Homosexuality* (Baltimore: Williams and Wilkins, 1973).

5. Saghir and Robins.

6. Virginia Prince and P. Bentler, Survey of 504 Cases of Transvestism, *Psychol. Rep.* 31, 1972, 903-917.

7. Richard Green and John Money, eds., *Transsexualism and Sex Reassignment* (Baltimore: Johns Hopkins, 1969).

8. L. Newman, Transsexualism in Adolescence, *Arch. Gen. Psychiat.* 23, 1970, 112-121.

9. Williams Masters and Virginia Johnson, *Human Sexual Inadequacy* (Boston: Little, Brown, 1970); Michael Goldstein and Harold Kant, *Pornography and Sexual Deviance* (Berkeley: University of California Press, 1973).

Chapter Thirteen

A Principal's Observations

Richard Baugh*

Although there have been extensive descriptions of the young child in school, we are just beginning to observe the primary and elementary school youngster in terms of his social and sexual identity.

Many of us, parents and teachers, are still unaware of problems in this area of development and are thus unable to help the troubled youngsters. Parents as well as teachers may still tell a young boy that his penis will fall off if he plays with himself, or may tell a young girl that a dragon fly will sew up her vagina if she exposes herself to others.

Children become interested in the differences between boys and girls at an early age. As a child becomes conscious of himself and others and expresses great curiosities about what he sees, he often will ask, "What is that?" pointing to the penis or "Where is yours?" pointing to the naked girl. Children are often curious about sexual intercourse because of their observations of animals and, many times, humans.

The world of little people is fantastic, rich in mysteries and adventures. It is truly an enlightening experience to teach and observe the small child in his private world. To illustrate this, I would like to tell you about a particular youngster whose progress I have been following for the past two years. He has hardly had a "normal growing pattern." His life has been one of utter confusion, mixed with apprehension as to who he is and what will happen to him next, and when. The youngster, Willie, still feels that at any time

*Former Assistant Principal, John Muir School, Berkeley.

something else could happen. His behavior hides his anger, fear, and frustration, perhaps about returning to the hospital or again becoming vitally ill.

He was originally referred to the school psychologist because he persisted in bringing pornographic pictures to school, although this seems to have been lost sight of amidst the total problems of this child's complex history.

At birth the doctor dropped Willie. At an early age the child developed a severe ear infection which resulted in meningitis. His parents didn't know that Willie couldn't hear until he was approximately three. In spite of ear surgery at that time, he continues to have a mild hearing loss, a factor in his speech problems, which include an extremely high-pitched voice. He has had speech therapy and some psychotherapy for the multiple emotional problems which he and his family present.

About a year ago, Willie fell thirty feet to some marble steps, receiving a hard glancing blow to his head, necessitating several days of intensive care in the hospital. He was out of school for weeks, and when he returned to us, there was still evidence of disturbance of his equilibrium and balance. His teacher noted a personality change as Willie became a risk-taker and a daring climber on the playground. He climbed to dangerous heights in the auditorium and on the play equipment.

Extensive psychological evaluation revealed that Willie operated within an average range of intellectual functioning, though his reading was at kindergarten level and his arithmetic was at the first-grade level. Most striking was Willie's extremely low frustration tolerance. His behavior ranged from destruction of objects and furniture to running away.

In the classroom Willie had much difficulty in responding to requests to perform academic tasks or to switch his attention from one task to another. He could not function productively in a large-group setting though he demonstrated a considerable fund of information and was generally curious about details.

Willie spent two years in kindergarten and though now finishing first grade, continues to function at the kindergarten level. He is distracted very easily and his gross motor coordination is poor.

With all this information, significantly, with all the people to whom Willie has been referred, there has been strikingly little discussion of any sexual problems.

My first contact with Willie as his principal came after a teacher confiscated some pornographic illustrations Willie was showing his friends. I asked Willie where he got his pictures. His initial answer

was "At home. In that guy's night table by the bed." When I asked him about the guy, he said, "My mother's husband, that's who." When I asked him, "Why do you call him 'guy'?" Willie responded, "He is not my real father." I asked him if his parents might know that he had such pictures and he said, "No, they'd really be mad and beat me." I asked Willie what he thought of the pictures, and he said, "They're okay, but I have better ones in my shirt." With that he pulled out a package of photographs, all of sexual situations.

Since this was his first encounter with me and his teacher concerning interest in the pornography, I asked him to take the material home and not bring it back to school again.

Our second meeting was two weeks later when a similar problem was reported. His teacher observed him with a ruler trying to poke two girls who passed his table. The teacher's note said, "Please hurry." On entering the classroom I observed Willie trying to penetrate the ruler between the legs of another girl, who, for a fleeting moment, thought it was all right until she noticed my approach and then started to yell at Willie to stop. Just before I placed my hand on Willie's arm, he quickly darted his hand under the girl's dress. There wasn't any embarrassment from Willie, but only his devilish grin as he walked with me to my office.

He revealed that he loved to feel the girls and watch them use the bathroom. He stated that his sister, a third-grader, always let him look at her using the bathroom. He also waited for his mother at times to observe her. He said that she only laughed at him and pushed the door "on his face." Willie complained, however, about the lack of response from the girls in playing his games. He said that girls were stupid, always cried, and ran all the time. He was angry because they always told the teacher on him.

The very next day Willie returned with more of his parents' pictures, showing them to some girls in the yard, who ran into my office to report that Willie had some pictures showing people doing "the pussy." This time I asked Willie's mother to come to school for an interview. I explained our observations and the difficulties. Willie's mother listened and responded, "I am newly married again and Willie is having some problems adjusting to his new father; Willie's teacher should not pressure him, but teach him and leave him alone. As for the pictures we will try to keep them locked up, and keep our bedroom door secure." When I questioned, "What do you mean 'secured'?" she answered, "Willie was standing by our bed one night and inquired as to what we were doing. This really unnerved my husband, and he kicked Willie in his side, out of anger and embarrassment." It is obvious that Willie had often observed his

parents in sexual intercourse, and he told me that the "guy" always hurt his mommy.

I find that frequently parents do not admit responsibility for their children's behavior, often insisting that it's "just kid stuff" or more frequently saying that they will do something, but secretly hoping that the problematic behavior will just go away. It is also true that when I discussed this with a number of teachers, most indicated that they would respond by ignoring it and certainly would be reluctant to discuss it with the parents.

Having curbed his photo displaying, Willie started to bring his sister's dolls to school. His second teacher stated he would bring the dolls to class and tell some of his classmates that the dolls were his mother. He would then proceed to punch the dolls in the stomach. I, of course, knew that the mother was pregnant. Willie said that he would not like his new brother or sister and that he didn't want any other children in the house.

Willie had a following of four boys who would usually meet in the boys' restroom. Their meeting was to indulge in some "restroom" games including:

1. Sword fighting: touching their penises together.
2. Peeing for distance: standing away from the urinal and seeing who could reach it.
3. Playing snowball: one boy would take a bowel movement and mold it into a round ball, at which point it was thrown against the wall or placed on a nearby bench.
4. Backstairs play: boys would meet in the stairwell and see who could urinate farthest down the steps.
5. Snatch the booty: boys would run up and grab a girl's rear end.
6. Humping: positioning behind a girl and gyrating, or moving in and out, usually called "Doing the Pussy."

The following semester brought some alleviation of Willie's difficulties because he was raising rats at home. As each was born he would kill it. He clearly didn't want any babies around the house. Willie was able to reverse some of this behavior because he began to raise the rats and sell them to the local science lab.

Let's look at some other examples of sexual activity at the primary-school level. There is a variety of "Doing the Pussy" activities in this elementary school. Often you will see girls and boys together with the girl on the ground "stomach or back up with the boy on top." Both are fully clothed, simulating intercourse. Sometimes this is done standing upright, facing each other and gyrating

together. It is very rare to see this sort of activity between children of the same sex.

As an example of sexual role confusion, I'll describe six-year-old David. He would sit at his teacher's feet during group meetings and run his hand up and down her calf while staring into space as if in a trance. On several occasions he would slowly zip and unzip her boots, while staring out of the window.

He was an extremely artistic boy, making various objects out of construction paper. He once made a "pocketbook" to carry, and one time a "flying nun's habit," which he began to wear. The teasing by the other children didn't seem to bother him, for he was a loner. His movements were quite effeminate, and he progressively dressed more frequently in womens' clothes, his favorites being dresses and high heels.

He was referred to me when he was discovered habitually crawling under the porch of the school to urinate. After much questioning, he explained that he was quite concerned about the size of his penis and afraid to use the school's urinals.

Girls frequently expose themselves. One girl would stand on the desk and quietly pull up her dress, inviting all to see her underneath after she had removed her underwear. This particular girl had a deck of "nudie" cards that she enjoyed bringing to school to shock her friends.

Girls often provoke boys to chase them into the girls' restroom; then they scream and accuse the boys of trying to peek and of hanging around their toilet.

If one spends time in such an elementary school, one realizes that it reflects the lives of these children who live in crowded conditions, exposed to pimps, hookers, and drug abuse. They all know about the fifth-, sixth- and seventh-grade boys and girls who are "hustling," and often their sisters and cousins are heavily involved in drugs. Generally their mothers have several male friends who come and go, and the adults openly indulge in sexual activities, seemingly unmindful that the children are around. The children tell of their pregnant sisters and speculate who the fathers might be. Often it becomes a joke to try to decide which man has "hung around the house most." They attempt to emulate the adult behavior they see, and yet it is striking that with all of the "humping" that we see, we've never noted an instance where clothing was removed. Nonetheless we know that at home when the parents are away, or in hidden places around the schoolyard, even second- and third-graders actually try intercourse.

※ *Chapter Fourteen*

From the Vantage of the School District's Intramural Mental Health Consultant

Harriette Block Wasser, M.A.*

Mental-health specialists in the community sometimes fail to recognize that there are personnel working in the schools who are also trained and experienced mental-health professionals. The school psychologist and the school social worker have the training of their counterparts working privately or in agencies, and in addition are knowledgeable about the school as a system. They are credentialed to work in schools, just as teachers receive state certification. Often they have worked in clinics prior to becoming interested in public schools. Many of them feel that working in the schools is an ideal way to reach the broader spectrum of the population.

The school psychologist, skilled in assessing children developmentally, emotionally, and educationally, is a diagnostician of learning problems, a trained consultant in planning special education programs and curriculum, and a resource in the design and implementation of evaluation programs. The school social worker is skilled in the organization and coordination of educational and community services, the resolution of educational problems arising from economic and cultural diversity, and the intricacies of school-community relationships. They function in a variety of ways, dependent upon their skills and the receptivity of the schools and their administrators. Both have training and experience in group dynamics, can function as consultants to teaching staff, and are available for in-service training programs. They are in an excellent position to understand, and at times overcome, the resistance of educators in

---

*School Psychologist, Berkeley Unified School District, Berkeley, Cal.

109

acknowledging child and family needs, as well as to facilitate referral to community resources.

An emerging role has been the "mental health quarterback,"[1] who relates to the school system as a whole, providing educative, consultive, supervisory, and resource functions rather than solely giving direct child services,[2] thus focusing on a preventive rather than a pathology model.

The school-based consultant can deal with parent, teacher, and student concerns. Consultation within the school may be on an individual basis or with a group focus. Sometimes the difficulty can be dealt with on a level that succeeds in keeping the youngster in school, the teachers in a supportive role, and the administrator, if not supportive, at least not punitive and/or undermining the ongoing work.[3]

The system itself places much stress on the school mental-health professional. It is often a dehumanizing giant that doesn't utilize its classified and certificated staff. Job insecurity is always a problem, with the school-based mental-health worker frequently finding himself in an isolated, sometimes hostile situation. Even with tenure, whole departments representing social services can be eliminated. And even when the job itself is not threatened, there is seldom support for the concept of mental health, although it is given lip service.

NOTES TO CHAPTER FOURTEEN

1. E.L. Cowan, Emergent Approaches to Mental Health Problems: An Overview and Directions for Future Work, in *Emergent Approaches to Mental Health Problems*, ed. by E.L. Cowan, E.A. Gardner, and M. Zax (New York: Appleton-Century-Crofts, 1967), 389-455.

2. E.L. Cowe and R.P. Lorion, Changing Roles for the School Mental Health Professional, *J. School Psychology* 14, 1976, 131-138.

3. Nicholas F. Rayder, John C. Larson, and Allan I. Abrams, *The Effect of Socio-Contextual Variables on Child Achievement*, unpublished, 1976.

Chapter Fifteen

The Effects of Family Disruption on Sexual and Gender Development

Charles Walton, M.D.*

Life is a process of change and development, a series of disruptions the successful surmounting of which leads to growth. Although they are inevitable, disruptions and changes of too great a degree or of the wrong kind at the wrong stage can be disastrous to the normal development or even the survival of a child. Recent studies have shown, for example, that several life-change events of almost any kind, from a death in the family to a changed job or residence, if too intense and too compacted into a short period of time, may result in actual physical illness.[1]

It appears that in general, a child's gender identity, gender role, and psychosexual maturation are likely to develop best in a relatively stable, predictable, enduring relationship with caring "good enough" parents of both sexes. Changes and disruptions of this environment or losses of significant persons from it at any stage of the child's development may seriously interfere with normal development.

Family disruptions and losses may affect almost any aspect of a child's development. A child's reactions to any event depend upon many factors, including gender, age, and the particular phase of development he or she is in, as well as particular adaptive strengths and weaknesses, the personalities of the parents, and the nature of their relationships with the child. Some effects on the sexual and gender development may be indirect, as in a reduced drive or generalized inhibition of activity or aggressiveness, or in a tendency

*Faculty, Extension Division, San Francisco Psychoanalytic Institute.

to avoid all kinds of close relationships with other people, while some disruptions may affect specific sexual development by, for example, interfering with normal sexual role identification.

The specific ways in which the child experiences this disruption or loss depend on his or her cognitive developmental level, how he or she comprehends the event, and on the particular stage of psychosexual and psychosocial development, which determines what the disruption or lost person means emotionally to the child.

Disruptions have two major characteristics, both involving loss to some extent. The first characteristic is the change or loss of familiar patterns of life. Even a move from one house or neighborhood to another produces a disruptive effect in children and adults—disturbed sleeping patterns, anxieties, various regressions in development—any of which may occur temporarily even under the best-managed circumstances. These effects are very often minimized if parents are themselves not too disturbed or anxious about the changes and are able to continue to be comfortably confident in their behavior. A degree of parental equanimity in the face of change may be the key to ameliorating the bad effects of disruption and change.

A second and usually more profound aspect of disruption, however, is the loss of people to whom the child has an emotional attachment. Loss may be by physical separation, as in divorce or prolonged hospitalization, by death, or by marked change in a parent's behavior, as in depression or psychological withdrawal.

Childhood mourning and depression as a reaction to loss produce a general disturbance of development and thus may indirectly affect sexual and gender development. Although children react intensely to the loss of a significant person from their lives, it appears that they are unable to complete a normal mourning process due to their developmental immaturity. Bowlby and others have described in children responding to loss a sequence of behaviors in which there is a protest phase, a phase of despair, and then a phase of detachment. The subsequent effects of this kind of experience may be profound.[2]

Childhood depression may be totally overlooked by teachers, parents, and others, especially if the child is in the protest phase. The child may seem a behavior problem or to have developed a school phobia. In the protest phase, the child refuses to accept the loss or disappearance of the parent and cries, fights, struggles, and demands the reappearance of the parent. In the detachment phase, the third stage of this process, the child seems to be daydreaming, inattentive, unmotivated, or even contrary. In fact, the child lacks the energy to pay attention or to be involved.

In the second phase of this childhood mourning process, the phase

of despair, the child may appear sad; this is easier for the adult to understand, and therefore the adult is more likely to be responsive.

One of the severe results of childhood loss of important adult relationships is that the response to a subsequent loss, however slight, may be as severe as if it were a repetition of the original event, although occurring many years later. Toman observed that individuals who have suffered losses of parents in childhood often attach themselves to unsuitable partners who have also suffered losses and are similarly suffering from unresolved grief for a lost attachment.[3] He believes that parental loss in childhood causes some adults to continually repeat the loss experience. They are attracted to people whom they will lose, almost as if reenacting or trying to master the trauma.

Disruption or loss of significant relationships in infancy and the first two years of life may interfere with the smooth development of gender identity, which is firmly established by the end of this period, because of drastic changes or discontinuities in the experiences that contribute to the sense of gender identity. In addition, disruptions and losses during this period may interfere with the development of the early tie to the mother and may thus interfere with the future ability to trust or feel safely close to another person. Or the child may be deprived of experiences of being dependably cared for and gratified in his or her needs to be held, cuddled, satisfied, and sensually gratified. Such interruption and deprivation may interfere with the future adult's ability to give or to enjoy such experiences in relationships with others.

The loss of a parent in the years after infancy often, if not always, causes a child to feel guilty for his rageful, destructive, envious, or competitive feelings. It is often as if the child believes the disappearance is caused by the power of his feelings, and ensuing deprivation or suffering are accepted or even sought as just punishments.

Attitudes about gender roles or attitudes about sexual roles are likely to be severely affected by disruption in the ages of three to six years. A study by McDermott on parental divorce and early childhood described a tendency in some children to identify with the more extreme character traits of the parent with whom the child was identified at the time of the loss.[4] For example, some little girls became extremely serious and acted like pseudomature sad little mothers, while some boys imitated an aggressive, domineering, blustering adult male. This premature adoption of an imitative identification with behavior of a parent may in some children seriously interfere with the development later of the complete normal identification.

When losses occur after the age of three, the lost parent is most likely to be experienced as a rival or as a loved person to be won or held on to. Since the child has an emotional attachment to both parents, the experience, for example, of winning the love of the mother exclusively for himself or herself will be accompanied by feelings of guilt and grief for the loss of the love of the other parent, as well as sometimes fear of retribution and punishment. The complex fantasies and feelings produced in the child by the loss of the parent in this stage of development may affect his future sexual and love relationships. It is quite common for a man or woman to consciously or unconsciously anticipate that his or her own love relationship or marriage will break up in the same way each imagined his or her own parents' relationship was disrupted.

Some kinds of disruption may be beneficial, as when a benign, loving person enters a child's life or an excessively malevolent or destructive caretaker is eliminated. Yet even beneficial changes are not without their complexities. For example, suppose a mother and child are afflicted with a father and husband who hates both of them, stays away, comes home only to beat them up, and doesn't support them. The mother finds a loving, caretaking husband who loves both her and the child; he moves in and begins to take care of them. Although this change would undoubtedly be extremely beneficial to both mother and child, a boy of four or five might very well feel that he had finally gotten rid of his father, and that he had the power to remove him and destroy him. Such a boy might be left with a feeling of guilt and fear of his own aggressive impulses and wishes. At the same time he might experience his mother's devotion of love and attention to this new man in her life as a deprivation and perhaps as a punishment. In other words, even though it might in the long run be beneficial to the little boy to have a loving father substituting for a bad father, he might still suffer considerable conflict over it, to the extent that he saw his original or substitute father as a rival or his mother as a loved person to be won.

Similar conflicts are frequently seen with girls. When a mother leaves the household for one reason or another, many girls from the age of three on to puberty enjoy fantasies of being wives to their fathers, but it is only an enjoyable fantasy if safely within the context that the mother is really the wife. Experiences such as these may jeopardize future love relationships for both men and women who fear the same fate as their parents suffered, sometimes as a punishment, sometimes because of identification with the parent.

In summary, disruption and change, however beneficial, risk interference with the normal development of gender identity, sexual

identifications, and love relationships. The less anxious and desperate the caretakers are, the less danger of bad effect or the greater possibility that the bad effects will be ameliorated. If the remaining parent or whoever is involved in caring for the child can provide this steady, supportive, relatively unanxious protection, then the negative effects may be minimized. Some problems related to the loss of a loved person can only be corrected if the lost person can be replaced soon by an adequate substitute.

NOTES TO CHAPTER FIFTEEN

1. Richard Rahe, Jack Mahan, and Arthur Ransom, Prediction of Near Future Health Changes from Subjects' Preceding Life Changes, *J. Psychosomat. Res.* 14, 1970, 401-406.

2. John Bowlby, Childhood Mourning and its Implications for Psychiatry, *Am. Journal of Psychiatry* 118, 1961, 481-498; John Bowlby, *Childhood Psychopathology.* ed. by Saul Harrison and John McDermott (New York: International Universities Press, 1972).

3. Walter Toman, *Family Constellation* (New York: Springer, 1961).

4. John C. McDermott, Parental Divorce in Early Childhood, *Am. J. Psychiat.* 124, April, 1968, 118-126.

Chapter Sixteen

Some Observations Regarding the Effects of Divorce in the Psychological Development of the Preschool Girl

Judith S. Wallerstein, M.S.W.*

The investigation of the effects of father absence on the psychological and social development of children has centered primarily on the study of boys in father-absent families. Many fewer studies have addressed or included the effect of father absence on little girls. The emphasis on boys has derived, in part, from a long-standing interest among social scientists in exploring causal links between a delinquent population that was largely male and the stresses of growing up in a fatherless household. Furthermore, from a psychological perspective, the primary psychological concern of researchers has been with the processes of continuity and disruption in same-sex imitation, modeling, and identification.

The results of several decades of these studies were summarized in 1970 by Herzog and Sudia in a comprehensive and by now classic review entitled "Boys in Fatherless Families."[1] Finding serious methodological flaws and limitations throughout the fifty-plus investigations which they examined, the authors concluded, in regard to findings that bear on the consolidation of masculine identity in these boys:

The evidence here is so fragmentary and so shakily based that it is difficult

*Lecturer, School of Social Welfare, University of California, Berkeley; Principal Investigator, Children of Divorce Project. This research has been supported since 1971 by the Zellerbach Family Fund. The project staff consisted of Mrs. Wallerstein, principal investigator; Joan B. Kelly, Ph.D., co-principal investigator; Angela Homme, Ph.D.; Doris Juvinall Schwarz, M.S.W.; Susannah Roy, M.S.W.; Janet West, M.S.W.

to achieve or to claim judicious perspective . . . our best efforts to analyze the studies and findings reviewed, with allowances for refraction through the lenses of the observers, yield a negative conclusion: that the evidence so far available offers no firm basis for assuming that boys who grow up in fatherless homes are more likely, as men, to suffer from inadequate masculine identity as a result of lacking a resident male model.[2]

Regarding studies that relate boys in fatherless households to juvenile delinquency, Herzog and Sudia stated:

It seems likely that even if all sources of bias were adequately controlled, including bias in apprehension and treatment of boys from low-income homes, these boys would be somewhat over-represented among juvenile delinquents. However, it also seems likely that the differences, if found, would be dwarfed by other differences, especially those relating to socio-economic status and to home climate.[3]

Although this highly critical evaluation of the conclusions yielded by so much work on father-absence is disappointing, it is not surprising. A great many unresolved conceptual and methodological problems attach to the investigation of father absence. For example, very little is known of the factors that mediate differences found between children with absent and present fathers, once such a finding is made. Furthermore, the problem of establishing adequate norms and the development of appropriate comparison groups for the assessment of findings is complex and worrisome. Hetherington *et al.* poke fun at the unrealistic models employed by the researchers for comparison with children from fatherless homes: "How can children, particularly boys, be expected to exhibit normal cognitive and social development or sexual typing or self-control if they don't have the field independent, quantitative, problem solving, instrumental, self-controlled, masculine model of the father to imitate?"[4] Moreover, father-absence is not a phenomenon that can be treated separately. The absence of a parent not only affects the direct models provided for the child and the relationships with the child, but has a ramifying influence on all aspects of family life, including at the very minimum the condition of the remaining parent, the sibship relationships, and the complex crisscrossing strands of social, economic, and psychological stress and gratification within the entire family. The absence of either parent profoundly influences the presence of other adults and the place and role of the extended-family members. And all of these multiple and shifting factors are brought into interaction with the idiosyncratic patterning and individual variation in each child's vulnerability and competence, as

well as with more generalizable factors relating to the age of the child, the timing, the circumstance, and the significance of the lost relationship.

Assessment of the effects of divorce on the child's development within a framework of father-absence or father-loss demands special caution from the observer. Divorce may represent loss to a very circumscribed or to a marked degree. Moreover, the pattern of the availability of the departed parent and his relationship to the growing child is subject to variation over time. In the only longitudinal studies reported regarding the effects of divorce on the parent-child relationship,[5] there is agreement that relationships between the father and the preschool child tended to improve in the year following the parental separation. Many fathers seemed able to generate less conflicted, more giving, more loving, and more gratifying relationships with their young children after the severance of the unhappy marital tie. It is also of considerable significance that the same studies report more deterioration and greater conflict in the postseparation relationship between the custodial mother and her preschool children. Some of these new difficulties in the parent-child relationship reflect the many pressures and demands on the single parent who has newly become the head of the family. These empirical findings that the relationship between the child and the parent who is present may deteriorate, and the relationship of the preschool child with the absent parent may indeed improve, bring a new and unexpected dimension to the investigation of the effects of divorce on the young child.

Only three studies have paid systematic attention to issues of sex difference in studying the response of young children to divorce.[6] McDermott recorded the changing school behaviors of sixteen nursery-school children at the time of the parental separation, as observed by teachers in a blind study.[7] In his admittedly small sample, he found significant differences between the boys' and the girls' reactions following the parental separation. Noting acute behavioral change in ten of the sixteen children observed, he grouped the responses of the changed children into three subgroups: eight children, including seven boys and one girl, whom he described as "sad, angry children"; two children, a boy and girl, whom he characterized as "lost and detached children"; and three children, all girls, whom he described as "pseudo adult and constricted." These little girls showed little general behavior change following the parental separation but became more constricted, querulous, and "bossy." McDermott was especially concerned at the constriction, the quarrelsome attitudes, and the pseudomaturity he observed in

these children as their way of dealing with divorce-engendered conflict and loss. He thought that these behaviors might augur major characterological change and "a premature, sudden, distorted freezing of personality traits."

In an ingenious experiment with seventy adolescent girls, Hetherington attempted to distinguish responses to men and women of girls from intact families, from divorced male-absent families, and from male-absent families in which the father had died. She found significant differences in the behavior of these three groups of adolescent girls with respect to male interviewers: girls whose mothers had been widowed appeared relatively shy, uncomfortable, and withdrawn with male interviewers; daughters of divorcees appeared more overtly flirtatious and seductive in their behaviors; whereas girls from intact families behaved in what appeared, by contrast, to be a relatively straightforward manner with the same male interviewers. These differences were exacerbated in youngsters who had lost their fathers before the age of five, both among the daughters of the divorcees and the daughters of the widows. Although these attitudes are suggestive of underlying personality and relationship differences, both along the dimensions of self-concept and relationship with the opposite sex, caution needs to be exercised in extrapolating from this adolescent behavior into adult life and adult relationships. The experimental findings, however, are strongly suggestive of fixation at early levels of development among the daughters of divorcees and a continuing restlessness, hunger, and somewhat driven search for the departed father or a replacement for him.

In 1971, Wallerstein and Kelly began a five-year clinical study of 131 children drawn from a normative population in northern California who were between two-and-a-half and eighteen at the time of the parental separation.[8] They reported significant age-related differences in response. Sexual differences in the response of children appeared in their study at approximately the age of four and seemed particularly striking in the kindergarten-age children, where the decline in functioning at a year following parental separation was most striking among the little girls. Of a total of fourteen children (nine boys and five girls) between five and six years old at the time of the parental separation, five children looked significantly worse at follow-up a year later by conservative clinical and developmental measures. These children showed troubled and symptomatic behaviors, including sleep disturbances, phobias, compulsive eating, aggressive outbursts, difficulties in peer relationships, and a driven seeking of physical contact and attention from adults in their environment. Of the five children who looked significantly worse at

follow-up, four were little girls. The composite psychological picture of these children which emerged at the year's mark was a prolonged intense investment in oedipal fantasies, diminished self-esteem, a general neediness and emotional hunger, and searching for contact with adults, sometimes almost at random. All of the more troubled little girls in this group also showed at the end of this first-year postseparation moderate to severe learning difficulties and inhibitions and poor peer relationships.

Ann is a little girl seen in this study whose behavior over the years that we followed her illustrates some of the particular responses of the little girls who seemed vulnerable and whose general behavior and functioning had deteriorated a year following the parental separation, as well as at the second follow-up mark four years after the separation. Ann illustrates particularly the use of fantasy to deny loss and grief, the extraordinary importance that these fantasies came to occupy in the lives of these children, and the almost real quality that attaches to these fantasy elaborations. Although these fantasies often occupy a considerable part of the child's energies, unfortunately they often fail to stave off the sadness, the sense of abandonment, and the accompanying low self-esteem that so many of these little girls experienced following the father's departure from the household. The intensity of the attachment to the absent father remains, if anything, more intense with the passage of time, as seen in many of these children. The infrequency of visits may, in fact, foster and encourage the increased romantic idealization of the departed father, which may consolidate and increase in importance with the passage of time. Finally, Ann's case significantly illustrates the frequent unavailability of the remaining parent to the child following the loss of the departed father. It may, indeed, be that divorce is followed not infrequently by a diminished capacity to parent or a diminished willingness to do so.

Ann was five years and two months old, the youngest of four daughters, when her parents separated. She came willingly to her initial interviews, where she presented herself as a pretty and well-developed child who was age-appropriate in her verbalization and in her play. She was considered to be achieving at age level in kindergarten, where she was well liked by friends and by her teachers. Her capacity to maintain her developmental achievement was particularly remarkable in that, prior to the divorce decision, her household had been in a frightening and sometimes violent turmoil. As the youngest child, Ann had enjoyed some protection. She was identified openly as her father's favorite child.

Although we saw Ann initially at a time when there was considerable agitation in her home, she greeted the interviewer with sweetness and charm and reached out very quickly to be hugged and kissed and held, at her request, on the interviewer's lap. She denied all sadness and worry in response to questions about her life, maintaining throughout an overly bright, cheerful surface and announcing gaily and loudly, "Everybody loves me." A number of indications of significant need to hold any inner distress, sadness, or anger under strict control were noted. For example, when the child was asked for her three wishes, she volunteered that she would like three masks—a funny face, a spider face, and an old witch's face.

A year later, at the first follow-up, when Ann was six years and two months old, we learned of a significant fantasy which, in the intervening year, the child had presented to her teacher in daily installments as an ongoing reality in her household. In these stories, Ann's mother had given birth to a new baby, and it had become the responsibility of Ann to help her mother in the care of this child. Ann described in minute detail how she and her mother regularly rose at midnight to minister tenderly and carefully to the crying baby. Toward the year's end, the teacher made a home visit and was startled to discover that the new baby was entirely the child's invention.

There are many meanings to this rich and poignant fantasy. Clearly, the unhappy child has represented herself in the newborn baby. The joint caretaking expresses the fantasy fulfillment of the child's unmet need for nurturance and care. Furthermore, the fantasy speaks of an addition to the family, and in so doing not only ingeniously obscures the loss of the father, but by adding to the family, undoes, reverses, and replaces the father's departure by providing for the arrival of the new baby. The fantasied good care of the baby is juxtaposed by the child against the real figure of the all too busy mother and represents the child's desperate effort to find and identify with the loving and caring mother and to deny the daily pain inflicted by the real mother who was, in reality, too preoccupied with her own needs to supervise the child's care. Finally, the fantasy of the new baby also represents the erotic age-appropriate longing for the father, and the fantasy of the oedipal child brings Ann and her departed father together.

The reality of the child's adjustment during the intervening year was one of increased difficulty in learning at school and gradual withdrawal from relationships with friends. Her teacher described her increasingly frozen, smiling façade and her driven, chattering monologues. During this same year, Ann's mother had reorganized her own

life, largely around her own postponed needs. Although Ann's mother was functioning reasonably well in a gratifying job, the central aspect of her life was an accelerated dating schedule with a great many boyfriends. The mother's hectic schedule hardly included time for the care of little Ann, and the child at age six was responsible for getting herself to school in the morning, as well as providing for her own meals and bedtime routines. Ann's father had, during this time, left for another city in the state, and although he maintained telephone contact, he had not visited at all during the intervening year.

It is important to point out that Ann used her fantasy resourcefully to make real contact with the real, concerned teacher, and in this way made an attempt to find a substitute parent and friend in the teacher, in order to cope with her own loneliness. Nevertheless, at the first year's follow-up, despite the teacher's warmth and genuine concern, the child was finding difficulty in maintaining herself at an age-appropriate level in school and with her peers and was showing increasingly what we have come to recognize as childhood depression.

Ann was seen by us again at age nine-and-a-half, at which time she appeared to be approximately twenty pounds overweight. Ann told our interviewer that she remembered very well coming to the office. She seemed happy to see the interviewer, and they sat companionably on the bed in the room in her house as she confessed that she hadn't done too well in school the previous year. She hoped to do better in the forthcoming year. She referred enthusiastically to her many friends and spoke rapidly of a variety of activities that engaged her attention regularly. Not unexpectedly, most of these achievements and relationships were fantasy. Ann was asked by our interviewer regarding the imaginary baby she had once described, and at first the child did not remember, and then she added quickly, "Oh yes, I made that up because I just hated being the youngest child in the family." She explained that her mother never went with her to any school activities and meetings and always offered as an excuse that she had already gone to these meetings with the older sisters. (The fantasy thus additionally was a way for the child to encourage the mother's interest and attendance at school and other places on her behalf.)

When asked about her father, Ann brought out a box containing all of the letters he had written to her during the past three years. These letters, possibly fifteen in number, were dog-eared, folded and refolded, and the interviewer couldn't help but be reminded of a precious collection of love letters that had been read and reread with tears. The father had actually visited only once in the past two years.

Her teacher, a gentle, soft-spoken man, expressed his concern for Ann. He found her lacking in self-confidence and low in self-esteem. "She doesn't believe she can succeed in anything. She's a grade level below in her reading, math, and language skills. She's so cooperative that if I told her to run through the wall I'm sure she'd try without any hesitation. She's always generally smiling. She is friendly, but harmless. She has a hard time reading, because the words don't make any sense to her." He added that he had never seen Ann show any anger.

There is little that is encouraging or heartening about this child's social or psychological condition. On the other hand, it is impossible to separate the child's neediness in regard to both of her parents from her suffering, which resulted from the loss of her beloved father. It is quite clear that the child's fantasy life and emotional preoccupation have crystalized around the father and seem fixated there. And it is not difficult to conjecture that the child's present and future development is severely burdened, and in fact imperiled, both by the loss of her father and by her mother's limitations in her capacity to parent.

The middle preschool group in our study included eleven children, five boys and six girls, who were approximately between three and four at the time of the parental separation. Children in this group seemed painfully bewildered by the departure of one parent. They became irritable, whiny, and tearful, and their aggressive behavior and fear of aggression increased. The central finding with this middle preschool group is that, although there was no overt family turmoil accompanying the divorce, nevertheless seven of the eleven children, five girls and two boys, were in obviously worse clinical condition at the time of the follow-up. Wendy was the one little girl in this group who seemed to be maintaining her good developmental pace when seen at follow-up a year after the initial assessment.

Responses similar in many ways to those of Ann, and particularly the use of fantasy denial to cope with the loss of the oedipal father, are also illustrated in some of the detailed interview material with Wendy, who was three-and-a-half years old when her parents separated. Nevertheless, the outcome is entirely different, and Wendy, unlike Ann, emerges intact and happy in our second follow-up, despite her undiminished hope that her father will return and her continued intense and idealized attachment to him. In this case, as in the case of Ann, one sees the effort to make use of fantasy denial to cope with the loss of the beloved and exciting oedipal father as the child soberly avows, in response to the father's absence, "Daddy sleeps in my bed every night." The very quick reaching out to the

strange examiner for comfort and affection is also reminiscent of Ann and reflects the little girl's neediness. There is a possibility that the behavior we have described as neediness in these little girls may be developmentally linked to the inappropriate flirtatiousness and seductive behavior that Hetherington found in her sample of adolescent girls from male-absent households.

Wendy, age three years and eight months when first seen, was at first shy but quickly made herself comfortable on the therapist's lap, saying, "You look like a mommy." First arranging the dollhouse family each in his own separate apartment, Wendy mentioned that her daddy lived in his apartment, and that she loved to go to visit him there. She followed this by placing the parents together, with the father's arm around the mother. Shifting quickly to animal play, Wendy expressed fear of the ferocious lion, reprimanding the therapist for accidentally placing the lamb beside the lion: "You shouldn't do that. He's scared stiff of the lion." To the therapist's inquiry, Wendy asserted, "He needs to sit on your lap." Asked if anything frightened her at home, Wendy replied, "Yes. There's a monster around my house that comes all the time." Asked what she would do when the monster comes, Wendy said, "Next time I'll run to your house." Wendy was reluctant to leave and tried to delay her departure at the end of each session.

In her second session during the initial examination, Wendy talked of being fearful of the wicked old witch who appeared after she scared the monster away. But she scared the witch away, too. While drawing her family, in response to the therapist's request, Wendy talked about her father. "Yes, I see him. He lives with me. He sleeps in my bed every night."

The examiner countered, "You wish he slept with you, and that he still lived at your house, don't you?"

Laughing, Wendy agreed. "Yes. But someday he really will. He promised me he would."

In the same interview, Wendy volunteered that her sister was a baby because she cried all the time. "She wants her daddy to come back home." In the third session, the examiner told Wendy that she had been talking to Wendy's daddy and had conveyed to him Wendy's wish that he would visit more often. Wendy said, "Don't say that. It makes me very sad."

"Why?"

"Because," said the child, "I don't get to see him very much."

In these sessions it is clear the child is struggling with concerns about her own vulnerability and about the protective and the threatening aspects of her parents and her relationships with each of

them. She has considerable difficulty, still, in separating reality from fantasy, and this differentiation is burdened by the divorce experience and her efforts to master the divorce, both cognitively and emotionally. Her sadness about her father's failure to visit appears in the guardedly disdainful description of her crying sister and emerges more clearly in the third session when the child confesses directly, "I don't see him very much."

A year later, at follow-up, fantasies regarding the father appeared in full force in our sessions with this child. Wendy, by then aged four years and ten months, greeted the interviewer by taking her hand immediately and spent most of the hour playing a lively and exciting fantasy game she called "Wait Till Your Daddy Gets Home." The story involved very simply a household full of people (dolls in the dollhouse), all of whom kiss, jump for joy, and dance around with gay abandon when the daddy doll comes home. Wendy volunteered that she sees her father a lot, "Because he loves us so much." Later she said that he would return to live with them when he, the father, was all very big and grown up. Noting a little ivory Buddha as she left, the child rubbed its tummy, making a secret wish which she confided to the therapist: that her father would return home.

The undiminished preoccupation of the child, the perhaps intensified hope and wish of the child for the return of the departed father could not be more clear than in this hour. Her statement that the father will return when he is all grown up mirrors the child's oedipal wish that she will be united with him when she grows into adulthood. It seems quite evident that whatever the child's outer behavior, that within her inner world a year after the parental separation, the child has not accepted the father's departure, nor the divorce.

It is important to note that during this intervening year, the child's fantasy was not fueled by the father's real behavior. Wendy's father visited infrequently and irregularly. He was clearly preoccupied with his own concerns, and his interest in Wendy and the other children was secondary. Her mother worked full time, as she had throughout the entire marriage. The children were cared for by an excellent live-in housekeeper, who was referred to on occasion as "Mommy."

At the year's mark, although Wendy missed her father a great deal, she was managing developmental milestones appropriately and, although sad, was nowise depressed. She provided us with an extraordinary view of the capacity of a preschool child to use vivid, intense fantasy to master loss and to remain faithful to a loving commitment to a father who hardly reciprocated. However, she did so without detriment to other aspects of her life. She entered school

at the appropriate time, did well, and was described by her teacher there as "a lovely, charming, delightful child, a good reader, outgoing, well liked, musical, and artistic."

Wendy was seen at age seven by the same interviewer. She appeared tall, mature, and full of fun. Gradually, she recalled her previous interviews as she played with the toys. She talked cheerfully of her mother's new boyfriend, whom she liked. She explained that she did not see her father enough and was disapproving of some of his conduct and of his many girlfriends. She referred with some humor and tolerance to her "kookie" dad. When asked for her three wishes at this time, she said: "I would like to see you a whole lot more; I would like to see my daddy a whole lot more; and I would like my mom and daddy to get married again." During this three-year intervening period, the mother had become a happier person; her health, her work, and her social life were much improved. She continued to work full time, building a very demanding career. The father maintained the same erratic relationship with his children that had been his pattern prior to the divorce and subsequent to the separation.

We lack, at the present time, sufficient knowledge and perhaps sufficient theory in order to distinguish the course and outcome of Ann from that of Wendy. And we are far from explaining, and very far from predicting, the effects of divorce on the long-term development of children, either in terms of their self-image or their identifications or their capacity for relationships. It is certainly possible to suggest a connecting link between the intense, erotic fantasy surrounding the departed father, the vigorous denial of his absence, the pervasive neediness and searching that both these little girls and other little girls of this age showed following the divorce, and the intense activation of yearning and erotic feelings that might well become central at the time of adolescence and could find reflection, behaviorally, in the maladroit seductive behaviors described by Hetherington.

Adolescence itself can provide these children with a second chance and another opportunity to develop a more realistic and straightforward assessment of themselves and their relationships with men and women. For all youngsters, adolescence carries the potential for new integrations and better resolutions prior to entry into adulthood and maturity. For some of these children, on the other hand, the fixation may remain in place or be reinforced by the vicissitudes of the adolescent experience. An unknown number of these children will require psychological intervention in order to unlock developmental processes. For both groups, it seems reasonable to suggest

that the clinging to the fantasy of the departed father and to the romantic expectation of his return can have both a positive and a negative impact on their femininity.

One major distinction between Wendy and Ann is the quality of the caretaking in their daily lives, as a separate dimension from the family disruption and the departure of their fathers. Both fathers were erratic, undependable, although not unloving figures after their departures. They both maintained some contact with their daughters. Both mothers worked full time and had their major emotional investments outside the home. Nevertheless, Wendy's housekeeper was a consistent figure from the child's infancy onward and remained with her as a constant caring person throughout the family disruption and afterwards. Unfortunately, this consistent care was not the good fortune of Ann. Whether the major distinction is to be found in the relationship of the primary caretaker and the organized routine of the one child's household, as compared with the disruption of the other; whether it can be found in individual variation in the children and differential response to stress; or whether it should be sought in the individual configurations of impulse, conflict, defenses, and available sublimations, we do not at this time know enough to separate confidently the central from the peripheral factors in the determination of long-term outcome.

NOTES TO CHAPTER SIXTEEN

1. Elizabeth Herzog and Cecelia E. Sudia, Boys in Fatherless Families, U.S. Dept. of Health, Education and Welfare, Office of Child Development, DHEW Publication No. (OCD) 72-33, Children's Bureau, reprinted 1971.

2. *Ibid.*, p. 62.

3. *Ibid.*, p. 61.

4. E. Mavis Hetherington, Martha Cox, and Roger Cox, Beyond Father Absence: Conceptualization of Effect of Divorce, Society for Research in Child Development, Denver, April, 1975.

5. E. Mavis Hetherington, Effects of Father Absence of Personality Development in Adolescent Daughters, *Developmental Psychology* 7(3), 1972, 313-326; Judith S. Wallerstein and Joan B. Kelly, The Effects of Parental Divorce: Experiences of the Preschool Child, *Journal of the Am. Academy of Child Psychiatry* 14(4) Autumn, 1975, 600-616.

6. Hetherington; John F. McDermott, Parental Divorce in Early Childhood, *Am. J. of Psychiat.* 124(10), April, 1968, 118-125; Wallerstein and Kelly, *op. cit.*, 1975.

7. McDermott.

8. Joan B. Kelly and Judith S. Wallerstein, The Effects of Parental Divorce: Experiences of the Child in Early Latency, *Am. J. of Orthopsychiat.* 46(1), January, 1976, 20-32; Judith Wallerstein and Joan Kelly, The Effects of Parental

Divorce: The Adolescent Experience, in *The Child in His Family; Children at a Psychiatric Risk* 3, ed. by E.J. Anthony and C. Koupernik (New York: Wiley, 1974); Wallerstein and Kelly, 1975; Judith Wallerstein and Joan Kelly, The Effects of Parental Divorce: Experiences of the Child in Later Latency, *Am. J. of Orthopsychiat.* 46(2), April, 1976, 256-269.

Chapter Seventeen

The Role of the Nursery-School or Day-Care Teacher with Young Children During Family Disruption

Millie Almy, Ph.D.*

Three major points require our attention:

1. The teacher often experiences considerable impact from the disruption or change in the child's life. Frequently, he or she bears the brunt of the child's concerns, and sometimes those of the parent as well.

2. Teachers and parents do many similar things for and with the child, but their roles are not completely interchangeable.

3. The teacher of young children needs emotional and intellectual support to do his or her job effectively. Such support becomes even more crucial when the children are experiencing change and disruption.

Any teacher who chose nursery-school or day-care-center work because he or she found young children appealing, pleasant to be with, and generally enjoyable has long since learned that young children can also be hostile, uncooperative, and even mean. Not all children who experience change and disruption express themselves in obnoxious ways; some, indeed, become passive and withdrawn, no trouble, but worrisome to a sensitive teacher. Others, with stronger inner reserves, continue to cope exceedingly well. What may appear to the teacher to be disruptive is not necessarily so perceived by the child or even the parent. Teachers have to distinguish between behavior upsetting to them and that upsetting to the child's family and/or culture.

When change and disruption are causing difficult behavior, the teacher faces a real challenge. Upset behavior is often contagious,

---

*Professor of Education, University of California, Berkeley.

especially when other children are also suffering from disruption. Unfortunately our notions of acceptable ratios of children to teachers often take little account of the characteristics, needs, and problems of the children being cared for. Many a teacher confronts a group that is unmanageable despite its "small" size.

If the group is reasonable in size and the number of children with special needs is not too great, the teacher is in a strategic position to help the child deal with his changing world. Provisions for play afford the child an opportunity to express and master hurts and confusions. At the same time the child's play helps the teacher to understand him and to plan for the child accordingly. In the setting of the school or center, which is less emotionally laden than the home, the child may raise questions that the teacher, with a perspective of other children and other homes, can help him to answer.

To serve the child effectively the teacher clearly needs a good understanding of the dynamics of child development and a strong sense of self. An integral part of a strong sense of self is *a clear understanding of the role of the teacher and the role of the parent*, how they are alike and how they differ. When young children are in day-care centers for long hours, their teachers assume many of the caretaking and instructing functions that traditionally belong to the parents. The difference between teacher and parent lies less in the functions they perform for the child than in the nature of the relationships they have with the child.

The tie between parent and child is characterized by an emotional intensity lacking in the teacher-child relationship. For the parents the child is, in a sense, an extension of them. The parent can never view the child with as much objectivity as the affectionate teacher. Also in different ways, the teacher inducts the child into the pleasure of learning about the world, learning to get along with peers and to deal with reality.

Failure to understand the differences in the two relationships and to recognize the priority and continuing significance of the parent-child relationship often leads to serious difficulty in the parent-teacher relationship. For example, the parent feels that the teacher is trying to take his place with the child, or the teacher tries to make up to the child for the lacks perceived in the parent.[a]

---

[a]Harriette Block Wasser, school psychologist in Berkeley, observed that the teacher generally finds it difficult to accept the less nurturant mother, even though a "friend" living within the child's milieu may become the child's true advocate, as might be the case where family disruption has occurred or where an alternative life style is being followed.

We know most about the rivalries that arise when the parent is the mother and the teacher a woman. I think, however, that the general principle of greater intensity and greater subjectivity on the part of the parent holds in any case. Furthermore, the teacher, whether male or female, is, or should be, constrained by the fact that his or her role in the life of the child is necessarily a temporary one. To attempt to build ties with the intensity of a parent, or to replace a parent, is to create for the child the inevitable disruption of another loss, for the tie must eventually be broken.

In addition to the rivalries that may arise when teachers and parents fail to differentiate their roles, the parent-teacher relationship is further complicated by the fact that teachers have all had parents, and parents have all had teachers. Accordingly, each may see in the other not the person he or she is, but the vestiges of some earlier relationship. The teacher may also be subject to the parents' hostility or anxiety, whether openly or covertly displayed.

Perhaps these misperceptions account, to some extent, for the fact that teachers do not always make parents feel comfortable in the nursery school or center. Granted, it takes a lot of planning and a lot of effort to create an atmosphere in which parents feel comfortable. How often, for example, does the center offer them a cup of coffee and a brief rest at the end of a long day or provide a pleasant place for them to share with other parents?

When the parent feels positively about the teacher and trusts him, the possibilities for a parent-teacher relationship that will be helpful to the child are greatly enhanced. Here again the teacher must understand and be clear about the limitations of the teacher role. The focus of that role is the development and well-being of the child, a focus shared with the parent. But the parent may seek more in the way of support, understanding, and personal help from the teacher than he is able to give. The teacher can and should be a good listener, but most teachers lack the counseling and therapeutic skills to deal with recurrent outpourings of parental feeling, particularly those only indirectly related to the child. Since teaching young children is in itself physically and emotionally demanding, it is a further demand on the teacher when he must cope with the emotional needs of parents who are upset and distraught.

I think the best situation for the child is where the parents and teachers see themselves as partners, with shared goals for the child, to whom each contributes in a specific way. When disruption and change in the life of the parent become unbearable so that the parent needs more than the reassurance of a concerned teacher, the teacher needs to recognize his own limitations and assist the parent in finding

appropriate help. It is essential to realize that the teacher of young children needs emotional and intellectual support if the job is to be done effectively. Peggy Daly Pizzo, in a penetrating analysis of the role of the teacher in child care, has pointed out that some women seek employment or further training today not only because they feel unfulfilled in the homemaker role, but because they find child care overwhelming.[1] Employment justifies their placing children in child care centers.

The child-care teacher has selected a profession that involves care for not one or two children, but rather a group of children. No one denies that in a well-equipped center most children quickly occupy themselves. There aren't the "no-nos" one finds in the home. Further, the presence of other children provides the teacher with a powerful reinforcement for acceptable behavior. Most children like being with other children and will conform to certain simple rules in order to maintain their place in the group. However, anyone in a child-care center knows that these general advantages of the group setting begin to wear thin after the children have been together four or five hours, to say nothing of eight or ten. Furthermore, if the center is a good one, the teacher is expected to provide some experiences that are educational.

Consider, then, the teacher's day. The job is physically demanding, with constant moving about, bending, lifting, kneeling, and squatting; and the job is emotionally demanding. Children don't mask their feelings, and the teacher must deal with love, affection, hostility, jealousy, rage, fear, anxiety, and sexuality, often in their naked forms. It is also intellectually demanding as the teacher attempts to recognize the way the children's thinking is qualitatively different from that of adults' and tries to see the world from the child's view.

Where are the gratifications? Most teachers would say that they enjoy watching the children's development and appreciate their affection. I submit that the satisfactions to be obtained with the children are not enough. If the teacher is to be warm and giving to both the children and the parents, he must be able to draw on a reservoir of inner good feeling. Ideally, the teacher is a person whose personal relationships are strong and satisfying. Unfortunately, the teacher, like parents, may also be experiencing disruption and change. It is important, therefore, that centers recognize the need all teachers have for emotional support from directors and from other teachers who know at first hand the demands of the job. Time must be found in the long day of child care to establish the team relationships that assure the teachers that they are not alone in either their problems or their triumphs.

The director and colleagues also provide essential intellectual stimulation. Though the teacher's job is intellectually demanding, it offers limited intellectual satisfaction. Teachers ruefully acknowledge that their conversation all too easily becomes geared to the level of the four-year-old. The educational experience the teacher provides the child is a reflection of the teacher's intellectual curiosity and interests. Although it is important for the teacher to *understand* the young child's thinking, I doubt anything very important happens in the classroom if the teacher does not think well beyond the child's level.

I have discussed some of the occupational hazards of being a teacher of young children, a complex role requiring continuing support. One might question whether the teacher's education and training provide adequate preparation. In fact, many individuals currently involved in child care and filling the teacher's role have had a minimum of preparation, for both nursery-school and child-care personnel tend to have less status and less pay than other teachers. Very often they move into these positions through circumstance rather than deliberate planning.

Even those teachers who have had a program of teacher education designed for early childhood probably have had less preparation for dealing with parents than other aspects of their work. I am not sure that this situation can easily be remedied. It seems likely that when one is learning to be a teacher, one's concern is mainly with the day-to-day realities of one's effectiveness with children. Perhaps it is only when one is comfortable in one's teaching that one can begin to be open to the needs of the parents. This is not to say that preservice education can ignore the teacher-parent relationship or, indeed, the relationship the teacher has with other adults. But it does suggest that preservice education alone is unlikely to be sufficient.

In summary, I think that nursery-school and child-care teachers are strategically placed to help children and parents deal with change and disruption. But we must not underestimate the responsibility that this adds to their already complex role, nor fail to provide additional support to them as they assume it.

NOTE TO CHAPTER SEVENTEEN

1. Peggy Daly Pizzo, *Operational Difficulties of Group Day Care* (Washington, D.C.: Day Care and Child Development Council of America, 1972).

✳ *Chapter Eighteen*

The Environment of Family Day Care

June Sale, M.S.W.*

Over 200,000 children in the state of California are receiving care in the home of nonrelatives for most of their waking day. This form of care is called family day care. It is an invisible, informal, neighborhood network which in fact provides the most integrated child-care program that exists in terms of culture, race, and socioeconomic background.

Family day care provides most of the out-of-home care for infants of working parents. It provides far more full-day child care than public and private day-care-center programs combined. It is the most flexible type of out-of-home care for children and their families, often providing for working hours that include swing shift, afternoon shift, and alternating working days. It is unrelated, for the most part, to most of the educational or welfare institutions that we know, other than the licensing process.

It is not connected to school districts, although more and more programs are becoming related. It is not babysitting. The adult-child ratio is usually 1:5, which includes the family-day-care mother's own children, up to the age of sixteen. Cross-age grouping is the rule rather than the exception.

Not only do family-day-care mothers provide quality care for children, but they also act as substitutes for the extended family or lonely, troubled, and alienated parents. The availability of a concerned family-day-care mother can be particularly significant during times of disruption. The stability of an established routine for the child can give needed security, as well as provide a parent support to

*Family Day Care Project; Pacific Oaks College, Pasadena.

handle his or her own trauma. In our observations in family day care, we have noticed a significant amount of family counseling. Family-day-care mothers, without any kind of professional orientation, give the kind of advice and assistance that one ideally would receive from a grandmother, older sister, or experienced friend. Whether it be with word or modeling, these exchanges may be viewed positively or negatively by the parents; however, there is no question about the care and concern involved by the family-day-care mothers. The advice may be rejected, but a standard, an idea, and/or a concern is provided.

Who are our family-day-care mothers, and what model are they assuming for the children and families for whom they provide needed child-care services? By and large, they are women who play a traditional role of staying at home and making their contribution by working with children. They represent a cross section of the United States. They are not in the vanguard of the women's movement, although in San Diego quite a few family-day-care mothers are members of NOW (National Organization of Women). They are the people who want law and order, who are against welfare fraud, who are worried about inflation. They may live in a poor middle-class neighborhood. They may be grandmothers or young women who want to stay at home with their own children and at the same time earn extra money. They usually have other means of support because they could not survive on money they earn through family day care. Family-day-care mothers generally assume all the duties of raising the child. They bottle feed and wean, change diapers and toilet train, provide tender care for a sick child, and sometimes take him or her to the doctor or dentist, or to get a new pair of shoes or a haircut. In other words, the basics of living, loving, and being are the threads that are woven into the eight- or ten-hour day that children spend away from their home. Needless to say, gender and sexual development is the warp that is ever present in this type of home environment for children away from home.

From the specific standpoint of sex and gender development, it is of interest to review a recent growth and development course designed by and for family-day-care mothers, offered by Pacific Oaks College. "X: A Fabulous Child's Story"[1] was read and discussed. This is a story of a child who was raised as neither a boy nor a girl, but as a healthy human being with no sex identity. The thrust of the article is that children are often forced into roles by adults because of their sex and therefore may not reach their intellectual, physical, and emotional potential.

It is of interest to review the discussion of the family-day-care

mothers. Questions were raised about the shoulds and should nots, dos and don'ts of sex-role assignments. The women wondered about the wisdom of expecting no tears from boys and many from girls. One mother said that she expected boys to wait their turn until the girls had theirs; the group questioned this practice. Another, an older woman, reported categorically that girls are toilet trained earlier than boys and that girls "come along faster." Most boys were encouraged to become involved in household chores such as washing dishes, cleaning, and vacuuming. Girls were involved with family-day-care fathers and fix-it routines, yard work, and car repairing as age appropriate. The family-day-care mothers were not too happy with the idea of girls playing football, but had no question about boys playing house and assuming the role of mother, at least for a brief time.

When we asked about what things they would do in the course of the day that their mothers would not have done, and what things they expected of male companions that their fathers would not have done, we found some interesting changes. Some of the family-day-care mothers who had been raised on farms reported that they shared many of the traditional male and female roles, i.e., women doing electrical repairs, men being responsible for changing and washing babies' diapers. The urban family-day-care mothers seemed to separate the duties in a much more traditional way. The husbands always did the electrical repairs and the women always cared for the babies' needs.

The implication of these attitudes for children of disrupted families makes increasingly clear the need for a good match in day care. Children in need of an open, permissive setting due to constraints and tensions at home might do well with a family-day-care mother who fosters creative, active, and problem-solving behavior; one who will permit the trying on of new roles. On the other hand, in a home situation that has few limits, a day-care arrangement with a family-day-care mother who understands the importance of boundaries may help a disruptive child develop self-discipline. Clarity in sexual roles may be comforting for this kind of child.

Another consideration in day care is length of day care. Children may be away from home for an eight-to-ten-hour day. A vulnerable child is made more vulnerable. When children are in crisis situations, the eight to ten hours away from home may be a mixed blessing. Away from the tension at home, the children may act out their anxieties, withdraw, or be just plain miserable. Family day care can be a comforting situation for such children, especially if there is communication between parents and family-day-care parents.

The crucial periods for such children seem to center around eating, sleeping, toileting, and discipline issues. Children find napping difficult during times of stress, and we have observed babies being rocked and cuddled, toddlers given a choice about where or when they want to sleep, and preschoolers permitted the privacy to daydream and rest quietly by themselves. In other words, these mothers intuitively allow the child to feel some control over his activities and body. Unlike some center settings we have observed, children don't have to keep their hands above blankets to prevent masturbation. Needed privacy is available in some homes, not all.

The need for individual attention, establishing sensible boundaries while allowing for regression during times of crisis for children and their families, is probably more easily possible in a family setting. Boys may cry, be whiny, and be cuddled. Girls may be angry, boisterous, and even sock a playmate without having shame or doubt being cast on their gender. The physical environment of a home gives distressed children all kinds of choices. Girls can climb trees. Boys can read quietly by themselves. In short, there are many natural opportunities to cross the traditional sexual role assignments without fear or anxiety.

A recent development in the early childhood field includes recruitment of young men into provider jobs with more direct work with young children, allowing for more male contact. This is considered particularly important with the increasing number of female heads of households. A recent study has shown that there are 500,000 women heads of households in the state of California now, with 1,500,000 children under the age of sixteen in this constellation.[2]

More young men are considering day-care jobs as a career, and, in fact, several male licensed family-day-care providers do exist. The future may, indeed, include more men in these positions, but the low pay and lack of status that seems reserved for women drive them into administrative or credential, tenured positions. A male presence seems to be of great importance to single women who are heads of households. They like having their children experience active male participation, including the presence of shaving utensils, pipes, tools, or a man leaving and coming home from work. Fortunately, studies of the natural networks of family day care have shown that there is a male presence in most households.[3]

Along with the greater involvement of more men in the care of children, there is also resentment. We found that it is often difficult to place male students in a practicum of family day care offered by Pacific Oaks College. Several women did not want to have a man in

charge of female day-care children. They did not think it was proper for a strange male to change the diapers and feed infant girls, toilet and change the clothes of toddler and preschool age girls. For cultural reasons, the Mexican-American families would not permit a male student in their homes. Generally, the older grandmotherly women were more reluctant to take male students into their homes. The question must still be raised among many working-class families, or many working families, "Would you want your daughter cared for by a male day care worker?" It would seem that despite much rhetoric to the contrary, we still live by the double standard. We can afford to be permissive with children, but openness narrows as boys become men. They are still suspect if they want to be a person who cares about young children.

I cannot overemphasize the potent role that parents have in shaping the direction in which family-day-care programs develop. Parents have the ultimate choice of the kind of day care program they wish, but parents need support in becoming aware of how to get what they want for their children and help in finding the right match. (The Child Care Switchboard in San Francisco, Bananas in Berkeley, and the Child Care Information Service in Pasadena provide such matching; however, there are few such services elsewhere in the country.)

In the area of sexual and gender development we must extend our knowledge, share it with parents and providers of day care, and listen attentively to learn from their on-the-line experience.

NOTES TO CHAPTER EIGHTEEN

1. Lois Gould, X: A Fabulous Child's Story, *Ms.*1(6), 1972, 74-76, 105-106.

2. Rita Gordon, personal communication from the Senate Office of Research, State of California.

3. June Sale, *"I'm Not Just a Babysitter,"* Pasadena, Calif.: Pacific Oaks College, 1971.

Chapter Nineteen

Alternative Family Patterns and Their Effects on Children's Sexual and Gender Development

Dorothy S. Huntington, Ph.D.*

A UNICEF report indicates that the major child rearing for half of the world's three-to-four-year-olds is being done by five-to-six-year olds.[1] Couple this with the fact that the divorce rate in the United States has increased as much in the past four years as it did in the entire previous decade, that there were sixty-three divorced persons in 1974 for every thousand married persons living with their spouses, compared with forty-seven in 1970 and thirty-five in 1960. During 1974, the divorce rate exceeded the highest level previously recorded in the United States, that of the immediate post-World War II period; the 1974 level of divorces is 109 percent greater than for 1962.[2] Divorces continue to increase: from January to September, 1975, 752,000 divorces were reported, 31,000 more than for the same period in 1974.[3] We are forced to think seriously about changes in our life styles that have occurred and that perhaps ought to occur in the future.

We have in the past held up as the ideal model for child rearing the isolated nuclear family consisting of two parents and 2.1 children. Father goes to work each morning, seeing little of the children; Mother stays home and cares for the house and children. The longer we hold to that model as our great American dream, and our only model, the longer we will be continuing our disservice to the real people who live in the real world of this country. Alternative life styles are a fact of life; Dr. Eiduson calls

*Child Development Specialist, Peninsula Hospital and Medical Center, Burlingame, California.

them emergent family styles and points out the rapid spread of ideas from these life styles to the "mainstream."

We need to consider some of the effects on children of being reared in varying life situations—to discuss some of the new norms for humans regardless of sex. One might ask what the optimal environment is for child development. Phrased this way, the question might seem to imply that there actually *is* one perfect environment for the fullest development of that mythical "perfect" child. Far from it; there is no *one* model of child development and no *one* "model" American child. We need to discuss the consequences of differing environments, of differing models. The questions might better be: Which environmental conditions enhance which kinds of development? What do you have to do to help children develop into the kinds of adults you want them to be? In addition, what are the differences between explicit goals—what we say we want—and implicit aims—what we really think is going to happen?

There is a multiplicity of goals for child development just as there is a multiplicity of ways of reaching those goals. Not only is there no *one* road to Rome, there is no *one* Rome.

Many so-called revolutions are occurring in this country now, and certainly the revolution in the care and rearing of our children is a major one. Perhaps some insights from other groups might give us some understanding of a way to go. We seem to need at this point to prepare our children for a new style of life, one in which they will be far more flexible and adaptable than ever before. Groups socialize their children for their special life circumstances; we must look at the totality of the experience in order to understand the adaptive meaning of the various behavior traits, in specific family forms, in specific communities. One of the basic questions is to what extent it is essential to a child's well-being that he be raised exclusively within the conventional setting of the nuclear family.

> All over the world infants are being cared for and reared in accordance with the traditional beliefs and practices of the cultural group to which they belong. What parents do to and for the infant, what they encourage or suppress, and how they induct the infant into their design for living inculturates and socializes the child and shapes his emerging personality for participation in group life. This expectation of what an infant should become and the insistent pressure to transform the infant and the child into the kind of personality which each group favors [is a fascinating field of study].[4]

It has long been held in American society that the mother-infant bond is of primary importance in the development of that child. No

one would deny this, but the question might be asked as to whether we have overemphasized it. Other people may be included in the family: the father, the grandparents, aunts, uncles, and other siblings. It is the women's movement position that "the heart of women's oppression is her child bearing and child rearing roles. . . . The power hierarchies in the biological family and the sexual repressions necessary to maintain it—especially intense in the patriarchal nuclear family—are destructive and costly to the individual psyche."[5] Further, the purpose of replacing the nuclear family with the extended or "organic" family is "to release the children from the disadvantages of being extensions of their parents so that they can belong primarily to themselves."[6]

"Although an occasional suggestion is made that it is a myth that the middle-class nuclear family is the only possible kind of family, and that perhaps child rearing is too complex for the individual small family unit to deal with, proposals of alternatives apparently evoke a kind of dread of tampering with the forces of nature."[7] It is in this context that people consider collective arrangements.

Behavioral scientists and clinicians, such as psychiatrists and pediatricians, encourage acceptance of the model in which the biological mother must provide the major portion of the stimulation, conditioning, and emotional satisfaction deemed essential for normal development of the child. Social scientists and clinicians have accepted as necessary and inevitable practices that are, in fact, culturally determined. It is suggested that changes in child rearing practices might reveal other methods to be biologically or socially more optimal for mother and infant, and more beneficial for promoting social change.[8]

Perhaps we can begin to evaluate the results in child development of different life situations.

NOTES TO CHAPTER NINETEEN

1. The Young Child: Approaches to Action in Developing Countries, United Nations Children's Fund, March 27, 1974.
2. National Center for Health Statistics, February 28, 1975.
3. National Center for Health Statistics, November 21, 1975.
4. Lawrence K. Frank, *On the Importance of Infancy* (New York: Random House, 1966).
5. Shulamitt Firestone, *The Dialectic of Sex* (New York: Bantam, 1970).
6. Germaine Greer, *The Female Eunuch* (New York: McGraw-Hill, 1971).
7. Zelda Klapper, The Impact of the Women's Liberation Movement on Child Development Books, *Amer. J. Orthopsychiat.* 41, 1971, 725-732.
8. Rochelle Wortis, The Acceptance of the Concept of the Maternal Role by

Behavioral Scientists: Its Effects on Women, *Amer. J. Orthopsychiat.* 41, 1971, 733-746.

✳ *Chapter Twenty*

Alternative Family Styles and Sex-Role Identity

Bernice T. Eiduson, Ph.D.*

One of the most interesting attempts to shape sexual attitudes and behavior of children in new and nontraditional ways has emerged as alternative life styles (single-parent families, living groups, social contracts, rather than legal marriages) have become part of the American culture.

These family forms emerged in the late 1960s and early 1970s as young people of parenting age looked for ways of living that expressed their humanistic orientation, their desires for closeness and intimacy, their desire to be at one with the environment—attitudes they considered no longer viable in the traditional nuclear family. They sought to replace the competitive strivings, disaffection, and alienation among individuals in mainstream society by more emotionally meaningful, warm, empathic relationships, in family forms that valued individual differences and gave each member the opportunity for creative self-fulfillment.

In line with this perspective was the issue of sex-role and gender identity. Some of the alternative families had actually emerged in response to the ideologies embodied by the women's movement. This

*Professor, Department of Psychiatry, University of California, Los Angeles. This work is supported in part by U.S.P.H.S. Grant NIMH I RO1 MH 24947-03, by Grant B-3694 from the Carnegie Corporation of New York, and by a Research Scientist Award K 05 MH 70541-04 from the National Institute of Health. The research is the work of the Family Styles Project, an interdisciplinary project, directed by the author as principal project investigator; Thomas S. Weisner, Ph.D., coprincipal project investigator; and senior investigators Jannette Alexander, M.S.W., Jerome Cohen, Ph.D., Max R. Mickey, Ph.D., and Irla Lee Zimmerman, Ph.D.

was the case for the young single mother who opted to keep her baby and become head of her household, and who was responding to the desire to have a child whether married or not, so that hers could be a complete feminine experience. The social-contract marriages similarly had been an outgrowth in some cases of men and women who had been interested in utilizing their marriage to fulfill the needs of each of the partners, with the woman being particularly motivated by the women's consciousness movement, which had suggested that child rearing and career could be combined, as the responsibilities of parenting became equally distributed between both parents.

In our pilot work[1] which served to identify and document parent values and behaviors in some of these families for our present systematic studies, we learned of some socialization practices likely to have important implications for sex-role and gender identity. For example, some of our alternative families expressed a preference for the words "parents" and "parenting," as opposed to "mothering" and "fathering" as a description of the interchangeable caretaking roles they preferred. A variety of multiple caretaking arrangements developed to permit fathers to share child responsibilities. These were aimed not only at presenting a sex egalitarian role perspective to the child, but also fostering an attitude of trust in other than the biological maternal parent.

We also found in informal pilot studies that sex-role equality and sharing is found in the two extremes, with little in between. For the most part there is a feeling that work, status, privilege, and responsibility ought to be equally distributed between the sexes in regard to all aspects of life. There is a breakdown of the stereotypical roles that parents have placed in regard to caring for their children. Fathers desire to participate more completely in the life of the child, in part because many are present a good deal more of the time than are traditional fathers working outside of the home area. Women seem concerned that they make a contribution toward family income whether it is a paycheck or a welfare check. This is a part of their inner feeling of equality as well as the actual expression of responsibility to contribute in a way that has traditionally been viewed as a function of the male role. It is also another way to break away from the patterns of the two-parent nuclear-family arrangements of differential responsibilities.

While aggression and violence are negated as ways to live, there is a general increase in the assertiveness that young children of both sexes are trained to articulate. In these families, assignment of passive-aggressive roles for males and females are consciously being recast. However, there are also alternative families in which there is a move

back toward a traditional sex-role differentiated life style. Examples of this orientation are to be found in both creedal and noncreedal living groups, as well as among members of the other alternative populations.

How do parents implement their values and attitudes around sex-role status in the formative childhood years? What is the impact on the socio-emotional development of the child of the changed parental behaviors influencing sex-role? Will alternative attitudes in this area make for identification problems as children grow older and are confronted with stereotypic cultural attitudes?

Seizing the opportunity for utilizing these naturalistically occurring experiments in family variations to study a number of such issues that have been raised in the child development literature, two hundred California children and their families were engaged as research participants in a longitudinal endeavor, with 150 children in specifically designed variations of the two-parent family, and fifty additional children in two-parent traditional families as a comparison group.

STRATEGY OF THE STUDY

All participants are Caucasian, whose families of origin are middle-class or stable working-class families. Minority groups have not participated to any extent in the alternative family movement.[a] Parents range in age from eighteen to thirty-five (mean age of mothers is 26.1 ± 3.85; fathers average 28.1 ± 3.9). They are compensated for their time and effort: five dollars for each interview, field visit, or assessment procedure, and the project pays eighty dollars a year toward each child's pediatric care. (The Pediatric Incentive Plan was developed both as a motivation for continuance in the project and to provide data about the use of organized medical services by alternatives. Many have espoused being opposed to organized medical and social services, whose practices reflect establishment attitudes. We were interested in knowing more about their patterns of health-service usage in regard to their children, and the

[a]The counterculture movement of the 1960s and 1970s was largely Caucasian. Minority families claim some prior experience with alternative family structures. However, their variations had been derived by default, rather than by choice, in the main. This situation encouraged their family variations to be perceived as deviances or deviations from the idealized nuclear unit. Only recently have the social and personal competencies attained by children who are reared in alternative families gained interest. In line with such interest, this project will attend to the competencies and adaptive skills, as well as the problems and conflicts, fostered by alternative child-rearing practices.

circumstances and symptoms under which prevailing perspectives about medicine might be cast aside. Thus the project pays the bill of the provider of services, once the latter has filled out an Encounter Form detailing such information.)

A multitrait, multimethod strategy is being utilized in conducting this large-scale longitudinal effort. Studies of the socialization processes in the child's family were initiated in the third trimester of the mother's pregnancy (and involved the father as well as the biological mother wherever possible); have been continued through the first two-and-one-half years of age; and it is hoped will be carried forward until the child has finished first grade. Assessments include studies of the family milieu—its physical, social, and functional aspects, using a variety of field and home observational techniques, as well as depth interviews and questionnaires.

Assessments of the child's physical, cognitive, and socio-emotional development beginning at birth were conducted and have continued at approximately six-month intervals. Standardized and semistandardized instruments have been administered at home and in project offices so that data on this population could be compared with data obtained in other populations in the current and past decades.

As part of the general strategy of this study, the child is the cohort-participant in the study, rather than his family or his living group. He is followed despite any changes in the family life styles. If his family life style changes, or moves geographically, such changes are noted and dated so data analyses can take account of such family changes. Numbers of moves or changes in life styles or in size of family thus become study data. Within the three family variations chosen, we tried to get as wide a range of family composition and structure as possible so that the child development issues of interest— such as multiple caretaking, fathering, sex-role egalitarianism—could be addressed with generality. Our position here was supported by our findings in the pilot work mentioned above that showed that there was no "typical" or representative commune or living group, or social-contract marriage or single-mother household.

Selected young women in the three alternative groups and in the controls were pregnant, preferably with their first child (though this proved not to be completely possible without increasing case selection longer than the one and a half years assigned to this task).

ANTICIPATORY SOCIALIZATION PRACTICES
AROUND SEX-ROLE

From the depth-interview data and field techniques (mapping, census, daily routines, and home observations) collected prior to the

child's birth, some of the parental attitudes and behaviors around sex-role and gender identity were explored. A number of questions were posed to fathers and mothers separately that related to their perspectives on sex-role egalitarianism, such as: preferences for a boy or a girl child; amount of involvement in caretaking; educational and vocational aspirations for the child; and attitudes toward sex-role typing and the women's movement. Responses to these questions plus data about household roles, functions, and responsibilities were also rated as a cluster variable for each parent, so that each could be scaled on the dimension: extent of sex-role egalitarianism. Subsequently actual child-rearing practices in regard to sex-role identity will be compared with ratings on this ideological stance, so that we can see how successfully our parents put their sex-role beliefs and attitudes into practice.

A few of the variables that showed statistically significant differences among our life-style groups have been singled out for presentation, more to show the trend of the data through the six-month period than to present final results. Collection and analysis of the six-month data are incomplete at this point, since a few babies are just reaching six months of age, while a few of our oldest children are approximately two-and-a-half.

Like many young adults today in traditional as well as the alternative groups, all of our mothers and fathers were determined to play down sex differences in their children. Most verbalized nonsexist orientations and planned to emphasize the fact to their children. Names for the anticipated child offer some change in thinking in terms of sex role. Some parents in alternative families, particularly living groups, gave children allegorical, symbolic, or religion-relevant names, so that it becomes impossible to tell from the name whether the child is a boy or a girl. A name specific to sex did not seem to be a relevant consideration.

The anticipated preference for a boy or a girl is usually based on personal, highly individual reasons. Some parents thought they would be more at ease or relate more easily with a child of one sex than the other. Traditional and experimental groups have shown no differences in this regard thus far. However, in line with conventional attitudes, traditional fathers preferred a boy in a larger (but not statistically significant) percentage of cases than in any of the alternative groups. Traditional fathers looked back on their childhoods more positively than did the other groups, and therefore a greater percentage significantly wanted their babies to have lives similar to those they experienced as children. These data are in line with the finding that traditional parents (mothers as well as fathers) perceived their families as more emotionally close than did the alternatives.

The alternative-life-style parents perceived themselves more often as unhappy as children than did those in traditional life styles, an attitude that must be viewed with awareness of their need to rationalize their becoming an alternative. Alternatives felt that their parents had pushed and directed them too much, and they were committed to sparing their children this pressure. They looked to their own peers and to the natural unfolding of the child's own talents to supply the essential basis for achieving self-fulfillment for their child. They were far less likely to want their children to identify with themselves or with grandparents as role models than were the traditional mothers, who saw modeling or direct teaching as primary ways of having their children identify with them. This suggests that alternative children are expected to draw their sex-role models from significant others.

Differences among family styles in attitudes toward the father's role in caretaking were succinctly embodied when we asked the father whether he anticipated having to change his life style when he became a parent: for example, in what ways would work, school, travel, or life style activities be affected by the birth of the child? As hypothesized, traditionally married fathers reported that they would not anticipate changing their life styles after they became parents. Forty-six percent of the traditional married fathers said "no change" to this question, compared to a significant difference anticipated by 18 percent of the social-contract fathers and 24 percent of the living-group fathers. Traditional married fathers were employed full time outside the home, more often than in other groups, which makes behavior more difficult to shift; but the difference in ideological perspective expressed here was predictive of other differences in the parenting area among father groups.

In line with this difference in outlook so far as their own activities were concerned, there was also less concern with traditional kinds of achievement orientation for children among the alternatives, although there is some question as to whether achievement orientation may be defined as life-style-relevant competencies. Most parents' aspirations for their child were expressed as maximizing his capacities and desires; yet the traditionals seemed to have more defined goals in terms of education and occupation than did the alternatives.

As we studied pregnancy behaviors, it was striking to note that fathers across the board tended to participate in preparatory programs and were present at birth. This is of interest since it suggests changing practices in the mainstream middle-class populations that our traditional marrieds represent.

CHILD-REARING PRACTICES DURING INFANCY

The most significant aspects of the birth experiences of our groups were found in the high incidence of home deliveries, in the increased use of Lamaze and other birth techniques, and in the frequent presence of the father and others at the birth of the baby. Life-style differences focused primarily on the incidence of home deliveries and the presence of the father or other individuals in the family at birth.

The emphasis on "parenting" of our population is reflected in the father's presence at birth. The father was present at the birth in over 60 percent of the cases, except for the single mothers. Fifteen percent of the single mothers had a male friend present, and 30 percent of the single mothers also had someone else present, usually another woman. Twenty-one percent, 20 percent, and 13 percent of social contracts, traditional married, and living group families respectively had someone else present. There were also some differences in the incidence of breast feeding across life-style groups. In general, however, we find a wide range of early infant caretaking patterns among mothers in all life styles, and there are no extreme or unusual practices relating to feeding, parental health, or caretaking patterns for any of our mothers, fathers, or babies.

FAMILY ROLES DURING INFANCY

One of the salient elements effecting sex-role and gender identity is the role model provided by parents for their child. In our studies, roles in the family were studied in terms of the distribution of work, assignment of typically male or female tasks, distribution of domestic vs. financial tasks, and the degree of scheduling around task performances. Living-group data show the strong effect of shared functioning in these large household units. Nearly all living-group families share nearly all tasks among the members. Even though social-contract and traditionally married families have the same opportunity (in terms of personnel available) to share tasks, it is nonetheless true that traditionally married mothers bear more of the task burden alone. This reinforces the general finding that social-contract families are more egalitarian in their sex-role attitudes and in sharing in a variety of ways in the family, including caretaking of children. This pattern is reflected in the task performance within the household.

Social-contract families were the only group that was, to a statistically significant degree, egalitarian in their task performance

and less likely to sex-stereotype domestic and financial tasks in the household. The data on father-caretaking patterns support this stance.

The role of the father in child care differs somewhat by life style but not a great deal. The greater change in life style altogether among social contract and living-group fathers resulted in a greater percentage of them no longer living at home with the baby. Actual data on family routines, play with baby, etc., have not been examined but if the extent to which fathers are involved in work outside the home is any index of extent of involvement with the child, we anticipate that the traditionals will be interacting less with the child. When home observations were conducted at six months during a typical morning period mothers were primarily caretakers in 95 percent of all families. When a second adult was present it was the father in 60 percent of the cases, and these were most often in living groups. Of interest in regard to the espousal of sex-role egalitarianism of many of our parents and their desire to model new parent roles for their child is that our inquiry into the number of other persons used as primary caretakers at that period showed a heavy preponderance of females.

CARETAKERS AS MODELS AT SIX MONTHS

It should be noted that home observations done at six months showed that the mother was almost invariably the baby's caretaker during the six-month observations. Occasionally, as when the mother was employed and used a full-time day-care mother or if she were hospitalized, other than biological parent caretakers were used at six months. However, we had the opportunity in the observational period to look at availability of other caretakers, people present and people who participated in caretaking; it appeared that living-group and social-contract family settings would offer more and different kinds of caretakers to the child than would the other two life-style groups. This was as we had expected from their multiple caretaking perspectives. Living-group babies averaged over twice as many individuals present in the immediate vicinity of the child across the entire observational period than the other three life styles. Social-contract families had more caretakers and individuals present than did either traditionally married or single-mother families. Living-group babies also experienced more change and variability in who was caretaking and how many different people cared for the baby during the full visit. In general, direct ratings and home observations confirm that at six months of age, living-group babies are being cared

for by more individuals than the other life-style groups, with social-contract babies being in the second position on this dimension. These data suggest the life styles in which multiple and diverse identificatory models during the formative years lie.

Our pilot studies had refuted the notion that all living groups and other emergent family forms tend to be opposed to the traditional sex-role model for their children; and our current, more systematic studies concur in this finding. Some living groups cling to traditional role models and even reinforce these in emphatic ways. Whether or not a living group clings to the traditional model seems related to the affiliation with a religious ideology or a charismatic leader. When a family group is directed by one of the formalized Eastern or Western religion communities, traditional role models are often emphasized. In one Eastern creedal group, for example, the woman's role is specifically that of serving the male; girl children are trained to subordinate their own desires and wishes to those demanded by the dominant group, the male priests. However, in another religious philosophy (not a living community but a sect found among the randomly selected traditional marrieds) equality between sexes is espoused, with the woman being regarded as a more important recipient of advanced education than the man, because she is the bearer of children, and thus her child's teacher and disseminator of family values.

Of course, a traditional role is not embraced only by living groups with a creedal ideology. We have been particularly interested to note in one stable community with a ten-year history, that boys and girls play in a rather free and egalitarian way until they are about six. When a boy reaches six years of age, his becomes the powerful, dominant, aggressive role, with the girl being taught those attitudes and activities that make direction by male wishes acceptable. In this community, sex-role model is one part of a return to a more glorious past in which dress, cultural activities, and life recapture fondly remembered times.

Most of our two-parent nuclear families share such traditional role models for children. Their rationale derives from the assertion that basic biological or physical attributes serve as determinants for certain personality characteristics; for example, the "natural aggressiveness" of boys or the "greater compliance" of girls is frequently reported by parents. Some single mothers, among them women's movement affiliates, also mention that inherent or biological tendencies direct later play and interests. However, some alternative families engage in interesting attempts to interrupt the automatic imposition of stereotyped sex roles.

In a living group committed to liberated child-rearing attitudes and group day care, fathers had to participate in the daily child-care activities, taking off half a day weekly from their professional roles outside the living group. When these fathers complained that they were not so good with children because they had not been around them and were less invested in caretaking responsibilities, the women questioned whether such attitudes were retreats from equal commitments to child care, and took pains to see that men "learned" how to care for the child. Members of this group have expressed surprise that despite their best efforts to break down stereotypic attitudes in nursery-school children—they take children to "watch women pumpers at the gas station," for example—boys tend to be much more interested in tinkering with the car or playing with trucks and automobiles and hovering near the male members of the group, while girls have been more concerned with housekeeping and playing house. Some parents have expressed doubts too about whether they should sensitize their children to cultural stereotypes when their school experiences will probably demand compliance with those roles.

Our one-year studies of exploratory behavior and attachment behaviors are too incomplete to report any sex-related differences. However, it will be of interest to see whether or not differences show up in the offspring of parents whose own caretaking styles show they are committed to modifying sex-role patterns.

SUMMARY

All of us are aware of the numerous diverse currents in contemporary society that are attacking cultural sex-role stereotypes for their limiting and inhibiting effects on personality, growth and development, and personal fulfillment. The experiments in family styles that I have been discussing may be one of the most fruitful of these; yet how successful they will be remains to be seen, for their success rests not only on conviction and determination, but also on a host of complex factors: the consonance between what parents say they do and what they actually do, their consistency over time, and the mitigating and attenuating influences of the outside world on their within-family behaviors.

For us as investigators, the significance of these longitudinal studies lies in the generic issues they address: To what extent can changes in sex-role and gender identity be effected under optimal conditions in the early environment? At what times or growth periods does maximum shaping take place? What is the impact of

new identificatory models on overall adjustment? If we can approach these questions, the conduct of these difficult but fascinating studies of alternative families and their children will have proved extremely worthwhile.

NOTE TO CHAPTER TWENTY

1. This research was supported by Grant No. OCD CB 166 from the Office of Child Development, and is reported in part in Bernice T. Eiduson, J. Cohen, and J. Alexander, Alternatives in Child Rearing in the 1970s, *Am. J. of Orthopsychiat.* 43, 1973, 720-731.

Chapter Twenty-One

Child-Rearing Research in Communes: The Extension of Adult Sexual Behavior to Young Children

Bennett Berger, Ph.D.*

Conceptions of child rearing and changes in age-grading generated by the conditions of communal living have been our major research focus. We are interested primarily in ideas and the relationship of those ideas to the social contexts that support or undermine them. What seemed most salient to us, particularly in rural commune studies, was the extension of the principle of equalitarianism to chronological age, age being pehaps the last major ascribed barrier, race and sex being successfully under attack already.

We noted age equalitarianism with respect to drug use, sexual behavior, work, a voice in the political affairs in the commune, and the rights of children to settle their own quarrels and resolve their disagreements without adult interference. We have at least two fully verified cases of sexual intercourse between six-year-olds and eight-year-olds; two not fully documented cases of intercourse between children and adults; and one instance of multiple rape of a small girl by several boys only slightly older. In this instance, the parents of the girl expressed anger, although not furious rage, at the boys, making it clear to the researcher that their anger was not about the sexual relations, but rather about the fact that the boys had forced her. She had willingly engaged in sexual intercourse previously.

Parents and other adults do seem to have mixed feelings about the sexuality of their prepubertal children. Coming from backgrounds where feelings about such matters are deeply socialized, it is not surprising that communal adults are sometimes surprised, even

*Professor of Sociology, University of California, San Diego

shocked, to hear about the sexuality of their children. Neither is it surprising that given their favorable predisposition to *natural* morality, they would examine their own shocked response and test it for *natural* virtue. Often they cannot explain their initially shocked response. If sexual behavior seems to do no visible harm to children, the burden of argument tends to fall on those who disapprove of it. Like the rationale for drug use by children, the appeal seems to be to some *natural* sense of propriety. The rationale expressed is that if we, as adults, believe that making love is a good thing, and if the children want to participate in something that we have found rewarding or beautiful, and if there is no persuasive evidence that what is good for us is bad for them, then "let us not obstruct erotic equality because of race, creed, color, or age."

In these circumstances communal adults accept childhood sexuality as part of the pattern of equalitarianism between the two generations. There is a strong predisposition by hip communards to assume that a relationship exists between a child's expressed interest in a given kind of behavior and a probable incipient competence to engage in that behavior. Fresh from the conflicts with campus establishments from whom they demanded "a right to participate in the decisions that shape their lives" and met with such rebuttals that they were too young, too inexperienced, too incompetent to shape university curriculum or to judge the competence of professors, hip communards might well be receptive to the idea of children's rights and children's liberation; at the very least, they are sensitive to the self-serving character of argument by elders for the exclusion of the young on the grounds of an imputed incompetence.

The process is complex because the interactions between ideological postures and the pressures exercised by social contexts sometimes weakens and sometimes strengthens ideological convictions. For example, the hip communal bias against technology may yield to the situational utility of the chain saw in a cold winter; and the ideal of hip brotherhood may be weakened by the need to exclude drug-abusers or frivolous hippies from serious communal enterprises. On the other hand, social contexts sometimes affirm and reinforce initial ideological convictions. For example, the development of primitive survival skills by rural communards may strengthen their belief in the imminent doom of urban middle-class life, and their possession of such skills increases their confidence in their ability to survive urban apocalypse. Similarly, the favorable predispositions of the counter-culture toward candor in interpersonal relations are reinforced by the close quarters and the dense interactional texture of communal living, which make it objectively difficult or impossible to hide or disguise feelings.

Much the same relations are applicable to what we call the inclusion-disattention patterns of child raising. In rural nonreligiously oriented communes, inclusion of the children (beyond the toddler stage) in the activities or rights of adults is general practice. Disattention because of the inclusion is routine, and the inclusive behavior is therefore not especially noted or notable. With the closeness of living quarters, the hippie children, like ghetto children, are exposed to sex between their parents and other adults at an early age. The physical setting reinforces the ideological feelings about candor and openness regarding sex. The parents and other adults are, themselves, young, and since stable nuclear family units are not modal, in the commune courtship and its equivalents are regularly in process. Moreover, babysitters are rarely used, so children get acquainted early with the erotic atmosphere of courtship.

Several of the communes we studied preferred home births where children are routinely present, watching fascinatedly as babies are delivered, sometimes assisting, and usually participating in chanting and other rituals accompanying the ceremony.

The pattern of inclusion of children does not seem to reflect any explicit and deliberate policy of child raising. It is, rather, seen as emerging naturally from the lives that they have to live, needing no explanation or justification unless questions are raised about it. The ordinary responsibilities of child care do not mesh easily with courtship or with the quest for a broadly defined personal freedom and other spiritual quests in which many in the commune are engaged. A philosophy of child care that diminishes the apparent need for, or even desirability of, child care itself, that emphasizes the natural intelligence or competence of children, reduces thereby the degree to which child care may be self-implicating for the parent. It reduces the degree to which one's reputation in the community is contingent upon how "successfully" one manages one's children, thus preserving the freedom and mobility of adults, even in the midst of fertility and poverty.

Conceptions of what children are and ideas about child raising almost always reflect the interests of parents, and these interests are likely to reflect the constraints exercised by social structures larger than the family. Most theories of child rearing assume the existence of middle-class families, and depend on the presence of full-time mother-homemakers, part-time fathers, functional equivalents like nurseries, day-care centers, schools, teachers, and other professionals who apply the principles of child rearing and do the deliberate work of socializers. Communards tend to believe in the benignity of nature's unseen hand; younger children are regarded as essentially healthy plants needing only a little sun and a little water to grow up straight and tall.

Therefore, it does not, in retrospect, seem remarkable either that prepubertal children show interest in sex or that some of them seem ready to seek sexual partners. Nor does it seem surprising that rural communal living should produce an apparent reversal of the hundred-year-old trend in Western industrialized societies toward the prolongation of childhood and other less-than-adult statuses.

We have been impressed with the tendency toward gravity and seriousness in the demeanor of boys, perhaps eight or nine years old, who ape the styles of their male elders in physical posture and linguistic patterns, at home during periods of leisure or in public places like cafés, taverns, fairs, and local dances. These eight- or nine-year-old boys are "very cool," indeed. Imputed with naturalism and spontaneity, childlike innocence combined with the tendency for children to ape their elders produces a minimum visual difference between them, reminiscent of a Breughel painting, a reversal of the modern trend of age-segregation and sharp differences in age-graded norms for behavior.

Our original research design did not include any special attention to gender differentiation, but the feminist movement in the counter-culture necessarily brought it to our attention. The extension of communal belief in equalitarianism, for example to the sexual division of labor, is complex and difficult. The conditions of creating primitive settlements obstruct the decline of stratification by sex in contrast to age stratification. A lot of the necessary work in creating primitive settlement involves heavy labor and the men "naturally" drift toward this work, and the women correspondingly toward traditional rural female roles. This does not happen by deliberate ideological design. Commune women who want to do so-called male heavy work, or to exercise strong leadership roles, are not discouraged from doing so by any pressures, subtle or not, that we were able to detect. Nevertheless, some anarchist communes have been criticized by feminists as being "male ego trips" in which women are systematically victimized by "macho" males who possess the important skills of survival in the country and hence command harems of dependent young women. There is some truth to this image.

In a pioneer generation, there is a lot of suffering, casualty rates are always high, and there are inevitably painful discrepancies between what one is socialized to feel and how one's ideological convictions constrain one to act. Very few communards live much above the level of bare subsistence, and although they may affirm female equality, they cannot afford the luxury of affirmative action programs. For women who go into communal scenes strongly qualified, there are no obstructions to their opting for "male" roles;

there is little or no gender prejudice. However, when they come in confused and unskilled, they tend to drift toward the kitchen.

Part of the strength of the religious movements, such as the Jesus movement in what used to be the counterculture, rests on the traditional protections they provide to vulnerable and unskilled young women. My impression is that the Jesus movement and some of the Eastern religious movements have attracted the kinds of young men and women who are more deeply alienated, who have been most hurt by bad drug and sex experiences. One of the things that these traditional religious communities do for victimized and exploited young women is to give them the traditional protections afforded women.

Chapter Twenty-Two

Sex Differences in Agonistic Behavior of Communally Reared Children

Elizabeth A. Missakian, Ph.D.*

The origins of human behavior have been both poorly studied and popularized during recent years. The general attitude among psychoanalysts, psychologists, and biologists has been that human behavior is too complex and motivational variables too sophisticated to be studied with the same tools one uses to study animals. Blurton Jones has suggested that this may reflect inexperience and naiveté on the part of the observers, rather than a real problem in applying ethological tools to the study of human behavior.[1]

The purpose of this study is to apply ethological methods of behavioral observation and analysis to the study of agonistic behavior among communally reared children living in Synanon (see p. 166). This is a preliminary report on the question of sex differences in agonistic behavior.

Aggression and dominance relations among children have been studied on a very limited basis.[2] The general conclusion following these studies has been that dominance is not a useful concept in describing the social relations of young children. In the case of children from three to five years of age, only boys participate in a sufficient number of aggressive encounters to allow construction of a hierarchy.

The specific questions asked in this portion of the study were:

1. Is there a difference in the frequency of aggression of boys and girls?

*Research Associate, Synanon Research Institute

2. Is there a difference in dominance position/rank of boys and girls?
3. What parameters of agonistic behavior do and/or do not reflect sex differences (i.e., physical contact, interactions involving priority to incentives, etc.)?

The Synanon School is a children's community within the larger Synanon community. Synanon Foundation, Inc., began with approximately twenty individuals in 1958 and has grown into a community today housing more than 1300 men, women, and children. Synanon has become a natural experiment involving the reconfiguration of environmental space, community health practices and delivery systems, and communal rearing of children. Synanon's primary business and concern remains the rehabilitation and reeducation of character-disordered individuals.

The Synanon School began in July of 1966. It is a twenty-four-hour-a-day situation for children ranging in age from birth to eighteen years. At the time of this study, there were more than 240 children in the school. The two groups studied were the infant program, six to eighteen months, and the two-to-four-year program. During the period of study, the population in the two programs ranged from twenty to twenty-four children.

An agonistic interaction was defined as a dyadic encounter in which an aggressive and submissive behavior were both observed. Dominance was reflected by the outcome of the interaction, not by the winner of an object or piece of property. This criteria is virtually identical to that used in studies of nonhuman primates.[3] A total of sixty-five separate aggressive gestures and forty-seven submissive gestures were delineated.

In addition to recording the aggressive and submissive behaviors in such dyadic interactions, records were also maintained of physical contact during the interaction and the role of property or space. Over 490 hours of observations of a total of 3538 individual interactions were recorded, and dominance matrices were prepared for the infant program and the two-to-four program. Highly predictable and stable matrices were found for both programs.

This chapter deals only with information relating to sex differences on measures of agonistic behavior. There was no difference in the aggression frequency of boys and girls in either the infant program or the two-to-four program. The positions boys and girls occupied on the dominance matrix were also analyzed. There was no difference in the rank of boys and girls in either of the two programs studied. In other words, boys did not tend to occupy positions of higher rank than girls. These findings are in sharp contrast to previous literature cited.

Agonistic interactions were divided into two gross categories: those involving physical contact between the children and those not involving such contact (vocalization, gestures, displacements, verbal threats, etc.). Again, there was no difference between boys and girls in the type of agonistic interaction. This breakdown of physical vs. nonphysical interactions is fairly gross.

The only parameter revealing a difference between boys and girls involved the analysis of agonistic interactions involving objects or space. It should be pointed out that significantly fewer interactions do not involve property. However, within the two-to-four program, in those encounters which did involve property, boys fought significantly more over objects than girls did. This was not true for the infant program. The reason for this difference is unclear.

In summary, this is a preliminary report on the agonistic behavior of communally reared children ranging in age from six to forty-eight months. The focus of the report is sex differences in social structure and dominance relations. The results of the study indicate that: (1) there was no difference between boys and girls on the measure of aggression frequency; (2) there was no difference between boys and girls on the measure of dominance rank or position in the hierarchy; (3) there was no difference between boys and girls in terms of whether their aggression involved physical contact; and (4) boys in the two-to-four-year program fought significantly more over objects and property than girls did.

The Synanon community is a culture that does not share the typical stereotypes of gender-specific behavior. Thus, the population of children raised in a communal situation in Synanon offers a unique opportunity for study of gender differences in aggression.

NOTES TO CHAPTER TWENTY-TWO

1. N.G. Blurton Jones, An Ethological Study of Some Aspects of Social Behavior of Children in Nursery School, in *Primate Ethology*, ed. by D. Morris (Chicago: Aldine Publishing Co., 1967), 347-368.

2. *Ibid.*; Ewan C. Grant, Human Facial Expression, *Man* 4, 1969, 525-536; C. Hutt and W.C. McGrew, Effects of Group Density upon Social Behavior in Humans, Symp.: Changes in Behavior with Population Density, Assoc. Study Animal Behav., 1967; W.C. McGrew, An Ethological Study of Agonistic Behavior in Preschool Children, *Proc. 2nd Int. Cong. Primat., Atlanta, Ga. 1968* 1 (New York: Karger 1969), 149-159.

3. Elizabeth Missakian, Genealogical and Cross-Genealogical Dominance Relations in a Group of Free-Ranging Rhesus Monkeys (*Macaca Mulatta*) on Cayo Santiago, *Primates* 13, 1972, 169-180; D.S. Sade, Determinants of Dominance in a Group of Free-Ranging Rhesus Monkeys, in *Social Communication Among Primates*, ed. by S.A. Altmann (Chicago: University of Chicago, 1967), 99-114.

Part III

**School Observations, Curricula,
Materials, Programs, and
Planning Related to the
Sexual and Gender
Development of
Young Children**

Chapter Twenty-Three

We Followed Them to School One Day: Sex-Role Socialization in the Pre-School

Diane Ehrensaft, Ph.D.*

> If each generation were left entirely to its own devices, . . . without even an older generation to copy, sex differences would presumably be almost absent in childhood and would have developed after puberty at the expense of considerable relearning on the part of one or both sexes.[1]

Here lies a major controversy of our generation. Are boys and girls inherently different in nature or in behavior, or are the sex differences we so often observe primarily a function of a complex socialization process enforced by the larger society?

Certainly socialization as the key factor in the development of sex-linked behaviors represents a predominant current of social and psychological thinking today. Growing numbers of social scientists are involved in analyzing and understanding the development of "femininity" and "masculinity" within Western society. This is no historical accident. We are witnessing a rapid growth of technology in Western culture, increasingly effective forms of mass-distributed birth control, and a growing use of institutions other than the home in which children are socialized (day-care centers, schools, etc.). These factors have helped create social conditions in which brute strength is no longer the crux of our economic system and women no longer spend their lives pregnant and in the kitchen.

The recent emergence of a women's liberation movement has increased public consciousness that perhaps the traditional role division of instrumental male and expressive female is obsolete,

---

*Department of Education, University of California, Berkeley

counterproductive, and psychologically damaging to both males and females. The underlying assumption is that such role division is a product of socialization and can thus be replaced by *new* forms of socialization. Talcott Parsons describes the division of the nuclear family (and, in fact, the society at large) into the "expressive" female, the one who performs the emotional, nurturant, and supportive functions, as contrasted to the "instrumental" male, who goes out into the world, makes a living, and deals with functional issues (fixit repairs, politics, and what have you). In essence, what he puts forth is the internalized world of women in contrast to the externalized world of men.[2]

A review of anthropological, sociological, and psychological literature certainly offers strong evidence for the importance of socialization in the differential molding of males and females.[3] Biological and psychological research also suggest that innate sex differences may have some bearing on certain sex differences in cognitive and social functioning, but are not pervasive enough to explain the immense behavioral differences and cultural variations in male and female roles.[4]

This chapter represents an observational study of an aspect of the teacher-child socialization process within a preschool setting, focusing on the ways in which adults interact with children in preparing them for their positions as males or females within our society. This setting was chosen because for most children it is the first contact with the outside institutional world, a world of paramount importance in shaping these young children into social and "socially acceptable" persons. Also, while other investigators have uncovered processes of sex-role socialization in middle and late childhood[5] and in early infancy,[6] a research gap remains for the developmental period of ages three to five. Further, as Walter Mischel points out, a study of sex-role socialization during this age period "would have to extend beyond parental modeling and parental practice to include relevant behavior of peers and other significant social agents."[7] This led me to choose the day-care setting, with its "other significant social agents."

I decided to focus on the verbal and physical interactions of teachers and children: talking, touching, and proximity-seeking. Verbal and touching behaviors are two areas in which males and females are known to differ later in life and that have been found to be sex-differentiated in early mother-infant interactions, with mothers talking to and touching girls more than boys by six months of age. Seeking proximity is another area in which infant studies have demonstrated a sex difference, with female toddlers seeking more

contact with mothers than males.[8] Are such early interactional patterns foreshadowings of the later development of the "affiliative" female and "instrumental" male normative in our culture?

Behaviorists emphasize the importance of learning processes in the acquisition of sex-role behavior, so within that context, it is important to look at the reinforcement contingencies set up for girls and boys in the classroom and the opportunities that exist for modeling and observational learning. Focus also must be not only on the teacher's shaping of the child, but also the child's shaping of the teacher, with the understanding that socialization is a mutual interactional process. But it is important not to stop here. Cognitive theorists, particularly Kohlberg, stress the importance of the child's cognitive organization of his or her social reality, guided by self-categorization as boy or girl. Thus, one must go beyond identifying the behavioral contingencies within the classroom and consider the effects of teacher-child interactions on the child's cognitive organization of sex role concepts.

WE FOLLOWED THEM TO SCHOOL ONE DAY: THE CASE STUDY

The setting for this study was a day-care center for three-to-five-year-olds in Montreal. Naturalistic observations were done in four different classrooms and include nine female teachers and sixty-five children, thirty-four boys and thirty-one girls. Using an interactional coding system, observations were collected over the 1972-73 academic year. Teachers and children were aware that my female assistant and I were watching classroom interactions, but did not know that we were specifically focusing on sex-linked patterns.

The center was typical of many modern preschools that emphasize structure and intellectual development while at the same time providing a certain degree of freedom for the children and close emotional relationships between children and teachers. Most of the families served were either working or student parents, and consisted of a large ethnic variety, ranging from Canadian and American to Moroccan and Jamaican. The teachers also reflected ethnic variety. Despite large cultural differences in background, both children and teachers appeared quite assimilated into North American culture. Children attended the school from 8:00 A.M. to 5:00 P.M. and were cared for within an egalitarian atmosphere in which all children were encouraged to develop themselves to their fullest potential. This egalitarianism carried over into teachers' *expressed* attitudes toward boys and girls, with all teachers reporting they treated both sexes

very similarly and encouraged both boys and girls to participate in *all* activities.

Despite these self-expressed equalitarian stances of the teachers, the study revealed that in actual practice, teachers related *very differently* to boys and girls in the classroom. The teacher *initiated* significantly (in the statistical sense—$p < .05$ or less) more contact with boys than with girls and in general paid more attention to boys than to girls. In fact the teachers tended to blatantly ignore girls more often than they did boys. On the opposite side of the coin, boys were found to be more "behaviorally active" than girls; that is, in quantitative terms, they emitted more touching, talking, and proximity-seeking behaviors than girls did, but only because boys were reacting to the greater amount of contact directed toward them by teachers. Boys themselves did not initiate any more contact with teachers than girls did. As we looked at specific interactions, we discovered that in contrast to the teachers' tendency to interact with girls less, girls approached the teachers more and asked the teachers more questions than did their male peers.

The major implication of the above findings is that teachers are more likely to engage in activities with boys than with girls. We will later discuss if this was so because the boys' actions in the classroom demand more teacher attention than did girls'. However, regardless of the causal factors, that girls may desire interaction from the teacher as much as or more than boys but with less response might possibly engender in the girls feelings of "invisibility."

We must consider, however, not only the *quantity* of attention that the boys and girls receive from teachers, but also the nature of that attention. Let's look at the "affiliative" relationship between the teachers and children. Boys received both more "glad" and more "mad" messages from teachers than did girls. Compared to girls, boys engaged in more mutual cuddling and were physically "stroked" and praised more often by teachers, but these "affectionate" interactions were tempered by the greater amount of *negative* interchanges with the teacher (in the form of teacher commands, "Stop this!" "Don't do that!" "Go there," etc.) These findings coincide exactly with those of a preschool study at SUNY-Buffalo.[9] The consequences of this "glad-mad" pattern may be the establishment of an approach-avoidance conflict for boys in social relationships: "In the adult world your friends may also be your enemies and you had best keep your guard up."

Although girls received fewer positive behaviors from the teacher than did boys, they also received fewer of the direct negative messages. The negative message to girls was of a much more subtle

nature. For example, girls' bids for physical affection were most often ignored by the teacher. Girls were *never* engaged in mutual cuddling with the teacher, and the only time girls were noticed as much as boys was in free play situations when girls had the opportunity to actively approach the teacher for attention.

From the standpoint of the social relationship between the teacher and child, we also looked at the nature of the teacher's control of the child, including commands, reprimands, and physical directing of the children. The study revealed that boys received much more teacher control than girls, particularly during sit-down activities, when children are more likely to become restless and inattentive. In response to these control attempts, boys rebelled far more often than did girls, by either ignoring teacher's directives or talking back. Girls tended to be much more compliant. Here lies the incipient stages of boys' warring relationships with authority structures, particularly in school situations. That girls aren't involved in this same power struggle may be a reflection of innate differences in behavior, particularly aggressive or "active" behavior. It might also be a function of prior socialization in which girls, even by age three, have already been more appropriately prepared for compliant classroom behavior. Boys may also experience themselves as being "picked on" more by the teacher, which might in fact be the reality in accordance with teacher's implicit expectations of the "naughty" boy and may ignore her in an attempt to discontinue any further negative interaction. Informal discussions and observations with parents and teachers revealing cultural expectations and behavioral practice would lead me to support the last two possibilities. The prototypic quote from a parent in the study—"I'd much rather have a little girl because they're so much more cooperative"—perhaps reflects a self-fulfilling prophesy of the stereotypic "ever-so-sweet" little girl pitted against her pugnacious male counterpart.

FROM WHENCE COME THESE PATTERNS AND WHITHER WILL THEY GO?

In reviewing this observational study, I developed the following hypothesis to explain the revealed teacher-child sex-linked phenomena in the classroom, particularly the greater amount of attention received by boys: Boys enter the preschool developmentally more immature than their female age-mates. They lag behind girls socially, intellectually, and emotionally, and therefore require more guidance and direction from teachers. Girls, on the other hand, are perceived as more independent. A report from a volunteer worker,

informal interviews with the teachers and center directors, and the classroom field notes of both observers substantiated the above supposition of maturity level differences and their effects in the classroom.[10] The finding of Gessell that from ages 0 to 5 girls score higher than boys on child development scales offers further corroborating evidence.

An important implication of the above interpretation is that age-grading in preschools and perhaps also in grammar schools may be destructive to both boys' and girls' social growth, given the divergent maturity levels of the two sexes. Boys' perception of their social reality may be that they feel picked on and bossed around while at the same time experiencing themselves as more noticeable than girls. Girls in this same peer group may feel more "invisible," less noticeable, may experience themselves as having to try harder to gain social recognition, suggestive of later self-perceptions commonly reported by grown women. This female self-concept of invisibility may develop even though the objective reality is that teachers notice girls less only because teachers give girls more credit for being able to do things on their own. That reality may be totally irrelevant to the little girl, for small children are often superbly perceptive of the behavioral aspects of interpersonal relationships, but terribly inaccurate in interpreting their meaning.

Not only do the differential levels of maturity between male and female age-peers force them into a different relationship with the teacher and set the stage for sex-linked differences in self-concept, it may also put them into a debilitating relationship with one another. I am particularly thinking of the tendency of little girls to fall prematurely into the maternal role with their male peers, reprimanding them and making sure they do not get out of line.

Educators might well think about putting younger girls with older boys or abolishing age-grading completely at the preschool level, as is done in the Montessori schools and in many "open classroom" structures. By such a procedure we could balance out the different maturity levels of the two sexes, perhaps opening up the possibility for healthier relationships between boys and girls and between teachers and children. By affording children the opportunity to group themselves according to their level of developmental maturity rather than their chronological age and sex, we might avoid the situation where the contrast between the disruptive boy and the conforming girl was the glaring dynamic of the classroom.

I would not, however, attribute sex-linked teacher-child patterns to maturity factors alone. Prior socialization and strong cultural expectations of male and female functioning may also interact to

affect the way teachers relate to boys and girls. I have cited previously in this chapter incidents of differential adult socialization of boys and girls as early as the infancy period. Even before birth many mothers assume that a very active fetus will most surely be a boy. By the preschool years a child has had two to three years of direction on appropriate male and female behavior, behavior that may in turn shape the teachers' relationships to the children. For example, if the boy has already been encouraged to be a "little man," assertive and self-determined, this pattern may be in conflict with the normative functioning of a well-structured classroom and push the teacher into more male-directed "control" interactions to keep her class in order.

Then we must consider also the ongoing expectations of male and female behavior that teachers bring with them into the preschool classroom, expectations that may be based both on direct experience and cultural stereotypes. Teachers in this study revealed in questionnaires that they had no strong culturally defined expectations of what boys and girls are like. Yet informal discussions with teachers indicated otherwise, with three teachers agreeing that women do not have the emotional capacity to become engineers, two other teachers expecting rowdiness from an almost all-male classroom, and a sixth teacher explaining that she did not provide dolls for water play because only boys were in class that day. Such attitudes can very likely carry over into the teachers' actual practice with the children, channelling boys and girls in very different directions. For example, *expectations* of rowdiness rather than rowdiness itself might dictate the greater attention showered on boys to "keep them in line."

At the Symposium, Dr. Millie Almy, (Professor of Education, University of California, Berkeley) referred to Lee and Gropper's work[11] which indicated that to all intents and purposes, we have been inducting boys into one culture and girls into another. Girls from the viewpoint of the masculine culture are disadvantaged or deprived. But Dr. Almy emphasized that from the viewpoint of the feminine culture, boys are also disadvantaged or deprived. "The time has come, I think, to shift to a bicultural view, openly acknowledging differences, but not treating them as deficits. There is need to examine the curriculum of the nursery school to ensure that boys and girls have equal access to materials, equipment and all resources in accord with their individual differences in interest and aptitude. The goal is not to reverse male and female sex roles, but rather to make certain of equal opportunity and a range of options for both boys and girls."

If a goal of teachers and educators is to diminish destructive forms

of sex-typing in the classroom, the above phenomenon suggests the potential need for teacher self-awareness and sensitization to their own actions in the classroom. Even if teachers' actions are dictated by actual sex differences, either innate or socialized, in children's behavior, teachers may want to counteract these behavior patterns through conscious forms of intervention that will promote healthier functioning of both girls and boys, functioning that at this point may require differential encouragement and attention in the development of certain skills or abilities. For example, girls may need more direct encouragement than boys for engaging in gross motor activity (an area of functioning in which early sex differences have repeatedly been reported), while boys may need more nurturant attention in the development of small muscle control in "sit-down" classroom activities.

The sex-linked differences of teacher behavior suggested in the data of this study were yet so subtle as to remain unnoticed by either observer during the actual classroom observations, and the teachers themselves reported no awareness of differences in treatment of boys and girls. It was only when the behavior counts of classroom interactions were tallied that these patterns became clear. Those of us who wish to break down destructive forms of sex-role stereotyping must study and sensitize ourselves to these subtle but potentially subversive processes which might potentially hamper boys' and girls' optimal social development, and we must begin to develop programs for change in the classroom.

NOTES TO CHAPTER TWENTY-THREE

1. Herbert Barry, Margaret K. Bacon, and Irvin I. Child, A Cross-Cultural Survey of Some Sex Differences in Socialization, *Journal of Abnormal and Social Psychology* 55, 1957, 329.

2. Talcott Parsons, The American Family: Its Relations to Personality and Social Structure, in *Family, Socialization and Interaction Process*, ed. by T. Parsons and B.F. Bales (Glencoe, Ill.: Free Press, 1955).

3. Barry, Bacon, and Child; Jerome Kagan and Howard A. Moss, *Birth to Maturity* (New York: Wiley, 1962); Margaret Mead, *Sex and Temperament* (New York: Dell, 1963); John Money, Psychosexual Differentiation, in *Sex Research*, ed. by John Money (New York: Holt, Rinehart and Winston, 1965).

4. Diane Ehrensaft, Sex Role Socialization in a Preschool Setting, unpublished doctoral dissertation, University of Michigan, 1974.

5. Patricia Minuchin, Sex-Role Concepts and Sex-Typing in Childhood as a Function of School and Home Environments, *Child Development* 36, 1965, 1033-1048; Patricia C. Sexton, *The Feminized Male* (New York: Vintage Books, 1969).

6. Susan Goldberg and Michael Lewis, Play Behavior in the Year Old Infant;

Early Sex Differences, *Child Development* 40, 1969, 21-31; Howard A. Moss, Sex, Age and State as Determinants of Mother-Infant Interaction, *Merrill-Palmer Quarterly* 13, 1967, 19-35.

7. Walter Mischel, Sex-Typing and Socialization, in *Carmichael's Manual of Child Psychology*, 3rd ed., ed. by P.H. Mussen (New York: Wiley, 1970), 3-72.

8. Goldberg and Lewis.

9. Lisa Serbin, K. Daniel O'Leary, Ronald N. Kent, and Ilene J. Tonick, A Comparison of Teacher Response to the Pre-academic and Problem Behavior of Boys and Girls, *Child Development* 44, 1973, 796-804.

10. A. Gessell, H.M. Halverson, H. Thompson, F.L. Ilg, B.H. Costner, L.B. Ames, and C.S. Amtruda, *The First Five Years of Life: A Guide to the Study of the Preschool Child* (New York: Harper and Row, 1940).

11. Patrick C. Lee and Nancy Gropper, Sex Role Culture and Educational Practice, *Harvard Educational Review* 44, August, 1974, 369-410.

Chapter Twenty-Four

Sex Information Among Nursery-School Children

Betty Cohen, M.S.W.* and
Susan Parker, M.S.W.[†]

Literature written since the Freudian formulation of the theory of infantile sexuality has been vast and provocative.

However, there have been few studies on the responses of young children to different kinds of family sex education. Noteworthy are the work of Kreitler and Kreitler and of Kendall and Moore, which stimulated our research. Both studies attempted to discover, through formal testing, the quantity and quality of the preschool child's sexual information and to examine this information in the light of Freudian and Piagetian constructs.[1]

Expanding their methods of research, we added the play interview in our attempt to examine the relationship between sexual information and attitudes apparently held by the parents and the ability of the children to talk and play freely around these themes. Though our findings are inferential, our results offer some suggestions for the nature and kind of sex education that is useful and understandable for young children.

POPULATION SAMPLE

We studied twenty-five children 4.1 to 5.3 years of age and their parents. The children (fifteen males and ten females) attended one of two schools in the San Francisco Bay area: a parent's cooperative and a private nondenominational nursery school. On the basis of private interviews and observation of the children within the school, we felt that all twenty-five were developing normally, both physical-

---

*Bananas, Child Care Referral Service; Berkeley.

†Vice-principal, Tyrrell Jr. High School; Hayward, Calif.

ly and psychologically. The parents, too, were seen as adequately adjusted adults functioning within a normal range.

The parents represented a young, upper-middle-class, well-educated, and financially solvent group. They ranged in age from 24 to 49 with the mean age for the mothers 30.8 and the fathers 33.7. Of the fifty parents, forty had B.A.s or advanced degrees. Of the remaining ten, all had completed high school and five had attended college. Seven of the fathers were associated with one of the universities in the area. All the fathers were employed, while only four mothers worked outside the home. Twenty pairs of parents were married and living together at the time of the study; two sets were divorced, two sets separated; and one father was deceased. Of the fifty parents, forty were American born, thirty of these having come to California from other parts of the country.

Of the twenty-five children, two were Oriental, two were of mixed Oriental-Occidental parentage, and twenty-one were Caucasian. Five were in families in which they were the only children, fourteen each had one sibling, and six had two siblings. Nine of the children with siblings were the eldest child; eight were the youngest; three were middle children. No family had more than three children.

METHOD

The research method included a semistructured interview with each child's parents, followed by a semistructured play interview with the child at nursery school. Each family was subsequently telephoned to determine the study's initial effect, if any, on the family. The study concluded with an interview with each teacher. All interviews were conducted by two second-year graduate students in social welfare at the University of California at Berkeley.

The parent interview included what information parents had provided their children regarding sex differences and human reproduction (intercourse, conception, pregnancy, fetal maturation, birth); what other sources might have influenced the child on sexual matters; what general parental attitudes existed about sex within the context of child rearing; and what retrospective thoughts the parents had about the handling of sexual issues in their own childhoods.

Following this interview, the parents were each instructed to inform their child of a special play session in a special room at school. At the beginning of the interview the child was introduced to a portable playhouse equipped with family members and various pieces of furniture. The child was asked to arrange the furniture and explain the sleeping arrangements for the family. Through play and a

stated series of questions, the nature and depth of the child's sexual information was explored.

The child was also asked to draw a self-portrait and a family portrait. The interviewer terminated the play session; however, the child was free to leave at any time or, in fact, to decline to play at all.

The final contact with the family on the telephone centered around three questions: What effect did the study have on you (and your spouse)? Did your child ask you any questions after being interviewed? What effect do you think the study had on your child?

After the family interviews were completed, the nursery-school teachers were interviewed using a questionnaire designed to obtain specific information about the individual participating children as well as general information about the nursery school's policies on toileting, sex play among the children, organized and spontaneous discussions of animal and human reproduction, and the teachers' own ideas and plans for sex education within the school.

ANALYSIS OF THE DATA

All sex information given by the parents or expressed by the children was organized into three major categories: intercourse-conception, pregnancy-intrauterine growth, and childbirth. Within each major category, parents were scored from 1 to 5 (5 representing maximal information), depending on the amount of information they reportedly had given.

The children's play and answers were scored in the same manner. Scores were derived independently by the two interviewers and then compared. Where differences existed, a collaborated score was agreed upon after reexamining the case study and particular areas of disagreement.

FORMAT CONSIDERATIONS

In the two previous studies designed specifically to elicit sex information from young children, the interviewing had been tightly structured in setting and format. One question followed another, and failure to answer any specific question would terminate the interviews. Although we wanted to ask many of the same questions, we developed a format through which children might express their ideas, fantasies, thoughts, and perhaps information about their own sexual identity, as well as about human reproduction. We also wanted to examine the children's responses related to what their parents

reportedly had told them, or what they might have assimilated from the environment.

INTERVIEWS

The parent interviews were straightforward; the children's play interviews became the most demanding aspect of this project. Questions in the earlier studies had been presented to the children in a developmental progression—from sexual identity and questions related to toileting, moving toward reproduction. With this model, we designed a play interview that would consider verbal answers to direct questions, play, drawings, and clinical impressions. A group of children was randomly chosen to be interviewed as a pilot project, the analysis of which would lead to a workable interview. Difficulties arose almost immediately.

The first articulate four-year-old answered: "No one in my family goes to the bathroom, silly" to an initial question, effectively closing that section of the interview. The interviewer tried again: "How do a mother and father get a baby?"

"Well, it's clear, don't you know; mother and father lay down very close together and mate and then later a baby is born who lived in the mother's uterus and comes out her vagina and that's that. Couldn't we talk about *Tyrannosaurus rex*?"

All the children in the pilot study either joked about or refused to talk about toileting and training. One child locked the play toilet in the garage, while another suggested that family members "went once a week." Anxiety, denial, and joking behavior characterized all their responses. In comparison, the topics of growing up, having babies, creating families, being like Mommy and Daddy, were handled by the children without tension. It was clear that a change was necessary if we were to obtain the information we were seeking. In fact, even with the revised interview, all play disruptions occurred during the toileting discussion. These children were too close to the mastery of self-control to deal with this anxiety-provoking area.

THE PARENTS

In all but three interviews, both parents were present. (In the case of a parental separation, both parents requested interviews because of their interest in the study.) Parents were talkative, interested, and involved.

There was little evidence of personal embarrassment, but it must be remembered that these parents felt free enough to volunteer. In

almost 50 percent of the families, the husband was the more articulate, even though it was clear that the mother would be providing more of the sex education for the children. This was true because of the mother's closer daily proximity to the children, but may also have been the family preference. Both parents were obviously concerned about the topic, and some asked the interviewers for advice as to how to proceed.

Contrary to findings in the previous studies,[2] girls and boys seemed to be receiving the same amount and kind of information. Some parents deliberately included their boys in discussions of pregnancy. Parents indicated that they would continue this practice in the future and that distinctions between kinds of information offered to boys and girls should be eliminated altogether.

Children with younger siblings generally received more sex information; typically, their curiosity was emphasized during the mother's pregnancy. At that time, mothers gave especially specific intrauterine and developmental facts. This was particularly true at the cooperative school. A number of children there had also seen adult and children's books about intrauterine growth and birth, and there had been periodic animal births at the school. None of the children had actually seen a human birth, although some of the parents were contemplating such deliveries in the future. All parents had, more or less, removed the concept of pain from birth—using words like "hard work," "pushing," "pulling," "breathing hard."

Parents expressed the greatest concern about presenting their children with the facts of sexual intercourse. Even so, one-third of the parents had already given their children some of the biological terms. One-half of these, however, expressed their difficulties. One mother described her dilemma quite vividly:

> Without any warning one day Robbie came to me and asked how babies were made. I didn't know whether he had heard something or not. I couldn't think of what to say so I asked him to let me think what I wanted to say and come back. I was really upset although I tried not to show it. The next day when he came back and asked me again, I was better prepared, although uneasy, and he came back every day for about a week until he felt satisfied that he had the entire story. I just chose to tell him the truth.

This mother seemed to manage, despite her anxiety, to convey the facts in an understandable way to her son, who was patient and persistent enough to keep reminding her each day that he still wanted answers. The child, a boy of five, was one of the four children who was able to convey the information to the interviewer.

Several other parents, however, felt categorically that their children were "too young" and "too vulnerable" to hear about sexual intercourse, and they hoped that the question would not arise. In fact, two families stated clearly that they would divert their children's attention rather than answer directly.

Almost 80 percent of the parents were providing their children considerably more sex information than they themselves had received. Only two said that they had received any information at their child's age. Three-fourths of the parents reported that they remembered absolutely no sex information from their parents, while the others recalled "one talk," usually in early adolescence. Similarly, they recalled no additional information from the school except a film strip shown in junior or senior high school in sex-segregated physical-education classes. Three-fourths of the parents claimed that peers had provided more sex education for them than had their parents.

Despite the wide diversity among families, the common denominator for all became the belief that parents are responsible for their children's sex education; that, despite some embarrassment, the parents expected to live up to this obligation; and that as the children grew older the parents would feel less anxious and embarrassed. They did not feel that the responsibility rested with the schools, nor did they want their children to receive the bulk of their sex education from their peers.

Even though these parents represented a rather specific slice of American life—upper middle class, well educated, and employed—they presented a rather broad spectrum of ideas, opinions, and beliefs. For example, with reference to nudity within the home, we found some families with a policy of parental nudity before children of all ages, as well as one family in which the mother insisted that the daughter never see the father nude. This mother was adamant on the issue, even though in the course of the interview, she related her own frustration and anxiety during her preschool days at not being able to "catch my father in the bathroom." Thus, we found some of the parents making changes based on their own experiences (over 80 percent) while others remained unsettled or unsure of their approach, yet willing to explore new models if they could find them.

THE SCHOOLS

In addition to family diversity, it is useful to consider the philosophical and practical differences between the two nursery schools. Parents' attitudes toward child rearing are expressed in their choice

of schools. At the cooperative, sharing an interaction between parents was an integral component of the school. In the private school, parents appeared not to know each other and had little opportunity to communicate within the school setting. Most problems were handled at the parent-teacher conferences.

Toilets at the private school were separated from the play area and there was little, if any, bathroom play. Nudity was discouraged. At the cooperative, however, the bathroom area was open; children of both sexes frequently visited with each other while using the toilet, and nudity during water play was common.

At the private school, the teacher was responsive and open when answering spontaneous questions about animal and human reproduction, but there was no curriculum planning around these issues. At the cooperative, children had observed nursing mothers, had played with various animal babies, and had in their library a few books on reproduction, like *How Babies Are Made.*[3]

THE CHILDREN

It is interesting that although these observations point to significant differences between the schools—the cooperative promoting more information and a freer atmosphere—the parents of each school supporting these different philosophies (Figure 24-1), the children themselves present a strikingly cohesive picture (Figure 24-2).

All the children, with one notable exception, were clear about their gender identity, clear about the visible sexual characteristics of the opposite sex, and verbally confirmed their belief in what their identity would be in the future. (The exception, a boy of four, gave no indication that he knew sex difference and demonstrated in play that he was convinced little girls also had penises.) The desire to grow up was reflected in the children's natural and matter-of-fact handling

	Conception	Intrauterine Growth	Childbirth	Total
Private nursery school parents	1.9	3.0	2.7	2.53
Cooperative nursery school parents	2.9	4.0	3.5	3.46

5 — Maximum amount of information given

1 — No information given
(no parent gave their child misinformation)

Figure 24-1. Amount of Information Given Children By Their Parents

	Conception	Intrauterine Growth	Childbirth	Total
Private nursery school children	1.97	2.76	2.5	2.41
Cooperative nursery school children	1.93	2.5	2.83	2.42

Figure 24-2. Amount of Information Reported By Children

of the general facts about intrauterine growth and childbirth. Both verbally and through play they were able to communicate and fantasize about the future and their personal roles in it. They were reflecting, we feel, their parents' generally open attitude about these facts. As previously mentioned, the parents had adopted a dosage technique, answering just those questions that were asked, and consequently had not dealt with sexual intercourse. However, 90 percent of the children did feel that the father had some role in the birth of the baby, if nothing more than the transportation, diaper, or babysitting services. There was a naturalness and interest expressed by many of the children upon not being able to answer questions. A typical response was: "I really do wonder, don't you?"

Of the eight children whose parents reportedly had told them about the father's role, four communicated that fact to the interviewer. These children were able to relate details in a simple factual manner, without anxiety. One of these children (a boy, 4.8) had been told by his divorced mother about sexual intercourse, but not about its relationship to birth and babies. She had felt this was necessary information for the child, since she often had male guests who spent the night with her. The child presented a confused picture, however: "Mothers wish for babies and that's how they get them" and "Little babies come out the penis." A marginal answer was: "Daddy carries something around, but I forgot what it is."

For the other children, the baby had always been in the mother in some miniature form, the most elaborate presentation of this being: "I was a teeny tiny baby inside my mother when she was a teeny tiny baby inside my grandmother." Several of the girls suggested that they themselves had these little babies inside them.

All accepted as natural fact the baby's life in the mother's womb. Responses in this regard included, "cosy," "warm," "the baby is just in there growing and growing," "the baby is getting bigger and bigger," "waiting to be born," "eating and sleeping." Darkness was perhaps the only frightening concept. Three children had less naturalistic notions: "Baby eats little things like raisins and is running around"; "The baby is eating the yolk"; and "The baby

grows and grows until it gets ready to crack the shell." Some anatomical uncertainty existed, however, with two very imaginative variations: "Well the baby drinks milk from the mother's breast from the inside" and "The baby isn't in the dark all the time; it gets light when the mother opens her mouth." This last child, a girl of five, had received a great deal of anatomical information from the family doctor.

In discussing childbirth, only three children reported that the mother goes to the hospital to get the baby, just as she goes to a store. Three children who had been given extremely specific anatomical explanations maintained absolutely, "The baby squeaks out the bottom" or "slides down the butt." The other children stated that the baby left the mother, not through the stomach or through the mouth, but from a special hole. For those who were vague it was "bottom"; more precisely for the rest, "vagina." Both boys and girls seemed comfortable with this information and, in fact, appeared proud of their knowledge of the specific anatomical term.

Despite the differences between the nursery schools and the differences among families and the amount of information they had provided, the children appeared to hold quantitatively similar misconceptions about sex. Fifty-seven percent of the children from the cooperative nursery school and 54 percent of the others held at least one misconception, the strongest and most common fantasy being that the baby had always been inside the mother. The total amount of knowledge reported was also almost identical for the two groups. This is true despite the fact that the cooperative nursery-school children received more information at home and at school. We can only speculate at this point as to the reasons for this, but we base our conclusions on a developmental framework. Children at this level can understand, cognitively and emotionally, only a certain amount and a certain kind of sex information; beyond this level, it is repressed, denied, and in a variety of ways not understood. (Bernstein and Cowan say: "Children actively construct their notions about babies; they don't wait to be told about procreation before they have an idea of how it occurs. What is often taken as misinformation may largely be a product of their own assimilative process at work on materials with too complex a structure for them to understand."[4]) Talking about their family roles does not cause undue anxiety; however, in the instance of toilet training, the defensive nature of the responses was evident. We also found the children stoically unwilling to verbalize oral or anal pregnancy fantasies.

None of the adults or children in the study expressed any misgivings about having participated. Sixteen parents, in fact, felt the

interview had a positive effect, facilitating communication between spouses about sex education for their children. None of the children seemed upset, unhappy, or unusually curious about sex after the play interview. Eight reported to their parents that the play had been especially fun. The nursery-school teachers felt the study had been interesting and worthwhile to them personally, beneficial to the parents, and perhaps helpful to the overall welfare of the school.

NOTES TO CHAPTER TWENTY-FOUR

1. Hans Kreitler and Shulamith Kreitler, Children's Concepts of Sexuality and Birth, *Child Development* 37, 1966, 363-378; James Moore and Diane Kendall, Children's Concepts of Reproduction, *J. of Sex Research* 7, 1971, 42-61. Bernstein and Cowan have since presented particularly well-documented research on children's concepts of sex and birth in terms of children's cognitive levels which develop according to a Piagetian sequence (Anne C. Bernstein and Philip A. Cowan, Children's Concepts of How People Get Babies, *Child Development* 46, 1975, 77-91. Also, Anne C. Bernstein, How Children Learn About Sex and Birth, *Psychology Today*, January, 1976).

2. Kreitler and Kreitler; Moore and Kendall.

3. Andrew Andray, *How Babies are Made*, (New York: Time-Life, 1968).

4. Bernstein and Cowan, p. 90.

Chapter Twenty-Five

Ecological Patterns in the Schools—Some Observations

Rosalind Singer, M.A., M.P.H.*

Since there is a real question about the extent to which the schools should or should not teach little boys to behave like boys and little girls to behave like girls, these observations should not be labeled positive or negative.

We know, of course, that there is a great deal of sex-role stereotyping in classroom materials, textbooks, readers.[1] The bulk of classroom materials portrays girls as more passive and less inventive than boys. Men are portrayed in a variety of roles while women are almost always portrayed as mothers. There are, however, organizations and individuals working on these instructional materials with a view to doing the same things in regard to sex-role stereotyping as has been done with racial stereotypes.

There are various ways in which a teacher establishes an atmosphere in a classroom regarding gender development: choice of classroom decorations, choice of reading and other materials, reward and punishment of sex-stereotyped behavior, sex-differentiated activities, attitude toward sex competition, and sex division for classroom management and discipline.

The following table is a useful tool in classroom observations of atmosphere and teacher attitudes regarding sex and gender development:

*Health Education Consultant, Albany Unified School District, Albany, California.

Checklist for Classroom Atmosphere and
Teacher Attitudes Regarding Sex and Gender Development

1. Classroom decorations   Yes   No   Comments

    Equal attention to the sexes

    Girls and women in stereotyped roles

    Boys and men in stereotyped roles

2. Reading and other materials

    Books show only sex-stereotyped roles
    and activities

    Equal selection of reading books with
    male and female main characters

    Teacher has made effort to find non-
    sexist material

3. Reward and punishment of sex-stereotyped
   behavior

    Is there praise and reward for docile
    passive "female" behavior?

    Is there punishment and criticism of
    aggressive, "male" behavior?

4. Sex competition

    Do boys and girls compete with one another:
    a. Academically
    b. For attention
    c. In sports
    d. Other

5. Sex-differentiated activities

    Do boys and girls participate equally in:
    a. Dollhouse corner
    b. Blocks
    c. Sewing
    d. Active sports
    e. Room clean up
    f. Verbal lessons and games
    g. Math lessons and games

6. Sex division for room management and
   discipline. Where it is necessary to group
   students, is it done along sex lines?

    Examples: a. Walking to recess
                    b. Dismissing class
                    c. Free time vs. lesson time
                    d. Getting wraps, etc.
                    e. Room management chores
                    f. Other

The following observations were made during visits to randomly selected classrooms in Berkeley elementary schools. It is not implied that these classrooms are typical; they are only examples of classroom atmospheres.

KINDERGARTEN

The children were sitting on the floor in front of the teacher. She asked all of the boys to stand and line up along the side of the room. A girl was selected to count the boys. The process was then reversed when the girls lined up to be counted by a boy. Next a giant abacus was brought out and beads were counted out for the boys, next for the girls, and then all of the beads were counted for the number of children in the class. Question: What is the value of this activity other than learning numbers? Is there a learning experience involved in girls counting boys and boys counting girls?

At recess all the boys were sent for their wraps while the girls sat in front of the teacher. When the boys returned, the girls were sent out. The teacher took one boy and one girl by the hand and two lines were formed, all the boys behind the lead boy and all the girls behind the lead girl as they walked out to the playground. Question: What other ways are there to divide a group if division is necessary? Can a teacher use a variety of ways to make divisions for classroom management?

During free play time four children went to play in the doll corner. Three of them, girls, were inside the compound playing with dishes and dolls while the little boy took a broom and was sweeping outside. One of the little girls kept telling him it was time for the daddy to go to work, but the little boy just kept sweeping the floor. Another little girl wandered over into the doll corner and then a slight altercation began. Apparently there is a rule that only four children can be in the doll corner at a time and the little boy had worked his way over to the sink and was doing something with the dishes. The teacher came over to mediate the dispute and asked what was going on. One of the girls said the boy was messing things up at the dishes. The teacher then said to the boy, "Now daddies don't do things like that. Can't you just act like a daddy?" Question: What does the teacher mean when she says "act like a daddy?" How does the little boy perceive this command? Does the little boy have a daddy at home as a role model?

Only boys were using the blocks during free time. Both boys and girls were painting at the easels, but only girls were sitting at the tables and drawing. Question: Can one assume that these activities

are self-selected by the children's preferences or are they teacher inspired?

THIRD GRADE

In this classroom a chart was made by some of the children that showed the heights of all the children in the class with different colors used for boys and for girls. The chart clearly indicated that the girls are generally taller than the boys. Question: What could have been the purpose of this exercise? The chart was posted by itself on the board.

FOURTH GRADE

In this classroom there was a list on the blackboard of all the children who had to stay after school. All the names were boys'. Question: What kind of behavior is being punished? Is it stereotypical male behavior?

A mixed group of children sitting at a table were discussing "Where did you come from?" in terms of place or geography. One child said, "You came from your mommy's tummy," and another said, "But who took you out of her tummy?" To the reply, "I don't know," the question came back, "What was *his* name, you know, the doctor?" Even in fourth grade the children know that all doctors are men.

ANOTHER FOURTH GRADE

In this classroom the desks were arranged in rows, unlike the other fourth grades where the tables or desks were grouped. Listed on the blackboard were three stories that the children had read and were prepared to discuss. The stories were *Houdini*, *Robert Bruce*, and *Daedalus*. Question: Is it a coincidence that all the stories were about males? Are there many good stories about girls and women?

COMBINED FOURTH AND FIFTH GRADE CLASS

In this classroom *Free to Be You and Me*[2] was prominently displayed on the blackboard as suggested reading. On the bulletin board was a display of sewing projects done by different children with just as many done by boys as by girls, and equal in quality. Two advanced children, a boy and a girl, who had finished their arithmetic work, were playing chess while others were finishing their lessons. I wondered who the chess-playing role model was for the girl. This was

a most relaxed but very active classroom with a student teacher and a parent aid helping the teacher. Question: Was the teacher's obvious attitude toward eliminating sex-role stereotypes in part responsible for the relaxed atmosphere?

SIXTH GRADE

In this classroom the teacher was a young male dressed in P.E. clothes. There was an array of sports equipment in the corner of the room as well as the teacher's bicycle. Books and pictures around the room were predominantly of sports and sports heroes. The teacher stated that the boys are terribly behind the girls academically and particularly in verbal skills. He said that the girls used imagery and complex sentence structure while the boys could hardly write a simple declarative sentence. The teacher also decried the fact that girls were so hesitant to participate in sports. Question: What effect did that teacher's "rugged masculinity" in dress, appearance, and attitude have on the children in his classroom? With sports heroes as role models, what motivation did the boys have to learn to write?

CONCLUSION

In reviewing these observations, I can only conclude that generalizations are difficult to make. What I saw was a variety of atmospheres, ranging from a rigid and old-fashioned classroom to a very relaxed and modern one, as well as much in between. It was striking how some of the teachers consciously and unconsciously stereotyped gender roles. Since every teacher's teaching style is different, we can assume that there is also a great variety in attitudes toward sex-role stereotyping.

With regard to sex education, my experience leads me to make certain generalizations. First, girls are generally more willing to ask questions than are boys. This, I suppose, is because in our society it is still considered all right for girls to be ignorant about sex, while boys are supposed to know all the answers. Second, we learn that despite the enormous amount of time and space given to sex in the media and the availability of information through books, the students have a very poor command of the basic facts and maintain much misinformation.

Additionally, it is important to note the uneven rate of development we observe in children in all aspects of growth, including physical, sexual, and social-sexual development. A major problem is in designing course work to meet the needs of a diverse group. In the

academically heterogeneous classroom, we individualize instruction to meet the developmental needs of the children, but in sex education much of the class work is done as a whole class and with discussions. Why can't this kind of instruction be individualized so that it meets the needs of the students at a particular time?

In teaching teachers how to present sex education, the same sort of diversity exists as among the young students. A recent post graduate education class consisted of fifteen teachers and nurses involved in grades one through twelve. The group was mixed in race and age composition with blacks, Chicanos, Asian-Americans, and Caucasians, and ages from twenty-seven to sixty-two. In addition to the diversity in race and age was a remarkable variety of sexual sophistication. At one end of the spectrum was the second-grade teacher who asked in an anxious voice: "What do you do with a little boy who is playing with himself when he is doing his arithmetic?" She could not use the word "masturbate." In the same class was a teacher who had attended all sorts of lectures and symposia on sexuality and was easily at home with the concepts and jargon of sex education.

In conclusion, the answer to the question "What are the schools doing in the field of sex- and gender-role development?" is that they are doing a multitude of different things, most of which are dependent upon the personality of the teacher and his or her own sexual and gender feelings, awareness, and ideas. As to what the schools can do in this field, the answer lies in how much time, effort, and money we want to put into preservice and in-service training for the teachers who are ultimately responsible for these tasks.

NOTES TO CHAPTER TWENTY-FIVE

1. See Judith Stacey, Susan Bereaud, and Joan Daniels, eds., *And Jill Came Tumbling After—Sexism in American Education* (New York: Dell Publishing Co., 1974).

2. Marlo Thomas, *Free to Be You and Me*, (New York: McGraw-Hill, 1974).

Chapter Twenty-Six

Sex Education in the Intermediate Grades: A Course Description

Joyce Evans, M.A.*

Four years ago I was asked by the headmaster of our school to develop and teach a sex-education course for the fifth grade. The course described here has evolved out of research, study, experience, and course work. I hope it can serve as a model and resource for others as they develop programs that fit the needs and levels of the students and the personal style and philosphy of the individual teacher.

Approximately three weeks before the course begins, a letter is mailed home to all parents outlining the general topics to be presented each week, with the dates attached so that the parents know specifically what and when a topic is being taught and discussed. They are encouraged to discuss the class with their children, using this opportunity to present some of their own values and beliefs. Questions and comments are encouraged. In addition, a time is set for a parents' gathering at the conclusion of the course, so they can hear in detail the content that was presented, the methods for doing so, and some of the general reactions of their children.

In teaching this course, some of the goals are:

1. To dispel fears of the unknown by discussing and learning about bodily changes before they occur.
2. To enable the children to accept and respect a broad range of normal development and feelings, which, as a result, will make them more comfortable with their own.

---

*Fifth-grade teacher, Marin Country Day School, Corte Madera, California

3. To create a sense of wonder and excitement about their own sexuality, accepting it as an important, positive, integral part of their lives.
4. To establish an atmosphere of trust where their questions and feelings will be regarded with utmost care and concern.

The course is taught to groups of fifteen boys and girls together, meeting for weekly sessions of eighty-minute periods for five consecutive weeks. The students know each other, for they are together regularly for classes each day, and as their English teacher, I have established a rapport with them before the sex education sessions begin.

The classes meet during the regular school day and become part of the standard fifth-grade curriculum during this five-week period. Parents could request that their child not be involved, as is their prerogative in any subject, but thus far this has not occurred. Since it is treated administratively as part of the fifth-grade curriculum, it is accepted by parents as such.

SESSION I

The first session has a dual purpose: to establish an atmosphere where there is a high level of trust and to examine the masculine and feminine roles in our society, noting how they will affect the lives of the students in the class. The trusting atmosphere builds as the course progresses but is enhanced in the first session by sitting in a circle so that discussion can take place naturally and the teacher, as part of the circle, can sense nonverbal messages. It is vitally important that the teacher assume the role of facilitator or guide, not the traditional imparter of wisdom. In this first session I enjoy using a poem by R.D. Laing entitled "Knots." It seems to express the feelings pervading this first session:

> There is something I don't know
>   that I am supposed to know.
> I don't know what it is I don't know,
>   yet am supposed to know,
> And I feel I look stupid
>   if I seem both not to know it
>   and not know what it is I don't know.
>
> Therefore I pretend I know it.
> This is nerve-racking
>   since I don't know what I must pretend to know.
> Therefore I pretend to know everything.

I feel you know what I am supposed to know
    but you can't tell me what it is
    because you don't know that I don't know what it is.

You may know what I don't know,
    but not that I don't know it,
    and I can't tell you.
So you will have to tell me everything.[1]

After sharing this poem, along with some nervous giggles, we establish several rules. I state:

1. No question is a "dumb" question.
2. No question is a funny question.
3. As the teacher, I will try to answer all questions and will search for answers to questions that I don't know.
4. What happens in these sessions should be considered private, and questions and comments are confidential.
5. Although everyone is encouraged to take part in the discussions and activities, no one *must* participate.

Each class is encouraged to add any rules for their group that they feel would help them feel more at ease or gain more from the sessions.

We spend some time discussing our feelings of embarrassment. Using the book *The Family of Man,*[2] we look at expressions felt universally and then spend some time analyzing how we as individuals express our various feelings. The intent of this whole discussion is to help the students understand that giggling, laughing, blushing, etc. are all "normal," acceptable ways to express a feeling. As long as the laughing does not involve another person's questions or comments, there is no reason to be concerned.

In order to involve the students and begin helping them feel comfortable in voicing their opinions, I use a "Values Voting" exercise taken from Sidney Simon's *Value Clarification.*[3] Some of the questions on which the children vote are:

1. How many of you are glad to have a sex education course?
2. How many of you are a bit nervous about the course?
3. How many of you discuss sex freely with your parents?
4. How many of you have questions about sex which you have been afraid to ask?
5. How many of you wish boys and girls were taught sex education separately?
6. How many of you have at least one book at home on sex that you are allowed to read?

7. How many of you think it is okay for boys to play with dolls?
8. How many of you think it is all right for girls to play football?

Using old magazines, posterboard, glue, and scissors, small groups of three or four children are asked to make a poster showing how society defines "masculine" and "feminine." After about twenty minutes the students are asked to share their posters with the others, and some of the stereotypes are listed on the board.

A "Values Continuum" is then placed on the board.[4] At one end is the statement: "I feel my own sex is outstanding and dislike everything about the opposite sex." The other end states: "I dislike everything about my own sex and think the opposite sex is ideal." The students are then each asked to place themselves upon the continuum, any place but in the middle. They are asked to explain their position, if they wish, while no comments or judgments are allowed.

Without further discussion Lois Gould's story "X: A Fabulous Child's Story"[5] is read. This is a story about a child who was brought up by parents who agreed, as a scientific experiment, to rear it as neither male nor female. The story presents role problems, and what confronted this child as it went to school, not knowing if it should line up with the boys or the girls, play house or football. Another story read is "Atalanta,"[6] an old-fashioned tale about a princess who was to marry the winner of a race, as determined by her father, the king. She agreed but only if she could also run in the race. A free-flowing discussion follows by my merely asking: "What comments do you have about the stories?" With their new insights, the children generally ask: "May we change ourselves on the continuum if we wish?" With the new freedom they gain from the discussion and the stories, they are willing to reveal more about themselves on the continuum.

SESSION II

The second session deals with the male. The purpose of this session is to learn about the forthcoming changes that will occur in the boy's body.

This class begins with an unfinished sentence sheet[7] which includes some of the following:

1. I sometimes worry about . . .
2. I enjoy my own sex because . . .
3. I like the opposite sex because . . .

4. I am afraid that . . .
5. I wish I . . .,
6. My parents are . . .
7. If I could only . . .
8. I often think about . . .
9. With boys I . . .
10. With girls I . . .
11. I often find myself . . .
12. It makes me feel uncomfortable when . . .

The students are asked to complete the sentences by writing the first thought that comes into their minds. They are assured that there are no right or wrong answers and that their statements are anonymous, not to be shared with the class.

On the board or on a chart the following terms are written so that they are visible throughout this and all other sessions: *penis, foreskin, circumcision, scrotum, testicles, pubic, erection, ejaculation, sperm, semen, nocturnal emission, adolescence, pituitary gland, masturbation, rectum, anus, urine, urinate, bladder, hormones.* Using a chart of the reproductive system, all of the terms are simply explained.[8] When a term such as *penis* is mentioned, we sometimes discuss briefly some of the other terms that are used at home or at school, stating that for many these are acceptable as well, but to insure clarity in discussion, we will use the same term throughout the course.

Before showing the film *Boy to Man*[9] I pass out question cards to direct the children's thinking during the film. Sample questions are: What is the cause of acne? At what age does the film say boys begin to produce sperm? and What is the function of the testicles? After the film these questions can be shared and discussed or simply handed in.

Since this is the first discussion that is emotionally charged, I find it important to give support to questions and comments as they are raised. I often state: "That's a question that is frequently asked" or "I can see why you would wonder about that" or "Many of the others are no doubt wondering about that too." Usually I pass out blank cards during any discussion so that those who prefer to write a question as it comes to mind may do so and later deposit it in the question box.

In answering questions I use the following guidelines:

1. I answer the question briefly with the idea that if the student wants more he or she will ask for more.

2. I restate the question and check to be sure I understand the intent.
3. If I sense a personal fear or guilt within the question, I try to speak to that as well.

For example, one girl asked hesitatingly, "If a girl already has her periods but a boy doesn't have sperms, can she become pregnant?" I surmised that the girl had recently been involved in some sort of sex play and was worried, so it was appropriate to answer the question and to mention the frequency and general harmless nature of most sex play in preadolescence.

Near the end of this session I distribute a simplified outline chart of the male body and ask the students to label the parts, using the vocabulary list from the board.

This period ends with some "I Learned" statements as explained in Sidney Simon's book. Some of the statements that I use are:

1. I learned that I . . .
2. I realized that I . . .
3. I relearned that I . . .
4. I noticed that I . . .
5. I was surprised that I . . .
6. I was pleased that I . . .
7. I was displeased that I . . .

By the end of this session, most of the students are open and willing to participate and discuss. The shyness and embarrassment returns for a few moments at the beginning of successive sessions, but generally the children are at ease.

SESSION III

The third session's purpose is to learn about the impending changes of the girl's body and to become familiar with the accompanying vocabulary. The class begins with the following terms listed on the board or a chart: *vagina, uterus, ovaries, Fallopian tubes, clitoris, hymen, menstruation, sanitary napkin, Tampon, pituitary gland, hormones, pubic, puberty, adolescence, rectum, anus, bladder, egg, masturbation, urine, urinate, acne.* As these terms are located on a pictorial chart, the students locate and label a blank dittoed chart.

The film, *Naturally a Girl*[10] is then shown, after which questions and comments are discussed. Sometime during the discussion I show a sanitary belt, a sanitary napkin, and a tampon, available in a special teaching kit.[11] Each girl is given the booklet "Growing Up and

Liking It,"[1][2] written for girls of this grade level. Classroom copies
are made available for the boys to read. An additional booklet,
"Boys: Have You Wondered What Happens When Girls Grow
Up?"[1][3] could be used but I have found the boys generally uninter-
ested in it but anxious to read the girls' booklet.

The following questionnaire from the California Youth Authority's "Family Life Education, Curriculum Guide"[1][4] is used next.
Adapted for this level it reads:

For each word listed, put a check in the proper column.

	Male	Female	Both
1. Fallopian tube			
2. Clitoris			
3. Testicles			
4. Penis			
5. Rectum			
6. Semen			
7. Erection			
8. Uterus			
9. Nocturnal emission			
10. Menstruation			
11. Ovaries			
12. Sperm			
13. Egg			
14. Anus			
15. Vagina			
16. Circumcision			
17. Hormones			
18. Ejaculation			
19. Masturbation			
20. Urinate			
21. Pubic			
22. Tampon			
23. Pituitary gland			
24. Scrotum			
25. Adolescence			

I allow this to be done or at least checked with a partner,
suggesting that changes be freely made until the list is correct.

SESSION IV

Session four deals with sexual intercourse and childbirth, becoming
familiar with terminology and gaining a sense of wonder about the
whole reproductive process.

New terms for this week include: *sexual intercourse, orgasm, fertilization, fetus, labor, umbilical cord, contractions, pregnancy, placenta, navel.* Again these terms are located on the chart and discussed with the class.

Children of this age are very interested in the act of sexual intercourse itself. In the television series *"Time of Your Life,"* Mrs. Marilyn McCurdy described it in the following manner:

> When a man and woman are married, they are closer to their husband or wife than they are to any other person. They trust each other and they can share things with their married partner that they could not share with anyone else. A man and wife have many ways of showing their love for each other. Some ways are being thoughtful and considerate of each other, or by saying "I love you." One very important way that they have of showing their love is by their physical contact and having what is called sexual intercourse. When a couple has sexual intercourse, this is physically the closest they can ever be. This is a beautiful way of showing and sharing the love that they have for each other. When a couple has intercourse, they are usually lying down very close to each other and usually in a bed. They often start by kissing and holding each other. Each person, the man and the woman, feel a very strong feeling of love for the other and excitement in being together. The man's penis has an erection and the women's vagina becomes moist or wet. At this point, as the couple is lying very close together and because the penis of the man is designed by nature to fit into the vagina of the woman, the man pushes his penis into the woman's vagina. He has an ejaculation and this is when the sperm are released into the vagina. They begin traveling into the uterus and up into the tubes. Their tiny tail propels them and they move quickly. At the time that a man's penis has an ejaculation, or when the sperm come out, they get a very strong but very good feeling called an orgasm or climax. After this happens the couple usually lie, still very close together, very quietly and still. They experience a very peaceful, warm and loving feeling toward each other.[15]

My description follows these lines, avoiding any sexist view and being sure to include the following points:

1. Intercourse is an expression of love between a man and woman, just as words, gifts, and special deeds are such expressions.
2. Intercourse is called the ultimate expression, in that it is the closest two human beings can be.
3. Warm, loving feelings accompany the act.
4. The strong, excitable feeling during intercourse is called orgasm.

After this discussion the film *Human Reproduction*[16] is shown. Since children of this age are fascinated by childbirth, questions

following the film abound. My general rule is to answer them all to the best of my ability, spending little time on the rare or unusual item such as Siamese twins, but rather on the majority of births and the feelings that accompany the birth.

This session is ended with "I Wonder" statements as suggested by Simon. Some of those I use are:

I wonder if . . .
I wonder how come . . .
I wonder about . . .
I wonder why . . .
I wonder whether . . .
I wonder when . . .

Normally I use these orally, allowing those who wish to participate to do so. They can be written, however, if that seems suitable.

SESSION V

The fifth and final session is a question period. The question box is used, questions from previous years are read and answered if the class so desires, and spontaneous questions from the students are encouraged as well. Some of the questions that are repeated by students over the years are listed here. From the questions asked one can surmise the maturity, the fear, the knowledge, the curiosity, and the concern of preadolescents.

1. How long does pubic hair grow?
2. Can people tell when a girl is having her period?
3. Does a girl have any warning before she has her first period?
4. Do you need both testicles to have sperm?
5. Does the size of the penis make any difference?
6. Does menstruation hurt?
7. What if you start your period at school?
8. How come the ovaries take turns releasing eggs?
9. Can you have intercourse right after the baby is born?
10. What causes twins?
11. Can you have intercourse before you have sperm?
12. Can boys have erections when they are not sexually excited?
13. What is in the water that the baby floats in?
14. Why is the baby bloody?
15. What would happen if a man urinated while in the middle of intercourse?
16. What if the woman has to go to the bathroom while delivering the baby?

17. How does the pill work?
18. Why don't people just not have intercourse if they don't want a baby?
19. What is a fag?
20. Why do parents get embarrassed?

These questions are answered with concern and care, trying to understand why they are asked while at the same time keeping the answers simple. Many of these things were discussed during the course but, as with other subjects, the students may have been "tuned out" or it may indicate a real concern in this area and a desire to have it "double checked."

At the end of this session I ask the students to write an evaluation of the course. The form includes the following questions:

1. Three things I like best about the course:
   a.
   b.
   c.
2. Three things I like least about the course:
   a.
   b.
   c.
3. If we were to have the course again I would suggest that . . .
4. The most important thing I learned for me was . . .
5. One thing we didn't discuss that I wish we had is . . .
6. One thing I would like to add is . . .

The closing discussion centers around the parents' meeting. It is from the students' advice and suggestions that I plan what I will share and the manner in which it will be expressed. I assure them that I will not reveal anything that anyone said specifically, but will instead share their general reactions, concerns, and questions.

NOTES TO CHAPTER TWENTY-SIX

1. R.D. Laing, *Knots* (New York: Pantheon Books, 1970).

2. Edward Steichen, *The Family of Man* (New York: Simon and Shuster, 1967).

3. Sidney Simon, Leland W. Howe, and Howard Kirschenbaum, *Values Clarification—A Handbook of Practical Strategies for Teachers and Students* (New York: Hart Publ. Co., 1972).

4. *Ibid.*

5. Lois Gould, X: A Fabulous Child's Story, *Ms.* 1 (6), December, 1972, 74-76, 105-106.

6. Betty Miles, Atalanta, 1 (9), March, 1973, 75-78.

7. Sidney Simon.

8. Reproduction and Human Development Study Prints (Instructional Aids, Inc. 1970).

9. *Boy to Man* (Churchill Films, 1962).

10. *Naturally a Girl*, Personal Products Co., Consumer Information Center; Box 6-GU; Milltown, N.J. 08850.

11. Personal Products Co., Milltown, New Jersey.

12. *Growing Up and Liking It*, Personal Products, Milltown, New Jersey, 1974.

13. *Boys: Have You Wondered What Happens When Girls Grow Up?* Personal Products; Milltown, New Jersey.

14. Family Life Education Curriculum Guide, Department of the Youth Authority, State of California, January, 1974.

15. William H. Ayres and Marilyn McCurdy, *Time of Your Life—Teacher's Manual*, San Francisco: KQED.

16. *Human Reproduction*, McGraw-Hill Films, 1965.

MATERIALS

Ayres, William H. and McCurdy, Marilyn, *Time of Your Life—Teachers's Manual*, Openheimer Management Corp., San Francisco, 1971.

Boy to Man, Churchill Films, 1962.

Boys: Have You Wondered What Happens When Girls Grow Up? Personal Products; Milltown, New Jersey.

Family Life Education Curriculum Guide, Department of the Youth Authority, State of California, January, 1974.

Gould, Lois, X: A Fabulous Child's Story. *Ms. Magazine* 1 (6), (December, 1972), 74-76, 105-106.

Growing Up and Liking It, Personal Products; Milltown, New Jersey, 1974.

Human Reproduction, McGraw-Hill Films, 1965.

Miles, Betty, Atalanta. *Ms. Magazine* 1 (9), (March 1973), 75-78.

Naturally a Girl, Personal Products Co., Consumer Information Center; Box 6-GU; Milltown, N.J. 08850.

Reproduction and Human Development Study Prints, Instructional Aids, Inc., 1970.

Simon, Sidney; Howe, L.W., and Kirschenbaum, H., *Values Clarifications: A Handbook of Practical Strategies for Teachers and Students.* New York: Hart Publishing Co., 1972.

Steichen, Edward, *The Family of Man* (New York: Simon and Shuster, 1967).

✳ *Chapter Twenty-Seven*

Dealing with Pubertal
Developmental Tasks in
the Classroom

Gale J. Brownell*

Family life education programs attempt to assist prepubertal and pubertal students in dealing with certain developmental tasks. As a teacher of a course in family life
education in a junior high school, I have developed a one-semester
course now required by our board of education, based on an outline
proposed by a community wide group of parents, students, clergy,
and teachers. All eighth-graders normally enroll in this program, but
there have been a few exceptions. Students may be excused from the
course for religious reasons or if the parents, teacher, counselor,
and/or the student feel the student would not benefit from the
course.

It is generally felt that these students need to know what is
physically happening to their bodies, how their bodies function with
these changes, and how to accept these sometimes exciting and
sometimes frightening changes. A small yet significant number of
youngsters lack accurate knowledge of the fundamental pubertal
changes taking place. A sizable majority understand that these
changes enable them to become parents, but they do not seem to
understand either how or why the individual parts of their bodies
function as they do. Providing them with opportunities to learn
about pubertal changes and reproductive function is relatively simple
for the students generally relish the opportunities to learn facts
about themselves. The classroom library provides books and other
materials at a variety of reading levels to encourage students of all

*Teacher, Family Life Education, Martin Luther King., Jr. High School,
Berkeley

209

reading abilities. (See pp. 213-216 for partial listing. In addition, my colleagues and I frequently rewrite materials to accommodate students of lower reading levels.) There is always a waiting list for some books, and many are kept by the students over an extended period of time. Students often report that they have lent the books to friends or relatives. The students are allowed to use whatever materials best suit them to find the answers to questions on the reproductive system and reproductive function. Many will check several sources for the information they seek.

Classroom discussions are frequently the most effective way to teach more about physical and sexual development. Once I introduce the subject, I can expect an avalanche of questions. Although some students are slow to begin asking questions, a generally relaxed atmosphere enables the students to pose their questions, these often being the vehicle for the entire unit on puberty. When students seem to have questions but are reluctant to ask them, I encourage them to ask *any* questions using any language they choose. Although I do not use "any language" to answer the questions, and sometimes choose not to answer personal questions, I feel that this freedom helps them to participate. It is important not to use a strict outline to structure the discussions, but rather to let an outline guide the teacher.

When it is appropriate to the subject matter, I may demonstrate issues by describing personal experiences or those of others. In addition, guest speakers are invited to make presentations in the classroom. The junior-high students find these visitors interesting and reap the benefits of being stimulated by another knowledgeable person, reinforcing the learning that has, it is hoped, preceded the visit.

Visual aids like movies and film strips are useful, as well. (See pp. 216-218 for a partial listing.) Good film strips, in fact, are an invaluable teaching aid, especially for students who learn more readily by means other than reading.

Students of this age seem particularly attracted to the bizarre, as noted by their interest in the *Guinness Book of World Records*, *Ripley's Believe It Or Not*, or Dr. Money's *Sex Errors of the Body*.[1] They avidly consume any accounts of developmental anomalies. I think this is part of the fantasy-reality-fear issue of children's development. Because of this, students need help in defining the normal range with respect to their own body organs and processes. They need help in determining what is fantasy and what is reality. This especially relates to their concerns with the time of onset of puberty and with the size of sex organs. Our society's equation of larger size with better quality sorely tests the self-esteem of many

young people. Even the most developed youngsters feel inadequate about their bodies, to say nothing of the late-bloomers. Since it is the exceptions rather than the normal range which receive the attention, especially in the media, I feel that we must concentrate on helping students realize how most are in the broad normal range rather than in the extremes.

Students enjoy participating in a classroom project that illustrates this issue. Each student's height is measured and plotted on graphs to aid in the understanding that the very short and very tall are part of the normal range, but that most are within a much smaller distribution. Discussions then help students apply this principle to all aspects of their developing bodies.

Junior-high students have three complex psychological tasks: establishing a sexual identity, establishing personal value systems, and finding comfortable ways to relate to others, especially to those of the opposite sex. Sexual identity is a difficult and crucial area with which to deal, especially these days, as young people are now confronted with society's confusions and transitions about male and female roles, as well as with the normal search for appropriate roles that occurs at this stage. The overlapping of sex-role identities makes it more difficult for some young people to achieve a clear picture of who they are. While this overlapping makes sex-role identity formation more difficult for some, fortunately, for others these changes provide a freedom to be more comfortable in directions not socially acceptable in the past.

Current events discussions inevitably bring up questions of female-male role identities. In these discussions students hear about wide ranges of acceptable role identities in different segments of the community. The media also presents a wider range of sexual role models. Women are appearing in many more areas of the work world, performing jobs that were once only in the male domain; men are in the news because some are becoming single adoptive parents, some are given custody of their children, some are working in the home while mates work elsewhere. Homosexuals and bisexuals are making their lifestyles known by demanding equal rights. Women may be seen as "strong" and men may be seen as being affectionate or vulnerable. Discussion of all of these issues in the classroom allows the pubertal students verbally to try on or test a variety of roles. This contributes toward a healthy resolution of the sexual identity conflicts that children in this stage experience.

Pubertal youngsters also need help in clarifying their values and developing comfortable patterns of relating to others. They seem constantly to check out ways of handling situations, and then to

question whether what they think, do, or say is acceptable to themselves and to their peer group. They are often careful to negate parents or teachers, in an attempt to lessen their dependence on their adult role models. Unfortunately there are few places or instances where most youngsters can discuss the values and relationship questions they are experiencing. I try to provide an environment in which it is safe to experience a variety of positions on these issues.

I frequently borrow from Simon and provide classroom activities that offer opportunities to work through some of these value issues.[2] I find that many of the activities can be utilized in the spare minutes just before the passing bell rings. I might ask students to state a one-sentence viewpoint on a specific issue or to tell what they are proud of having done in the past week. I also use "public interviews" of three to five minutes in which students volunteer to be interviewed by me and/or another student in front of the class. They are given the option of refusing to answer any of the questions, but the majority of the queries are answered. Public interviews seem to be a very successful device for getting to value-loaded issues in a way that lends dignity to each individual's viewpoint. They also seem to have carry-over value. I have frequently heard students continuing discussions that obviously had their beginnings in a value-oriented public interview.

Another stratagem that I employ is called "Coat of Arms." I ask the students to sketch a shield (stipulating that artistic skill is not a criterion for grade evaluation). The shield is to be divided into four or perhaps six areas, and a scene or symbol is to be sketched in each area. I specify what each area should signify: one might be the student's greatest achievement to date, one might be his or her biggest "flub." I might ask each to show what each is working to improve upon or to indicate aspirations for the future. These coats of arms illustrate the students' value decisions graphically, especially when they are posted around the classroom. They also serve as good points for discussion.

As part of the unit on personal development, I assign students the task of bringing in four letters, each to be descriptive of the individual student. One letter is to be written by the student about himself as he is now, *not* emphasizing autobiography. Another is to be written by a good friend; the third is written anonymously by a classmate who draws the particular name from a hat; and the fourth is to be written by a family member. Sometimes I hear the comment, "Nobody in my family is going to write about me." I find that if I suggest a family member write a note to that effect, for equal credit, the letter is written. It is often difficult to get the students to ask

others for the letters, but the dividends of the effort are evidenced when I return all the letters to the students. Many of them positively glow about themselves, especially when they read the letters from their families. They are pleased to see what people have to say about them, even if they are critical in some senses. Many parents seem not to take the time to tell their children how they feel about them, so this letter gives them the opportunity to talk to their children about what "neat kids" they are. I have had good responses from both parents and students about this particular exercise.

In summary, I see six developmental tasks for pubertal students. There are three relating to the physical realm: learning about their bodily changes, accepting those changes, and learning how their bodies, especially the reproductive system, functions. I see the psychological tasks as establishing a sexual identity, questioning and formulating personal values, and establishing comfortable patterns of relating to others, especially those of the opposite sex. Many stratagems must be employed in the classroom to assist young people in attaining these developmental tasks.

NOTES TO CHAPTER TWENTY-SEVEN

1. Norris McWhirter and Ross McWhirter, *Guinness Book of World Records* (New York: Sterling Publishing Co., 1975); Robert L. Ripley, *Ripley's Believe It or Not* (New York: Simon and Schuster, 1975); John Money, *Sex Errors of the Body* (Baltimore: Johns Hopkins Press, 1968).

2. Sidney B. Simon, Leland W. Howe, and Howard Kirschenbaum, *Values Clarification: A Handbook of Practical Strategies for Teachers and Students* (New York: Hart Publishing Co., 1972).

MATERIALS*

Books and Pamphlets

Personal Development

American Guidance Service, *The Coping with Books*. Circle Pine, Minn., 1970.

Gesell, Arnold; Ilg, Frances; and Ames, Louise, *Youth: The Years from 10-16*. New York: Harper and Brothers, 1956.

Hall, Elizabeth, *Why We Do What We Do: A Look At Psychology*. Boston: Houghton Mifflin Co., 1973.

LeShan, Eda J., *What Makes Me Feel This Way? Growing Up With an Emotion*. New York: Macmillan Co., 1974.

Lewellen, John, *You and Your Amazing Mind*. Chicago: Children's Press, 1952.

*In addition, although not listed here, are materials on drugs and related topics also used in the course described.

McBain, William R. and Johnson, R.C., *The Science of Ourselves: Adventures in Experimental Psychology.* New York: Harper and Row, 1962.

Menninger, William G., *How To Be A Successful Teenager.* New York: Sterling Publishing Co., 1954.

Smith, Sally L., *Nobody Said It's Easy.* New York: MacMillan Co., 1965.

Sexual Development

Bauer, William W. and Bauer, Florence Marvyne, *Way To Womanhood.* Garden City, New York: Doubleday and Co., Inc. 1965.

Corner, George W., *Attaining Manhood.* New York: Harper and Brothers, 1938.

_____, *Attaining Womanhood.* New York: Harper and Brothers, 1939.

Duvall, Evelyn Millis, *About Sex and Growing Up.* New York: Association Press, 1968.

*_____, *Love and the Facts of Life.* New York: Association Press, 1967.

Gordon, Sol, *Facts About Sex For Today's Youth.* New York: John Day Co., 1973.

Guttmacher, Alan, *Understanding Sex: A Young Person's Guide.* New York: Harper and Row, 1970.

Hettlinger, Richard, *Growing Up with Sex.* New York: Seabury Press, 1971.

*Hofstein, Sadie and Bauer, William W., *The Human Story: Facts On Birth, Growth and Reproduction.* New York: Lothrop, Lee and Shepard Co., 1969.

Jensen, Gordon D., *Youth and Sex: Pleasure and Responsibility.* Chicago: Nelson Hall Co., 1973.

*Johnson, Eric W., *Love and Sex in Plain Language.* Philadelphia: J.B. Lippincott Co., 1974.

_____, *Sex: Telling It Straight.* Philadelphia: J.B. Lippincott Co., 1970.

May, Julian, *Man and Woman.* Chicago: Follett Publishing Co., 1969.

Moore, Marcena and Moore, Trevor W., *Sex, Sex, Sex.* Notre Dame, Ind.: Ave Maria Press, 1969.

Pomeroy, Wardell B., *Boys and Sex.* New York: Delacorte Press, 1960.

_____, *Girls and Sex.* New York: Delacorte Press, 1969.

Schoenfeld, Eugene, *Dear Doctor Hip Pocrates.* New York: Ballantine, 1973.

Southard, Helen F., *Sex Before Twenty: New Answers for Young People.* New York: E.P. Dutton and Co., 1971.

Spock, Benjamin, *A Teenager's Guide to Life and Love.* New York: Simon and Schuster, 1970.

Tanner, James M.; Tayler, Gordon R., and editors of Time-Life, *Growth.* New York: Time, Inc., 1965.

Widerberg, Siv, *The Kids Own XYZ of Love and Sex.* New York: Stein and Day, 1972.

Wright, Erna, *Painless Menstrual Periods.* New York: Hart Publishing Co., 1967.

Pregnancy and Childbirth

Bewley, Sheila and Sheffield, Margaret, *Where Do Babies Come From?* New York: Alfred A. Knopf, 1973.

*Indicates Class Sets

Day, Beth and Liley, Margaret, *The Secret World of the Baby*. New York: Random House, 1968.
Ets, Marie Hall, *The Story of a Baby*. New York: Viking Press, 1939.
Flanagan, Geraldine L., *The First Nine Months of Life*. New York: Simon and Schuster, 1962.
Guttmacher, Alan F., *Pregnancy and Birth*. New York: Viking Press, 1956.
Mitchell, Robert M. and Klein, Ted, *Nine Months to Go*. New York: Ace Publishing Co., 1973.
Montagu, Ashley, *Life Before Birth*. New York: New American Library, 1964.
Navarra, John G., Weisberg, Joseph S., and Mele, Frank M., *From Generation to Generation*. Garden City, New York: Natural History Press, 1970.
Nilsson, Lennart, *A Child is Born*. New York: Delacorte Press, 1966.
Portal, Colette, *The Beauty of Birth*. New York: Alfred A. Knopf, 1974.
Sundgaard, Arnold, *The Miracle of Growth*. Urbana: University of Illinois Press, 1967.
Wright, Erna, *The New Childbirth*. New York: Hart Publishing Co., 1968.

Miscellaneous

Bauer, William W., and Bauer, Florence Marvyne, *To Enjoy Marriage*. Garden City, New York: Doubleday and Co., 1967.
Blanzaco, Andre, *VD: Facts You Should Know*. New York: Lothrop, Lee and Shepard, 1970.
Brownmiller, Susan, *Against Our Will: Men, Women, and Rape*. New York: Simon and Schuster, 1975.
Connell, Noreen and Wilson, Cassandra, eds., *Rape: The First Sourcebook for Women*. New York: New American Library, 1974.
Consumers Union, *The Consumers Union Report on Family Planning*. Mt. Vernon, New York: Consumers Union, 1966.
Editorial Research Reports, *Medical Issues*. Washington, D.C.: Congressional Quarterly, Inc.
Ehrlish, Paul, *The Population Bomb*. New York: Ballantine Books, 1971.
Fleming, Alice, *Psychiatry: What's It All About*. Chicago: Henry Regnery Co., 1972.
Fontana, Vincent J., *Somwhere a Child Is Crying: The Battered Child*. New York: Macmillan Publishing Co., 1973.
Gardner, Richard A., *The Boys' and Girls' Book About Divorce*. New York: Jason Aronson, 1970.
Gillette, Paul, *Vasectomy Information Manual*. New York: Dutton, 1972.
Gray, Marian and Gray, Roger, *How To Take The Worry Out of Being Close*. Oakland, California, 1971.
Hanna, John P., *Teenagers and the Law*. Boston: Ginn and Co., 1967.
Haverman, Ernest and editors of Time-Life, *Birth Control*. New York: Time, Inc., 1967.
Hyde, Margaret O., *This Crowded Planet*. New York: McGraw-Hill Book Co., 1961.
_____, *VD: The Silent Epidemic*. New York: McGraw-Hill Book Co., 1973.

Jay, Karla and Young, Allen, eds., *Out of the Closets: Voices of Gay Liberation.* New York: Douglas/Links, 1972.

Johnson, Eric, W., *VD.* Philadelphia: J.B. Lippincott Co., 1973.

Langone, John, *Goodbye to Bedlam: Understanding Mental Illness and Retardation.* Boston: Little, Brown and Co., 1974.

Lieberman, E. James and Peck, Ellen, *Sex and Birth Control: A Guide for the Young.* New York: Thomas Y. Crowell Co., 1973.

Lifton, Robert J. and Olson, Eric, *Living and Dying.* New York: Praeger Press, 1974.

Liston, Robert A., *The Edge of Madness: Prison and Prison Reforms in America.* New York: Franklin Watts, Inc., 1972.

Lobel, Suzanne, *Conception, Contraception: A New Look.* New York: McGraw-Hill Book Co., 1974.

Loeb, Robert H., Jr. and Maloney, John P., *Your Legal Rights As a Minor.* New York: Franklin Watts, Inc. 1974.

Mead, Margaret and Wolfenstein, Martha, eds., *Childhood in Contemporary Cultures.* Chicago: University of Chicago Press, 1955.

Montreal Health Press, eds., *Birth Control Handbook.* Montreal: Montreal Health Press, Inc., 1974.

Murtagh, John M., *Cast the First Stone.* New York: McGraw-Hill Book Co., 1957.

Nolen, William A., *Spare Parts for the Human Body.* New York: Random House, 1971.

O'Neill, Nena and O'Neill, George, *Open Marriage: A New Life-Style for Couples.* New York: M. Evans and Co., 1972.

Osborn, Fairfield, ed., *Our Crowded Planet.* Garden City, New York: Doubleday and Co., 1962.

Pierson, Elaine, *Sex Is Never an Emergency: A Candid Guide for Young Adults.* Philadelphia: J.B. Lippincott Co., 1973.

Reich, Hanns, ed., *Children and Their Fathers.* New York: Hill and Wang, 1962.

_____, *Children and Their Mothers.* New York: Hill and Wang, 1964.

_____, *Baby Animals and Their Mothers.* New York: Hill and Wang, 1965.

Steichen, Edward, *The Family of Man.* New York: Simon and Shuster, 1967.

Sundgaard, Arnold, *The Miracle of Growth.* Urbana: Univ. of Ill. Press, 1967.

Wyden, Peter and Wyden, Barbara, *Growing Up Straight: What Every Thoughtful Parent Should Know About Homosexuality.* New York: Stein and Day, 1968.

Audiovisual Aids

Personal Development
The Adolescent Experience: Understanding Emotions, Parts I and II. Guidance Associates, 1973.

Dealing With Group Pressure. Guidance Associates, 1973.

The Game. Contemporary/McGraw-Hill Films, 1966.

The Merry-Go-Round. Contemporary/McGraw-Hill Films, 1967.

Sex: A Moral Dilemma For Teenagers, Parts I and II. Guidance Associates, 1966.

Sexual Values in Society, Parts I and II. Guidance Associates, 1969.
Sixteen in Webster Groves. Carousel Films, Inc., 1966.
Teenage Rebellion: Challenge to Authority, Parts I and II. Guidance Associates, 1971.
Tom and Anne: Making Out. Perennial Education, Inc., 1970.
Values for Teenagers in the 1970s, Parts I and II. Guidance Associates, 1973.
Your Personality: The You Others Know. Guidance Associates, 1969.

Sexual Development
About You: Boys. Warren Schloat Productions, 1970.
About You: Girls. Warren Schloat Productions, 1970.
Achieving Adulthood. Henk Newenhouse, 1968.
The Acme Acne Factory. Teachers Library, 1973.
Becoming A Man: Maturation and Growth, Parts I and II. Guidance Associates, 1968.
Becoming A Woman: Maturation and Growth, Parts I and II. Guidance Associates, 1968.
Boy to Man. Churchill Films, 1962.
Girl to Woman. Churchill Films, 1966.
Growing into Manhood: A Middle School Approach, Parts I and II. Guidance Associates, 1968.
Growing into Womanhood: A Middle School Approach, Parts I and II. Guidance Associates, 1968.
Learning About Sex. Guidance Associates, 1968.
Love and the Facts of Life: A Series (in 7 parts), KQED Productions, 1967.
Masculinity and Femininity. Guidance Associates, 1969.
Sex Education: Understanding Growth and Social Development. GAF Corp., 1968.
World of a Girl. Modern Talking Picture Services, 1964.

Pregnancy and Childbirth
All My Babies. Columbia University Press, 1953.
Birth. Film-Makers' Library, 1968.
Childbirth. Henk Newenhouse, 1967.
Childbirth: The Great Adventure. Childbirth Education League, 1963.
Have a Healthy Baby. Churchill Films, 1969.
How Life Begins, Parts I and II. Contemporary/McGraw-Hill Films, 1968.
Human Heredity. Henk Newenhouse, 1969.
Human Reproduction 100. Guidance Associates, 1969.
A Normal Birth. Medical Arts Productions, 1951.
Physiology of Birth. Warren Schloat Productions, 1970.
The Wonder of New Life. Encyclopedia Britannica Films, 1967.

Miscellaneous
And They Lived Happily Ever After. Guidance Associates, 1967.
Beyond Conception. Population Dynamics, 1968.
Courtship and Marriage, Parts I and II. Contemporary/McGraw-Hill Films, 1962.

Do We Live or Exist? Guidance Associates, 1971.
Family Planning Today, Parts I and II. Guidance Associates, 1970.
Her Name Was Ellie, His Name Was Lyle. Louis de Rochemont Associates, 1966.
The Homosexuals. Carousel Films, 1967.
How an Average Child Behaves, Ages 1-5 (in 5 parts). Parents Magazine Films, 1968.
How Would You Like to Be Old? Parts I and II. Guidance Associates, 1973.
Juvenile Thief. Guidance Associates, 1972.
Kathy. Aims Association Instructional Materials, 1969.
Living With Dying, Parts I and II. Sunburst Communications, 1973.
Modern Women; The Uneasy Life, Parts I and II. Indiana University Audio-Visual Center, 1967.
Phoebe: Story of a Pre-Marital Pregnancy. Contemporary/McGraw-Hill Films, 1965.
A Quarter-Million Teenagers. Churchill Films, 1964.
The Squeeze. Henk Newenhouse, 1964.
Teenage Pregnancy. Sterling Educational Films, 1970.
Tomorrow Happens Today. Glenn Educational Films, 1968.
To Plan Your Family. Churchill Films, 1968.
VD—Name Your Contacts. Coronet Instructional Films, 1968.
VD: What you Should Know, (Series in 3 parts). Guidance Associates, 1973.
Venereal Disease: A Present Danger, Parts I and II. Guidance Associates, 1968.
What is Marriage, Parts I and II. Guidance Associates, 1971.
The Wheels of Justice. New York Times, 1972.
You and the Law, Guidance Associates, 1969.

Chapter Twenty-Eight

Sex Education in Sweden

Floyd M. Martinson, Ph.D.*

If any country in the world has tried to establish a program of sex education for all young people, it is Sweden. Sweden has had sex education in elementary schools since 1942, and it has been compulsory since 1956. Sweden has a strong commitment to equality of the sexes and high regard for the freedom of the individual in the area of sexual behavior.

The Swedish Board of Education published an official sex-education handbook for teachers.[1] The schools were to provide a unified course of instruction which paid attention to society's demands on the person; that is, the emphasis on respect for sex and respect for other people. Also the program was to relate directly to the concerns of youth. Teaching material was to be keyed to the level of the development of the pupils. As a result of this official action, sex education became a part of the curriculum at all three levels in the nine years of compulsory education that begin at age seven. Kindergarten schools have only recently been introduced.

At the lower level of the compulsory school, ages seven to ten, the pupils learn about the differences between the sexes, where babies come from, the father's role in conception, developments before birth, the process of birth, and how babies depend on their parents and their families.

At eleven through thirteen, the children study the structure and functions of the sex organs, puberty, menstruation, nocturnal emissions, masturbation, conception, pregnancy, traumatic experiences during pregnancy, development of the fetus, labor, sex determina-

---

*Professor of Sociology, Gustavus Adophus College; St. Peter, Minnesota

tion, twinning, and the infant's postnatal dependence on the mother. Information on some sexual "deviation," such as exhibitionism and homosexuality, is also covered in this age grouping.

Since 1956, *all* these matters have been taught in *mixed* classes. The handbook states that menstruation must be covered during the fifth year of school, so that girls shall be prepared for menarche. This instruction, like all sex instruction, is for both boys and girls. During this year, the teacher also discusses sexual intercourse. This is illustrated by using an overhead projector to show the woman's organs on one transparency with a transparency superimposed, showing the male with the erect penis, demonstrating how the penis fits in the vagina. This is explicit education. The lecture is followed by discussion and questions from the pupils.

The fourteen-to-sixteen-year-olds are taught sex education principally by the biology teacher, with the help of the school physician and school nurse. Subjects covered are verification of pregnancy, pregnancy, the development of the fetus, abortions, venereal disease, contraceptives, sterilization, and menopause. Contraceptives are brought into the classroom and their usefulness is discussed.

The biology teacher, however, is not the only teacher of sex education in the Swedish schools. Material is also covered by the social-studies teacher and the religion teacher. (Religion is taught in the public schools.) The social-studies teacher talks about social problems regarding sex, and the religion teacher talks primarily about ethical concerns. There is some overlap from one class to the other, and this is not inadvertent. The repetition takes into account that the individual child will learn according to his readiness to incorporate the material.

When Sweden had had compulsory sex education for ten years, a national commission to examine the ten-year experience and to make recommendations was established. The recommendations contained in an eight hundred-page study generally suggest moving all the topics to earlier age levels.

For instance, in the kindergarten, although there is not to be any specific sex education, all children's questions are to be answered factually and correctly. Also, the kindergartener is to get the impression from the teacher that masturbation is normal. If the teacher observes the children in school or during recess playing sex games, he is not to interfere. Sex play at this age is regarded as normal.

One of the subjects being moved down to the seven-to-ten age group is the study of menstruation, recognizing that some girls experience menstruation before they are twelve. If the recommenda-

tions are adopted, masturbation and contraception, sterility and adoption will be discussed at this level as well.

At eleven to thirteen, the children will have an elementary course in adolescent psychology in which they talk about coitus, sex ethics, venereal disease and discuss variations in sex behavior. For the fourteen-to-sixteen group, there is to be focus on abortion, pornography, sexual disorders, and prostitution. Other emphases reflect the fact that Swedes traditionally marry, and traditionally are loyal to their spouses.

Not all sex education in Sweden takes place in the school. Obviously children learn from peers, but what especially impresses a visitor to Sweden is the amount of sex education on radio, television, and in the newspapers. The American visitor to Sweden might be surprised at the extent to which sex is discussed in the daily newspapers and in weekly news magazines. Papers carry news reports and information articles with very explicit sexual content, often accompanied by pictures and diagrams; for example, pictures showing how a woman can examine her own genital area by crouching over a mirror and looking down.

Another aspect of the total sex-information program in Sweden that strikes the American visitor is the extent to which contraceptives are advertised in the newspapers, both for birth control and as a venereal disease control. I was in Sweden one summer when a National Condom Month was being celebrated. Emphasis was placed on the condom as a potential method for reducing the incidence of venereal disease. Along with newspaper advertisements for contraceptives, Sweden makes provisions for everyone to have contraceptives of some kind available if he or she chooses to use them. Contraceptives can be ordered through advertisements in the newspaper, and there are condom vending machines on the outside of buildings, so that condoms can be purchased twenty-four hours a day. Contraceptives are also provided free to anyone who cannot pay for them.

With emphasis in the school, in the mass media, and in the home (Swedes emphasize that the home is really where sex education should take place), one is justified in asking whether or not Sweden's sex-education program has been effective. This is difficult to evaluate. It is true that Sweden has a lower divorce rate than does the United States, and one of the lowest rape rates in the world. Sweden has effectively avoided the population explosion, and the rate of syphilis is considerably lower in Sweden than it is in the United States. The frequency of gonorrhea has risen for the population as a whole, but has decreased for teenagers fifteen to nineteen years of age. *"One* of many contributory factors to this trend is in all

probability to be seen in the instruction on sexual matters and interpersonal relationships provided by comprehensive school."[2] It is true also that the majority of Swedes use contraceptives beginning with the first time they have sexual intercourse, and 85 percent of Swedish young people report that their sex education was adequate, good, or very good.

Nonetheless, the Swedes are not satisfied with the results. They want to assure that much more than 85 percent will be satisfied with their sex education, that contraceptives replace abortion more completely as a birth-control method, and that venereal disease be under control.

Since I support sexual knowledge as opposed to sexual naïveté, I support Sweden's efforts. They are not satisfied with teaching anatomy and physiology of sex alone, but are now attempting to deal with the more difficult aspects of sex education by placing emphasis on interpersonal relations, ethics, and sociosexual problems.[3]

NOTES TO CHAPTER TWENTY-EIGHT

1. *Handbook on Sex Instruction in Swedish Schools* (Stockholm: National Board of Education, 1957).

2. Hans-Jorgen Karlsson, Sex Education in Swedish Schools, National Swedish Board of Education, May 5, 1974, p. 8.

3. Birgitta Linner, *Sex and Society in Sweden* (New York: Harper & Row, 1973); *Proposed Guidelines for Sex Education in the Swedish School System*, Stockholm: State Commission on Sex Education, 1974.

✳ *Chapter Twenty-Nine*

The Racial (Black) Issue and Its Relation to Sexism

Thomasyne Lightfoote Wilson, Ph.D.*

Three questions come to mind: To what social and gender modes are black "girl" persons and black "boy" persons socialized? By whom are they socialized? To what extent are these gender orientations consonant (or dissonant) with black children's historical and/or current sociocultural education?

My thoughts about these questions were diverse, especially after I reviewed our African precedents regarding gender differences and schooling, the residues of slavery in black lives, acculturative writings of sociologists and anthropologists, popular images of black males and females in the literature, and images of women and blacks in school texts. One thought struck me strongly: whites usually are mentally and institutionally entangled with the desire for hierarchical and competitive dominance of one person above another, while blacks are caught between this white reality of competition for human dominance *and*: the sexist but nonhierarchical conditioning of our historical-cultural precedents;[1] acculturative persuasions from schooling; and the current but ridiculous slogan "Let's push our men."

Our African precedents in sexist education are facts with which we must reckon. Many of the societies from which we came, in West Africa especially, rigidly maintained separate initiation schools for girls (Sande or Sandegi)[2] and boys (Poro or Porogi).[3] Another sexist practice was to require a "bride price" (dowry) to secure a wife, and sometimes women were used to secure debts or fines.[4] To verbalize

*Consultant, Ravenswood School District, East Palo Alto, California; Faculty, San José State University

these historically "sexist" black precedents is not to pass judgment. A thorough study of tribal education will reveal human complementary functions among and between women and men that were less sexist than the practices in industrial societies today.

The transmission of sexism through the schools has been pervasive and systematic. This acculturation toward human inequality has been through instructional materials and instructional processes.[5] In the former case, girls are portrayed as passive, conforming, "indoor entities" while boys are depicted as persons who think, problem-solve, contruct things, and enter business.

Our recent survey on sexism among black children indicates black girls conceptualize a much longer list of possible jobs for men than for women. This result was expected, for books, films, and other widely used educational materials stress fewer types of vocational and social experiences for girls and women. They mirror and make legitimate even fewer work, home, and socio-ethic living experiences of black women.

At the Sex and Gender Symposium, November, 1974, Ms. Emma Ford, Family Planning Consultant/Community Health Worker, Berkeley, presented an issue related to this stereotypic thinking, regarding the sexual behaviors of black children:

> It has been noted that black youth are often seen as youth of nature—simple, lovable, and giving way to every impulse. Therefore, questions of black students regarding sexual issues are often misinterpreted by teachers. Whereas the questions do not indicate sexual promiscuity, teachers seem to feel overwhelmed by the issues as they are influenced by the stereotype. Girls have been referred to me for sexual counseling because the teachers think the girls are sexually active, basing this opinion on questions asked in class. In reality, the particular students have explained that they are trying to find answers to questions stimulated by adults and by movies. The sexual curiosity of black adolescents is overreacted to, based on the myth about black sexuality.

An example of the devastating effects of sexism and racism occurred at the end of one of my teacher education seminars. (There were fifteen student teachers in this Cross-Cultural/Urban Teacher Education Program: eleven women, all Euro-American, and six men, one Afro-American.) A student teacher had just finished teaching a mini lesson to six black children, half of whom were girls. The student teacher said: "I think Dr. Wilson has something for you." Seeing the opportunity to check out some of the influences of sexism I said, "Children, go and touch Dr. Wilson." Each touched a man in our group. When the student teacher said, "You have touched

only men, and none of them is Dr. Wilson. Is it possible that someone else in this room might be Dr. Wilson?" The children then took turns guessing and touching all the women, except me, the only black woman in the room.

A student teacher finally said: "This is Dr. Wilson," pointing to me. A child with an embarrassed grin said in black English, "She ain' no doctor. She a woman. No woman ain' no doctor."

The example underlined the lack of belief among black children (and many black adults) that blacks and women can be and are in positions of "authority" or leadership. It is but one instance reflecting conditioning of limited opportunities for females and blacks and the implication that females and blacks are not leadership types. Both conditions can be inferred from the submissive-dominance syndrome in sexism and racism. The "inferiority" model implied in the male-female relationship can be inferred from the "deficiency" that Baratz and Baratz discussed as they talked about the pathology that many authors want to ascribe to "differences" in manner, cognitions, and cultures of blacks.[6]

We pretend to have equitable institutions, but the operations within our educational and social systems demonstrate "divide and conquer" processes between females and males, old and young, fat and thin, physically handicapped and nonhandicapped, fast readers and slow, and many other "different" kinds of persons. The institutional systems intentionally set up procedures that rank and stress gradations to value and devalue human beings. The processes that are set up tend to support and reward those who compete with and destroy weaker, powerless persons (e.g. women, children, blacks, Chicanos, and the like).

As you can see we are attempting actively to reject the acculturative persuasions in the schools. Furthermore, we are implying that the issue of sexism is symptomatic of a domination-subjugation value orientation, which we feel is destructive. Those tendencies include the acculturative persuasion of accepting the school as a mechanism for allocating places and superior-inferior variations for persons.[7]

We use the school as an institution that transmits the profit motive through rewarding the domination of one person over another, to transmit false images of men and women to children, and a place in which instructional processes constantly reflect preferences for certain girls or boys depending on the nation in which the schools are located.[8] In short, the school is accepted and used as a place for supporting privileges for the privileged through competitive human relations. Our aim for human equality is to move away from acculturation and the fallacious notion of an open classroom that

still prods children toward some designated social status expectations, roles, and competitiveness. Instead, we wish to offer the alternative of community-family-guided education as a process for *equality* and *quality* education for *all* girls and boys and their parents.

The concept of community-family-guided education is deeply rooted in the African tradition of the extended family.[9] It stresses interdependent and caring familial relationships between and among all members of the extended family, in contrast to stressing individualistic competitive achievement orientation *per se*. The community family concept includes humanely equitable processes and methods of education that aim to guide toward self-other caring and connecting. It aims to identify and use complementary skills of all persons who interact in and identify with the community-family of each group (or in the school, the school district as a whole, and/or among persons of a total geographic community). It aims to use intragroup decision-making, responsibilities, leadership, and evaluation in the process of expanding the physical, intellectual, sociocultural, political, healthful, emotional, and recreational aspects of all children and adults.

Community-family-guided education subscribes to those human relationships and methods that aim to bring about nondomination of one person above another. Males, females, the blind, the sighted, black, white, brown, readers and nonreaders alike would be valued. Community-family-guided education aims to bring about positive self-other contact and connections, humaneness, responsible groupness identity, and caring and sharing in the development of self *with* others. Its goal is to assure intragroup accountability, goal-setting, complementary interactions, and community building through positive child and adult development. Community-family-guided education seeks to increase one's awareness and valuing of differences— diversity of people's skills, languages, and cultures, as well as differences in conditions and learning styles.[10] Community-family-guided education rejects hierarchies among all people including those among persons of the same "paint job" or skin color. Community-family-guided education recognizes the reality that sexist and racist values are born from the same seed; namely, devaluing and rejecting different and unconventional persons with automatic exclusion, fear or other negative predispositional behaviors.

Black values of inclusion of everyone, as members of the extended family (as implied in the community-family context), will not brook sexism. Consequently, to return to the Afro-essence of complementarity and cooperative self-otherness means abolishing sexist talk,

terms, values, and predispositions. It means establishing the equitable human and humane connections that are aspects of our Afro culture. When applied, these Afro values offer directions toward nonsexism that can guide us away from sadistic competition and can lead toward beneficial definitions of and behaviors for equality and justice for all.

NOTES TO CHAPTER TWENTY-NINE

1. T. Lightfoote Wilson, Notes Toward a Process of Afro-American Education, *Harvard Educational Review* 42, August, 1972, 374-389.

2. Augustus Caine, A Study and Comparison of the West African Bush School and the Southern Sotho Circumcision School, unpublished master's thesis, Northwestern University, Evanston, Illinois, 1959; George Parker, Acculturation in Liberia, unpublished doctoral dissertation, Kennedy School of Missions, Hartford Seminary, 1944; George Schwab, *Tribes of the Hinterland*, Papers of the Peabody Museum of Am. Arch. and Ethnography 31, Harvard, 1947, 161-163.

3. T. Lightfoote Wilson, A View of Developmental Education, and the "Disadvantaged" in a National Perspective: Implications for International Education, *J. of Negro Education* 41, Howard University, Summer, 1972; James Gibbs, *Peoples of Africa* (New York: Holt, Rinehart and Winston, 1965).

4. T. Lightfoote Wilson, Different Patterns of Instruction in Liberia; Implications for Modernization, unpublished doctoral dissertation, Stanford University, 1971; George P. Murdock, *Africa, Its Peoples and Their Culture History* (New York: McGraw-Hill, 1959).

5. Carol Jacobs and Cynthia Eaton, Sexism in the Elementary School, *Today's Education* 61, 1972, 20-22; Carol N. Jacklin, Eleanor E. Maccoby, and Anne E. Dick, Barrier Behavior and Toy Preference: Sex Differences (and Their Absence) in the Year-old Child, *Child Development* 44, 1973, 196-200; Eleanor E. Maccoby and Carol N. Macklin, *The Psychology of Sex Differences* (Stanford, Calif.: Stanford University Press, 1974): Terry Saario, Carol Nagy Jacklin, and Carol Kehr Tittle, Sex Role Stereotyping in the Public Schools, *Harvard Educational Review* 43, 1973, 386-416; Wilson, 1971, 263-290.

6. Stephen Baratz and Joan C. Baratz, Early Childhood Intervention: The Social Science Base of Institutional Racism, *Harvard Educational Review* 40, 1970, 29-50.

7. Talcott Parsons, The Social Class as a Social System: Some of its Functions in American Society, *Harvard Educational Review* 39, Fall, 1959, 297-318; H. Peter Dreitzel, *Childhood and Socialization* (New York: Macmillan, 1973).

8. Ulf Hannerz, What Ghetto Males Are Like: Another Look, in *Afro-American Anthropology*, ed. by Norman Whitten and J.F. Szwed (New York: Free Press, 1970), 313-325; Ulf Hannerz, Soulside: Inquiries into Ghetto Culture and Community, in *The Best of Simple*, ed. by L. Hughes (New York: Hill and Wang, 1961.) George Henry, *Masculinity and Femininity* (New York: Macmillan, 1973);

Gerda Lerner, ed., The Myth of the "Bad" Black Woman, in *Black Women in White America* (New York: Vintage Books, 1973). Boys were attended to by teachers as "preferred persons" among some groups of African teachers, T. Lightfoote Wilson, 1971.

9. The Black College: A Continual Progression of "Community-Family Guided Education—A Process Toward Afro-American Continuity" in *The Black College in an Age of Ferment*, ed. by James Hudson (Tallahassee: Florida A & M University, 1974), 105-128.

10. T. Lightfoote Wilson, A View of Developmental Education and the "Disadvantaged" in a National Perspective, 276-290; *Toward Equitable Education; A Handbook for Multicultural Consciousness for Early Childhood—A Bicentennial Revolution?* (Redwood City, Cal.: Ujamaa Developmental Education Publications, 1976).

Chapter Thirty

Homosexuality: An Integral Part of Human Sexuality

Ronald D. Lee, M.S.W.*

In considering experimental sex-education programs, focusing on an adult program and on particular cultural attitudes not only helps to determine applicability to children, but most certainly will underline essential inclusion of a correlated attitude into curriculum for children. At the Center for Special Problems, one of the outpatient clinics within the Community Mental Health Services of San Francisco, we are particularly concerned about the questions of gender identity and sexual orientation as manifest in the problems of people struggling with these issues. About 40 percent of our clients are homosexually oriented to some extent, and about 5 percent of our clients are men and women sometimes referred to as transsexuals. In addition to the various forms of psychotherapy, we offer sex therapy for those who want to become more sexually proficient, and a sex-education program making extensive use of documentary films of sexual expression.

With the information and insights provided to us during the past few years by the women's liberation and the gay liberation movements, surely there is no longer any question as to the detrimental effects of sexist attitudes on the lives of millions of human beings. Many of the individuals seen in our clinic are objects of a destructive sexist attitude, homophobia, which I describe as an irrational fear of homosexuality. Homophobia particularly affects men, but also most women. It negatively influences the relationships that

---

*Clinical Social Worker and Director, The Center for Special Problems, San Francisco Community Mental Health Services.

men have with men, women have with women, women have with men, and men have with women.

Historically, our culture has developed within the Judaeo-Christian tradition, which condemns all forms of human sexual expression except that between a man and a woman who are committed to a lifelong monogamous relationship and whose goal is the creation of children. Masturbation, oral-genital sex, anal-genital sex, sex between unmarried people, and certainly sex between people with the same genital structure have come under this religious condemnation. Changes are beginning within the religious community as the theology of human sexuality is reconsidered and reevaluated. Gay women and men are beginning to see a growing acceptance of their humanity and their expression of sexuality among religious people.

Often certain codes of morality become institutionalized in our public and civil law and make a mandate for all people to follow. So we find within most jurisdictions of this country all forms of sexual expression except those between husband and wife who have in mind the creation of children are considered criminal offenses. These laws are not usually enforced against people who are heterosexually oriented, but vast sums of time and money are spent in enticing, entrapping, and harassing members of the gay community. In most civil-service jurisdictions in the nation, gay men and women cannot find employment if their sexual orientation is known and will be fired if it is discovered. In all of our public institutions, schools, prisons, hospitals, military services, housing and public accommodations, pervasive discrimination against homosexuality still interferes with the lives of gay women and men.

This homophobic attitude has permeated mental-health professions too. If you look at the historical development of psychological theory in reference to human sexuality, you will find that all forms of human sexual expression except between a man and a woman monogamously married with procreation in mind have been considered immature, disordered, neurotic, or pathological.

However, changes are taking place. Archaic laws are being changed, sexual orientation is being included in nondiscrimination clauses, and there is a growing recognition and understanding of the costliness of this form of discrimination; but the change is very slow.

The growing agreement within the religious community, civil and criminal law, and the mental health professions that loving other human beings of either sex and expressing that love sexually is a good thing will have profound implications for the education of children in terms of gender and sexual identity.

My work as a therapist and educator with extensive experience in dealing with gay people has led me to several basic assump-

tions that I believe will stand any therapist or educator in good stead in dealing with any age group. One assumption is that to have sexual feelings is a natural phenomenon at any age. We should assist human beings to be aware of and appreciative of their feelings. We should develop ways for individuals to value their bodies and be able to use their bodies as instruments through which they can experience liveliness.

Another assumption that I make is that, except for certain biological and physiological differences, there are no significant differences between men and women that have not been socially and culturally induced, and that sex-role stereotyping interferes with the ability of untold numbers of women and men to achieve and experience their full potential as human beings.

I assume there is no intrinsic differential value attached to heterosexuality or homosexuality. The important consideration is the quality of lives and relationships and not the particular sexual equipment that is possessed. I believe that we should develop environments that support and encourage cooperative relationships unhampered by competitiveness.

We should assist people of all ages in valuing the unique combination of femininity and masculinity and heterosexuality and homosexuality found in each of us. We should create environments that will assist people in discovering and being who they are, freely expressing love through sexuality with anyone of either sex, in private, whenever all persons involved agree.

These assumptions, of course, have implications for our entire social and economic structure. Sex plays an important role in every person's life, whether or not it is expressed. Sexual fantasies, desires, and dreams should be recognized as a valuable part of one's sexuality. Important is the right of individuals of any age to know all the facts. I think that any sex-education program that does not include the phenomenon of homosexuality is inadequate and propagandistic.

If we can educate according to these assumptions, I believe that we will be taking an important step towards the achievement of our full potential as women and men and that we will be making a profound contribution to the evolution of our culture and to the discovery of the full meaning of the nature of women and men.

Chapter Thirty-One

Implications for Children's Development in Sex-Oriented Adult Group Work

Joseph Gutstadt, M.D.*

There seems to be general agreement that the primary source of the affective and emotional education of children is the parents and other significant adults during the child's early life. The works of Harlow and Prescott,[1] among many researchers in the field, have proven quite conclusively the necessity of early touch and movement stimulation in the child and their relation to the predominance in later life of aversive or affiliative responses in interpersonal relationships. It becomes increasingly apparent in the study of subhuman primates, as well as other animal species, that sexual and aggressive responses fuse and defuse in a highly complex fashion and are related to many other behavioral functions beyond that of reproduction. Functions that have been so taken for granted until recently in the past twenty years have been subjected to much closer examination. The more accurate knowledge of the complex interactions of sexual anatomy and physiology has led to revisions of many of our older concepts regarding sexual functioning. In some cases concepts that have been adhered to with almost religious tenacity have been proven incorrect with a resultant clamor more reminiscent of a religious war than a scientific disagreement.

The new knowledge of sexual function brought to us by such researchers as Masters and Johnson, John Money, Hartman, and Fithian and many others, have also given us cause to reexamine our views, not just on sex education, but also on sex therapy. Innovations that twenty years ago were unheard of and would have been

*Member, San Francisco Psychoanalytic Institute; Community Mental Health Services, Marin County

totally unacceptable in a puritanical culture are now being accepted and widely used.

When one threads his way through the maze of current therapeutic approaches—individual, group, family, multiple, Gestalt, Reichian, neo-Reichian, and many others—one issue becomes patently clear. Education or therapy on a level that is mainly intellectual or insight focused, hopefully with significant affective components, is not always successful. This is particularly true if the therapy aims at altering behavior that can be subsumed under the heading of autonomous ego functioning. This alteration frequently requires a more active treatment to break up the autonomous ego patterns and provide room for change.

My own introduction to this field of interest was a workshop on human sexuality, the National Sex Forum, in San Francisco. Aware of the profound effects of the intensive exposure to films of explicit sexual behavior, I wondered about the potential of this particular medium, not only for sex education, but for sex therapy as well. Characterized as desensitization, the programs were unquestionably of value, not only as an aid for those involved in the counseling profession, but also as a potentially powerful approach to the education of the teachers or parents whose own comfort with sexuality was vital if they were to present to their charges, students or children, an attitude free of prejudice and personal neurotic distortion.

Many persons have viewed pornographic films in the commercial setting of the movie theater. The atmosphere frequently is pervaded with neuroticism, lewdness, and a feeling of participation in some form of clandestine activity with its associated guilt and anxiety. Given a different atmosphere, one conducive to warmth and acceptance, scientific learning, and the appreciation of the values of human contact, affection, and intimacy, similar films can and do lead to a greater openness to one's own sexuality, more acceptance of sexual behavior in general, and an often noticeable decrease in anxiety and tension.

Briefly, the program as we present it in our Human Sexuality Foundation programs offers an easy, humorous, and light introduction to sexuality, old myths, the semantics of sex, and films of explicit sexual behavior taking place in an atmosphere of affection and warmth. There follows a detailed discussion of sexual anatomy and physiology, with much opportunity for discussion and sharing of feelings and attitudes. All questions are answered as far as possible in a nonjudgmental and caring way. Later, subject matter dealing with masturbation and homosexuality is introduced, reviewed, and dis-

cussed, again with sharing of feelings and responses. Finally, such additional matters as communication, intimacy, sexual dysfunction, role confusion, and role stereotypes are discussed. The age of participants has ranged in our groups from sixteen to seventy-nine.

Early in the programs, our participants were asked to state their reasons for coming to the program. One middle-aged school principal stated that she had frequently had to deal with issues of sexuality with her teachers and students. She had come from a strict mid-western, rigidly Protestant family, and although she was satisfied with her own sexual responses, she realized that she felt uncomfortable and inhibited in dealing with others, professional associates and students, around these issues. At the end of the workshop, she acknowledged a loosening in her own attitudes. Incidentally, she and her husband were two of several participant couples who later, on their own, decided to meet regularly to continue the discussions, which they felt had been helpful to them.

A different form of sex education, sex therapy, as devised by Masters and Johnson and elaborated on by many other workers, serves in some ways a similar function, although it focuses on the treatment of specific sexual dysfunctions. A detailed sex history is taken of the two partners, separately by each of the two treating persons. The history is then discussed, with emphasis placed on the relationship between the persons' early experiences and the development of the dysfunction. The interaction of the couple is closely observed and communication problems and obvious areas of resistance are commented on and, at times, explained. Then, at appropriate times, various exercises are assigned that relate to specific dysfunctions and are aimed at overcoming certain areas of inhibition. The limited area of treatment, mainly sexual dysfunction, and the sanction, permission, and encouragement of the therapists serve to overcome guilt-induced responses and relieve anxieties associated with specific activities, encouraging a gradual, or at times not so gradual, change from previous neurotic anxieties and inhibitions to new values of self-enhancement, being good to one's own body and oneself, and the interrelationship of intellect to body function. These shifts enhance the individual's self-esteem and offer him possibilities of greater gratification.

Frequently, patients will spontaneously make connections between attitudes they have experienced on the part of their own parents and other significant adults and inhibitions of certain sexual activities. At times, they have volunteered comments about their changed attitudes on such activities as their children's masturbation or curiosity about their own or others' bodies. They express not only

a greater comfort about talking to their children about sexual matters, but also mark alterations in their own reactions. Being more accepting of their own needs for bodily pleasure, they find less need to inhibit such expression of need on their children's part.

One husband presented his wife with a vibrator as a Christmas present. The vibrator was discovered by their three-year-old daughter, who quickly learned that its use was pleasurable, although not using it in the same manner as an adult might. One evening as her parents were entertaining at dinner, she made an appearance with the vibrator, turned on, sported between her legs. Without any ado, the mother suggested calmly that the child's bedroom was a more appropriate place for her to use it. Later, in relating the story to us, the mother was pleased in what she felt was a new acceptance of such behavior that would never have been possible prior to her having participated in the sexuality workshop.

In one of the preorgasmic women's groups,[a] one participant reported that having come to the point of freely enjoying pleasuring herself, she found herself one day faced with the sight of one of her children masturbating. Instead of making an effort to stop or distract the child, she found herself able to freely discuss the pleasant feelings of which one's body is capable, and she could comfortably give the child permission to continue to investigate the pleasure potential of her own body.

Another member of the group spoke of the extreme inhibition and restriction on sex which she had experienced in her own life and how she, in turn, had transmitted this to her own children through the manner in which she had reared them. However, now she has made a firm resolve that she would discuss these matters with her children at this point, so that her young granddaughter would not have to experience the same difficulty in her growing up. Such an experience for both mother and child can only serve to enhance the warmth and closeness of their relationship, allowing the child in later years to enjoy a more profound and thorough experience of sexual pleasure.

The early childhood education through parents can later be assumed by the teachers, first in the nursery school and later in the elementary and secondary schools. As time goes by, education that was initially a totally experiential process becomes an increasingly intellectual and academic one, although the experiential factor continues to be very significant. In areas such as sex education, which are so intensely invested with emotion, teaching attitudes and the entire ambience of the teaching situation are of great importance.

It may be impractical and perhaps overly idealistic to advocate that all teachers of human sexuality be offered programs of desensiti-

[a]Groups of women who have never experienced orgasm, as described by Lonnie Barbach, Ph.D., Sex and Gender Symposium, November, 1974.

zation; we do not believe so. Further, we feel that possibly no education in sexuality at all might be preferable to that which would be presented in a highly sterile, clinical, or perhaps moralistic fashion that conveys the biases and inhibitions of the teacher.

As yet, our own experience and the reach of our programs is too limited to draw any real conclusion as to the benefits. The examples that I have presented are suggestive of the potential scope of this type of teaching. With the more wisespread use of sex-therapy techniques, we should have available to us information that will give us a more accurate picture of the effectiveness of the techniques, as well as their more indirect influence on the sexual attitudes and behavior of children.

Dorothy Baruch stresses that the process of sex education begins at birth.[2] The openness with which a mother can accept her new infant and in her caring exhibit a freedom of contact, touching, stroking, and loving is the first step in the process of sex education or education for loving that can continue throughout the child's early years and all his life. To the extent that these experiences are expressions of loving and caring, free from guilt and neurotic inhibitions, the child's emotional life is enhanced. We are certain that the opposite is also true. Parental guilt and inhibitions will detract from these possibilities and markedly constrict the child's potential for later body pleasure and the expression of love. To the end that the child's opportunities for ultimate fulfillment can be as great as possible, the newer techniques of sex education and sex therapy seem to have much to offer and hopefully will become increasingly widespread.

NOTES TO CHAPTER THIRTY-ONE

1. Harry Harlow, et al., The Maternal Affectional System of the Rhesus Monkey, in *Maternal Behavior in Mammals*, ed. by Harriet Rheingold (New York: Wiley, 1963), 268; James Prescott, Early Somatosensory Deprivation as an Ontogenetic Process in the Abnormal Development of the Brain and Behavior, *Medical Primatology*, 1970.

2. Dorothy Baruch, *New Ways of Sex Education* (New York: McGraw Hill, 1959).

Chapter Thirty-Two

Selecting Sex Education Materials

Derek L. Burleson, Ed.D.*

In this country we have available many sex-education materials in many formats: books, pamphlets, models, charts, film strips, eight- and sixteen-millimeter films. These materials are available for many audiences, from young children through adulthood, and are continually being published. We have materials with many points of view—religious, political, medical, psychological, cultural, and sometimes radical. One of the obligations facing us with the plethora of material is to make choices. Making choices involves judgment based on some accepted criteria. However, there are some dilemmas in this area, because we are not really sure of our criteria. We bandy about such generalities as "healthy attitudes about sex" and "achieving sexual maturity," but how confident are we in translating such generalities into the materials and education experiences we plan for children?

There is no question in my mind that we have made great strides in combating the ignorance, the superstitions, the prejudices, and the generally exploitative view of sex that pervades our culture. We have done quite well in dealing with sex as a problem, but I wonder if we are ready to deal with sex as a potential. This is the new frontier of sex education. Even though some instructional materials treat sex positively, we have yet to see what the full implications of some of these materials will be.

As a reviewer, I see most of the new sex-education materials

*Managing Editor, *Medical Aspects of Human Sexuality;* formerly Director, Educational and Research Services, Sex Information and Education Council of U.S. (SIECUS).

coming on the market. One of our problems I see is publishers and audiovisual producers who seem obsessed with bringing out still more material on how babies are made, how to live with pubic hair, what to do on that first date, and how not to catch VD. I don't condemn their efforts to try to do it better, but as a reviewer I am getting rather tired of watching that ovum come "bouncing" down the Fallopian tube. The children, in fact, are also rather tired of these approaches, in spite of some of the clever animation featuring Olly Ovum and Sammy Sperm.

The criteria of reality, accuracy, truth, appropriateness, and significance are legitimate guidelines in evaluating sex-education materials, but these guidelines, like most generalizations, have to be interpreted. Here are some candid quotes from reviews in a consumer newsletter of children's sex-education books that show how varied the evaluations can be.[1]

The True Story of How Babies Are Made by Per Holm Knutsen.[2] This is a Danish children's book that has been translated into English. The reviewer writes "not just another Danish pastry. This import depicts the reproduction story with a simple text that is vividly color illustrated, featuring graphic drawings of a man and woman having intercourse, fetal development, and birth. Everyone smiles all the time, so it looks like the whole thing is a good idea."

The Wonderful Story of How You Were Born, by Sidonie Guenberg.[3] The reviewer writes "This one has introduced 250,000 kids to the birds and bees over the past twenty years and it is beginning to show its age. Its vague illustrations and syrupy text may strike the Sesame Street generation as too dull to sustain interest."

Another young children's book is *Where Did I Come From?* by Peter Mayle.[4] The reviewer writes: "If you want to know, don't ask this book. A slick, cutesy piece written, indeed, for the red-faced parents of its dedication. Full of misinformation (babies grow in mothers' stomachs), feeble jokes (penis is pronounced like peanuts without the "t"), and silly analogies (an orgasm is like sneezing). If this is the only alternative, stick with the stork."

Sex and the Young Teenager, by Eleanor Kay,[5] is "crammed with technical detail on a wide variety of topics including masturbation and VD; it falls flat, however, when it attempts to treat the all-important emotional element. Even the language changes. Man and woman become male and female for the discussion of the act of intercourse. Stiff, shaded line drawings resemble no known human form. Mrs. Kay is a registered nurse and really knows how to anesthetize a good story."

More positive reviews included Eric Johnson's *Love and Sex in*

Plain Language and *Sex: Telling It Straight*,[6] "two versions of basically the same book; one for mass consumption, the other X-rated. Public and school libraries will carry *Love and Sex in Plain Language* and teens will buy *Sex: Telling It Straight* for themselves. It uses all the four-letter words yet invented, [and is a] direct, forthright approach to basic sexuality, [with a] particularly good discussion of the emotional and psychological aspects of love-making."

Overlooking the pungent "putdowns" that this reviewer makes, I wonder what a parent reading these reviews would think when trying to make a decision about which one to buy. The criteria of appropriateness and significance become unclear if one takes into account the parents' background, comfort with the subject, and value orientation. Even the criteria of reality or accuracy requires some modifications as new research creates new truths. It is my feeling that in the next few years all chapters in sex books on attitudinal differences about sex between males and females are going to have to be rewritten, as many of us recognize and accept the new social realities concerning man-woman relationships.

I raise these dilemmas to point up the reality of pluralism in our culture and the problem it presents in creating, selecting, and evaluating educational materials on sex. We are far from a homogeneous culture, especially when it comes to sex. Therefore, we are going to need good materials for many audiences; there can be no "best" materials.

Publishers, naturally, are looking for the widest possible audience for their products. In the process, they make compromises in order to cater to the widest possible market acceptability. I have seen, however, some real attempts by some publishers to meet the needs of various audiences, such as the two versions of Eric Johnson's book, *Love and Sex in Plain Language* and *Sex: Telling It Straight*. I have been impressed with the efforts of Churchill Films in their two new VD films.[7] One, *Half a Million Teenagers Plus*, is a revision of an older film. It would probably be acceptable in most communities. However, they have also produced a companion film, *Guess What's Going Around*, which covers much the same content, but is intended for slightly more mature students who are likely to be sexually active. It is more explicit and provides specific information about treatment and prevention.

Many teenage sex books have chapters on premarital sex that attempt to help the reader understand the consequences in an objective manner. One can see how the writers struggle to be nonjudgmental, with varying degrees of success. However, one recent

book called the *Sex Handbook, Information and Help for Minors*, by Handman and Brennan,[8] starts out with the basic assumption that many teenagers are sexually active and proceeds to inform them how to have good sex. Teenage books have not done this before.

Comic-book formats have been developed by Sol Gordon at Syracuse University[9] to present basic information in a humorous way, particularly for those youngsters who would never otherwise read a book. The Medical School at Emory University in Atlanta has published three issues of a magazine, *True to Life*,[10] written in a true-romance style. There are many young people, particularly girls, who read this kind of book or magazine. Although it looks like a true-romance magazine, it also includes situations within the stories to convey appropriate information and positive attitudes about sex.

Children's and teenage literature sources are beginning to treat sex in fiction. In an article, "The Hardy Boys Didn't Have Wet Dreams,"[11] Lorna Flynn discusses the treatment of sexuality in contemporary teenage literature. Today's fictional twelve-year-old girl begins to menstruate. Harriett the spy, in *The Long Secret* by Louise Fitzhugh,[12] gets her period and goes right on trying to solve the mystery. In the book *Are You There God, It's Me Margaret* by Judith Blume,[13] the heroine just wants to be normal; getting her period is a sign that all will be okay. Male adolescents are also beginning to be sexual in a few teenage books. In John Donovan's *I'll Get There, It Must Be Worth the Trip*[14] and Barbara Wersba's *Run Softly, Go Fast*[15] brief homosexual experiences are related, of the nature we know to be quite common among adolescents, which are blown out of proportion by the adults in the books who panic because of their own ignorance. However, neither of these books revolves around the particular incident. The book *Sticks and Stones* by Lynn Hall[16] is set in a small town and deals with a teenage boy who becomes close friends with a young man who has been discharged from the military service because he was homosexual. However, this is not a key point in the plot, as the teenager is actually never aware of his friend's past. In Paul Zindel's *My Darling, My Hamburger*[17] the heroine has an illegal abortion.

This isn't to say that including a sexual incident makes the book good teenage fiction, but there is recognition by these authors that sex is a real concern of youth. This conveys an authenticity to their writing, and the sexual episodes can be handled in a way that will be a source of guidance to young people.

Probably the next breakthrough in children's literature will be in the treatment of sex-roles, especially in younger children's literature. The analyses that have been done of children's books have sensitized

us to some of the rigid sex stereotyping. Some militant feminists would have us throw out all such books; my view is that we must write some new ones.

The Feminist Press of Old Westbury, New York, has produced an experimental packet of stories for children ages three to ten. These are either to be read to the children or for youngsters to read themselves. Too often these writers allow their ideology to interfere with their telling a good story for children; nonetheless, there are a couple of stories that impressed me. One is *My Body Feels Good*,[18] a little picture book for three-to-six-year-old girls, with a minimum of text. It tries to express the many sensuous and good feelings that the body can have through such activities as rolling down a hill, sitting on a sprinkler, swinging high in the air, having a bowel movement, and having one's back rubbed. The other is a story called *Peter Learns to Crochet* about a little boy who wants to learn to crochet, but cannot find anyone who will teach him. He finds that his teacher knows how to crochet and she teaches him basic stitches. He makes a bookbag for his books and school supplies, which, of course, is much admired by all his friends.

Most of us working in the field of sex education like to make the distinction between content and process. On the content side, there is a wealth of good material. In addition to Eric Johnson's books, there are Wardell Pomeroy's two books *Boys and Sex* and *Girls and Sex*,[19] and Sol Gordon's *Facts About Sex*[20] as just a few examples of solid informational content presented in a positive, not a problem context. There is no lack of good audiovisual material on anatomy and physiology that provides basic sex information. Content is, by far, the easiest kind of material to create and publish.

(In the symposium there was some discussion of the use of dolls for sex education and for general play. In considering how representative the genitalia of dolls should be, Dr. Jerome Oremland felt that the dolls can be sexually ambiguous, but should not be inaccurate. Dr. Albert Solnit expressed doubt about the value of dolls in teaching children about sex in that it is very difficult to get dolls that really do simulate the human body. He continued: "If we cannot have a doll that is fairly realistic, then why not allow children to use their minds to understand in their variety of ways, with gradually increasing accuracy and facts as needed. An insistence on concreteness perhaps is an unwillingness on our parts to accept our own uncertainties."

Dr. Mildred Sabath concluded: "We have found from work in nursery schools that the least structured materials, those which just give a general form and outline, are the ones which children enjoy

using the most, and the ones to which they impute a great deal of imagination and creativity. The total climate that the teacher establishes which provides opportunities for children to ask their questions, to make their comments, to interact with each other, and to be free enough to really explore what they want to know, gives the teacher a chance to move in and do the kind of teaching that needs to be done at any particular point.")

What about process? In the best sex-education classroom there is a free and trusting atmosphere where questions can be asked and answered fully, where attitudes and values can be examined, and where controversial issues can be debated and analyzed. Instructional materials alone cannot create this atmosphere. The teacher has to orchestrate this process, but materials can be developed to aid him or her.

An example of materials development is the Women's Studies Program of the Berkeley Unified School District, which works directly with students, teachers, and community consultants to research and develop multiethnic curriculum materials which explore the full range of female and male roles. These materials are then made available to classrooms throughout the school district, and, in addition, certain materials are available for purchase to persons outside the district. Workshops are also held periodically to assist teachers in utilizing and developing productive classroom strategies and materials around this theme. The materials available through this program are designed for early childhood through grade six, but may be adapted for other levels.

Two good examples of process-oriented materials are those developed by the Unitarian Universal Association called "About Your Sexuality,"[21] for junior highs and the United Methodist Church's program called "Christians and the Meaning of Sexuality"[22] for senior highs. Other examples are the high-school text *Patterns of Life* by Dolloff and Resnick,[23] with case studies and social issues to involve students in value-oriented discussions. Such audiovisual materials as those from Churchill Films, *The Searching Years*,[24] the Billy Budd series, *Circle of Life*[25] and the Paulist Productions *Insight* series[26] are good examples of open-ended discussion-oriented films that can lead to involvement in the process of sex education where human relationships are explored, values are tested, and vital social issues are studied and debated.

While there is greater need for teachers trained in the process of sex education, instruction materials can be a great help in making this process pattern. I would like to see a moratorium on materials about the biology and physiology of sex and more concentration on

materials dealing with emotions, feelings, values, relationships, the place of the erotic in our lives—both real and fantasy—marriage and its alternatives, anthropologic overviews of the family that help us to break out of some of our stereotypic views of family life, and changing and emerging viewpoints of male and female roles. If these kinds of topics are to be process-oriented, then they have to be developed in formats that lend themselves to open-ended situations, case studies, role-playing, psychodrama, values-clarification games, and self-awareness exercises.

Parents and school administrators are particularly uneasy dealing with values and moral and ethical issues. School administrators are sensitive because they are in a highly vulnerable position when the curriculum comes under attack. Parents tend to underestimate their influence on their children and overestimate the influence of a single textbook or film that might be used in the sex-education program. Nevertheless, parents, teachers, and school administrators are concerned about the implicit or explicit value orientation in materials dealing with such topics as masturbation, premarital sex, homosexuality, pornography, and abortion.

To illustrate, following are three examples of widely used materials that deal with the subject of masturbation. First is the *Boy Scout Handbook*,[27] which has sold over 28,000,000 copies in many editions over the years. In the most recent edition (1972) is a one-page discussion on sexual maturity:

> You may have questions about sexual matters such as nocturnal emissions, (also called wet dreams), masturbation, and even those strange feelings you may have. Talk them over with your parents and your spiritual advisor or doctor. Don't rely on the advice of friends who think they know all the answers, but may not really know as much as you do. In these matters, it is always smart to get the facts and not fiction.

I suppose it is progress that the *Boy Scout Handbook* even mentions the word masturbation, but it fails in providing the young reader any facts, and could very well create all kinds of fiction about those strange feelings which, I am sure, many eleven-year-olds wonder about. It is, of course, totally unrealistic in its recommendations, because masturbation is an area of behavior that most young people simply do not talk about, especially with parents.

Next, consider *A Boy's Sex Life*, by Father William Bausch.[28] It is directed to the Catholic boy. Father Bausch writes:

> Why do so many boys masturbate? One of the answers is that it is not because the boy is bad or really wants to do it. His masturbation is often a

symptom, a signal that he is not solving the real problems of growing up . . . . Like the cold, masturbation is normal in the sense of common, but not normal in the sense of right . . . . Masturbation is, as the doctors tell us, a really immature response to life and caters to an already existing selfishness and self-centeredness that none of us can afford to increase . . . . Therefore, to control this problem, as is highly desirable in developing a well balanced and manly personality, the problem must be dealt with and overcome.

Father Bausch then moves into a situation-ethic position, saying: "We never talk of sin unless we look to the person who is involved—his realization—his intentions—his understanding—his consent. Is masturbation a sin? The answer is no, not for the boy of good will." Father Bausch concludes with the advice to be positive about sex, but to beware of excessive masturbation.

Compare this approach to that of Wardell Pomeroy in *Boys and Sex*. He says, in coldly objective terms:

It is a pleasurable and exciting experience. The feelings it produces have been enjoyed by people universally from the beginning of history. . . . It is easy to do, requires no special place or time. Anyone can do it and of all sexual activity it is the most easily learned and usually the one first learned. . . . It releases tensions and is therefore valuable in many ways. . . . In itself it offers a variety which enriches the individual sex life. . . . It is not against the law as long as it is done privately. . . . It is taboo at some levels of society, therefore may arouse feelings of guilt which is an unhealthy state of mind. . . . It is condemned by some religions and again a conflict of guilt may arise which may undo any good resulting from the practice. . . . Medically speaking, it is not possible to masturbate to excess. The body knows what excess really means. It sets its own limits. When a boy has been masturbating a great deal, he can no longer get an erection. He has reached his particular limit for the time being. The body has to rest for awhile, but when the boy is young it restores itself quickly. He will know when it is restored, because he will then be able to have an erection again.

This contrast between the priest who is earnestly and sincerely trying to give some reassurance and guidance out of his particular religious tradition and the sex researcher Pomeroy giving straight objective facts (but not without some value stances) points up the difficulties in selecting educational materials. It also illustrates the ethical dichotomies teachers face when dealing with such topics in the classroom. Are they prepared to handle them? Can they help their students to understand the competing and conflicting positions? If we are truly a pluralistic society, do all positions get a fair

hearing in a public-school setting? I think they should. Further, children are and ought to be exposed to some of the controversies surrounding these ethical issues. They ought to grapple with some of the different kinds of authority that operate in our lives. This can happen in a process-oriented sex education classroom where process-oriented materials are being used, or it can happen in a discussion over the family dinner table.

NOTES TO CHAPTER THIRTY-TWO

1. "Sex Ed Books Which Screw Up Your Kids," *Moneysworth*, July 8, 1974.
2. New York: Children's Press, 1973.
3. Garden City: Doubleday, 1970.
4. New York: Lyle Stuart, 1975.
5. New York: Franklin Watts, 1973.
6. Philadelphia: Lippincott, 1974.
7. Churchill Films, 662 N. Robertson Blvd., Los Angeles, Calif., 90069.
8. Putnam, 1974.
9. Ed-U-Press, 760 Ostrom Ave., Syracuse, N.Y., 1974.
10. Emory University School of Medicine, Family Planning Program, Box 26003, 80 Butler St., Atlanta, Ga. 30303
11. SIECUS report, November, 1972.
12. New York: Harper & Row, 1965.
13. New York: Bradbury Press, 1970.
14. New York: Harper & Row, 1969.
15. New York: Atheneum, 1970.
16. New York: Follett Publishing Co., 1972.
17. New York: Harper & Row, 1969.
18. In *Story Packs*, Old Westbury, N.Y.: Feminist Press, 1974.
19. New York: Delacorte, 1968.
20. New York: John Day, 1973.
21. Boston: Beacon Press, 1973.
22. Nashville, Tenn.: Graded Press, 1972.
23. Phyllis B. Dolloff and Miriam R. Resnick, *Patterns of Life*, Columbus: Charles Merrill, 1972.
24. Churchill Films, Los Angeles, 1971.
25. Billy Budd Films, 235 East 57th St., New York, N.Y. 10022, 1972.
26. Paulist Productions, 17575 Pacific Coast Highway, Pacific Palisades, Calif. 90272, 1971-1974.
27. Boy Scouts of America, New Brunswick, New Jersey.
28. Notre Dame, Ind.: Fides, 1969.

MATERIALS

About Your Sexuality, Unitarian Universal Association, Beacon Press.
Bausch, William, *A Boy's Sex Life: A Handbook of Basic Information and Guidance*. Notre Dame, Indiana: Fides, 1969.

Blume, Judith, *Are You There God, It's Me Margaret.* Bradbury Press, 1970.
Christians and the Meaning of Sexuality. Nashville, Tennessee: Graded Press, 1972.
Circle of Life: A Series (in 2 parts). Billy Budd Film Series, New York, 1972.
Dolloff, Phyllis B. and Resnick, Miriam R. *Patterns of Life.* Columbus: Charles Merrill, 1972.
Donovan, John, *I'll Get There, It'll Be Worth The Trip.* New York: Harper & Row, 1969.
Fitzhugh, Louise, *The Long Secret.* New York: Harper and Row, 1965.
Flynn, Lorna, "The Hardy Boys Didn't Have Wet Dreams." SIECUS Report, November, 1972.
Gordon, Sol, Comic Strip Series. Syracuse: Syracuse University, Ed-U-Press, 1974.
_____, *Facts About Sex.* New York: John Day, 1973.
Gruenberg, Sidonie, *The Wonderful Story of How You Were Born.* Garden City, New York: Doubleday, 1970.
Guess What's Going Around. Churchill Films, Los Angeles, 1975.
Half a Million Teenagers Plus. Churchill Films, Los Angeles, 1975.
Hall, Lynn, *Sticks and Stones.* New York: Follett Publishing Co., 1972.
Handman, Heidi and Brennan, Peter, *Sex Handbook: Information and Help for Minors.* Putnam, 1974.
Hines, Frederick L. (ed.), *Scout Handbook.* Boy Scouts of America, 1972.
Insight: A Series. Pacific Palisades, Calif.: Paulist Productions, 1971-1974.
Johnson, Eric, *Sex: Telling It Straight.* Philadelphia: Lippincott, 1970.
_____, *Love and Sex in Plain Language.* Philadelphia: Lippincott, 1974.
Kay, Eleanor, *Sex and the Young Teenager.* New York: Franklin Watts, 1973.
Knudsen, Per Holm, *The True Story of How Babies Are Made.* New York: Children's Press, 1973.
Mayle, Peter, *Where Did I Come From?* New York: Lyle Stuart, 1975.
Pomeroy, Wardell, *Boys and Sex.* New York: Delacorte Press, 1968.
_____, *Girls and Sex.* New York: Delacorte Press, 1968.
"Sex Ed Books Which Screw Up Your Kids." *Moneysworth*, July 8, 1974.
Story Packs, Old Westbury, New York: Feminist Press, 1974.
The Searching Years: A Series (in 6 parts). Churchill Films, Los Angeles, 1971.
True to Life, Emory University School of Medicine, Family Planning Program.
Wersba, Barbara, *Run Softly, Go Fast.* Atheneum, 1970.
Zindel, Paul, *My Darling, My Hamburger.* New York: Harper & Row, 1969.

Chapter Thirty-Three

Problems in Selection of Materials

Walter Smithey, M.A.*

As educators now understand, different kinds of books and different kinds of experiences for different kinds of people are required to learn, depending upon the learners.

The California board of education has developed textbook commissions for the approval of materials and the state board lists Guidelines for Family Life Education. These bodies serve in the process of selecting materials. Several years ago the state board of education placed SIECUS on the "blacklist" to prevent the use of SIECUS materials in the classroom. Although this was only a recommendation, it was taken as law by educators throughout California.

In 1973 the state board of education rescinded that particular action and vindicated SIECUS, again granting it status as a worthwhile educational institution. In the interim many excellent materials were denied to educators. The original recommendation, as I understand it, was an attempt on the part of the state board of education to placate opponents of family-life education.

We need to study closely the different social class compositions, with regard to the selection of materials. People from lower socioeconomic classes generally have certain characteristics that we must be aware of and consider. They tend to be more suspicious of people in authority, people who have power, people who are educated, and people who are trying to do something to change their world. Tending to fear change, when changes occur too rapidly in their

*Psychologist/Coordinator, Family Life Education, San Mateo Office of education.

world, they become understandably upset. They are often concerned more with survival and material things than anything else, and not as concerned with educational programs *per se*. It is hard for people in the lower socioeconomic classes to come to school to participate in school activities. As an administrator for a Title I project, one of my obligations has been to develop training programs for aides, volunteers, and parent advisory committee members to help reach these people. We find that we have to train people in how to conduct meetings, how to verbalize their feelings, and how to express themselves in meetings. These are some of the problems that you have to consider when you are dealing with parents of children from these socioeconomic levels and selecting appropriate learning materials for them.

Persons from this lower socioeconomic level reflect a greater acceptance of orthodoxy. Perhaps a part of the faiths or religious systems that sustains and gives them hope lies in the myths and old wives' tales that circulate and flow in their neighborhoods. Schools must overcome these myths as the misinformation is passed from one person to another, as must also happen to a lesser extent in the middle classes as well.

Piaget and Jerome Bruner and many others in the field of child development report that young children think in very concrete terms. This points up another problem in the selection of materials. When you show children a picture, it gives them a dimension, but it does not give them the depth of dimension. From personal experiences in attempting explanations regarding the location of the uterus in the female body, I have observed that children often misinterpret this organ as being in the stomach. Very often the literature perpetuates this concept and misinformation. When you use abstractions in explaining the questions of young children, models may be helpful. The Dickinson models from the Cleveland Health Museum are excellent for showing the developing fetus, where it is, and how it eventually leaves the female body.

An excellent film, *A Baby is Born*,[1] presents a complete view of the birth of a baby. I have shown it to mixed groups from ages eleven to adulthood, and there is something for every age in it. I think it helps develop the respect of males for the whole process of birth and what females undergo. The film depicts a young couple awaiting delivery. Their anxiety grows and is felt as the labor is prolonged. Whereas other available films show a very sterile, very "perfect" kind of delivery, *A Baby Is Born* is much more realistic. This film includes an epilogue on contraception where the physician talks to the young couple about what they should do to plan for their future family.

Another graphic film dealing with the issue of population, *Tomorrow's Children*,[2] concerns our lack of resources to feed and provide for the world's population. Obviously, the aim of the film is to explain the need for contraception.

Selecting films in a county office of education is an extended process. The San Mateo County Office of Education fortunately has a Medical Society Family Life Committee to evaluate materials for authenticity with regard to medical issues and a County Family Life Committee that evaluates materials for content, age appropriateness, and specific lack or need within the instructional program. It is of interest to see the different ways people rate different kinds of materials. When we try to determine the criteria used for selection, we find often it is just personal preference. Slang or physiological terms may be objectionable, as might the way a narrator speaks. Parents have a different perspective from teachers and physicians, and thus bring still a different perspective to the task. Trying to purchase films and materials that are appropriate for children takes us through a long waiting process. I presume that every school district has some similar process for film selection.

School districts tend to look for materials that are not going to offend. This often leads to sterility in the kinds of materials selected. We have used parent committees effectively and extensively. Not to involve them at the onset of a program is asking for problems. If parents feel that they have been involved and their opinions and judgments have been considered, they become committed to the outcome of that process.

Today, most of the federal legislation that deals with additional funds for education requires parent advisory committees or school councils. If parents are involved, they learn a great deal through the process of helping select materials and determining the program's progress. In that learning process parents often express appreciation for what they learn and they respond by supporting programs. Too often parent advisory committees are abolished when the program is initiated. In this event opponents of family life or sex education programs direct their negative forces onto the school board. It is especially important to have the ongoing parent group's cooperation and support at that time.

Parents need direction. They come with stereotypical ideas, fears, problems, and axes to grind. They need to know the realities and the constraints, the costs of a program and materials, and the size of the budget available and what is appropriate for children at different age levels. Training sessions can equip the parents with the information they need for their task of assisting in the selection of appropriate materials.

In our county we have several permanent committees to evaluate materials. In addition to the Medical Society Committee on Family Life Education, we have the County Committee on Family Life Education, composed of representatives from various organizations and school districts within the county. They function in a fashion similar to the Drug Education Committee, a Health Education Committee, and the Social Studies Council. Some districts have their own evaluation teams on the district level.

A related subject is the policy of the public libraries concerning accessibility of sex-education materials for children. Our county library system is very liberal in this regard; however, some of the employees working at branch libraries have a policy of their own. They become "gatekeepers" as I refer to them (see pp. 266-267), who take it upon themselves to decide which people should have what available to them. Although our libraries are usually quite open and disseminate a great deal of material, there are some libraries with a closed system aimed toward keeping books off the shelves. Children have to ask the librarian for them, which in itself stops the circulation, because children usually don't ask strangers for books on sex.

It is gratifying that there are so many books and materials available for purchase. Unfortunately, the people who need them the most often don't have the necessary funds. There is still a great deal of overt and covert censorship in our free society, and we continually have to find ways to make materials readily available when people need information.

NOTES TO CHAPTER THIRTY-THREE

1. *A Baby Is Born*, Perennial Education Films, Inc., 1974.
2. *Tomorrow's Children*, Perennial Education Films, Inc. 1971.

MATERIALS

A Baby Is Born, Perennial Education Films, Inc., 1974.
Albrecht, Margaret, *Parents and Teen-agers: Getting Through to Each Other*. Parents' Magazine Press, 1972.
Auerbach, Aline B., *Straight Talk About Sex*. New York: Triangle Press, 1970.
Baker, Katherine Reed, and Xenia F. Fane, *Understanding and Guiding Young Children*, 3rd ed. Englewood Cliffs, N.J.: Prentice Hall, Inc., 1975.
Beserra, Sarah Senefeld, *Sex Code of California: A Compedium*, Public Education and Research Committee, California, 1973.
Bewley, Sheila, and Sheffield, Margaret, *Where Do Babies Come From*? New York: Alfred A. Knopf, 1973.

Biller, Henry B., *Father, Child and Sex Role: Paternal Determinants in Personality Development.* Lexington, Mass.: Heath, Lexington Books, 1971.

Blacklidge, Virginia Young, *Sexual Behavior of the Mentally Retarded.* Alameda County Retardation Service, San Leandro, 1971.

Blakeslee, Alton, *What You Should Know About V.D.* New York: Benjamin Company, 1972.

Bolmeier, Edward C., *Sex Litigation and the Public Schools.* Charlottesville, Va.: Michie Company, 1975.

Boston Woman's Health Book Collective, *Our Bodies, Ourselves: A Book By and For Women,* Revised edition. New York: Simon and Schuster, 1976.

Brenton, Myron, *The American Male.* Greenwich, Conn.: Fawcett Publications Inc., 1970.

California State Board of Education, *Moral and Civic Education and Teaching About Religion,* Sacramento, Calif.: 1973.

Chafetz, Janet Saltzman, *Masculine-Feminine or Human?* Itasca, Ill.: P.E. Peacock Publishers, 1974.

Chesser, Eustace, *Young Adult's Guide to Sex.* New York: Drake Publishers, 1972.

Child Study Association of America, *What To Tell Your Child About Sex.* New York: Hawthorn, 1968.

Collier, James Lincoln, *The Hard Life of the Teenager.* New York: Four Winds Press, 1972.

Committee on Sex-Education, Diocese of Rochester, *Education In Love.* New York: Paulist-Newman Press, 1971.

Dalrymple, Willard, *Sex Is For Real: Human Sexuality and Sexual Responsibility.* New York: McGraw-Hill, 1969.

DeLa Cruz, Felix and LaVeck, Gerald D., (eds.), *Human Sexuality and the Mentally Retarded.* New York: Brunner-Mazel, 1973.

Del Solar, Charlotte, *Parents' Answer Book.* New York: Grosset and Dunlop, 1971.

Emma Willard Task Force on Education, *Sexism in Education,* 3rd. ed., Minneapolis: Emma Willard Task Force on Education, 1972.

The Facts About Sex, Book 2, Albany, New York: Delmar Publishers, 1970.

Ferguson, Lucy Rau, *Personality Development.* Belmont, Calif.: Brooks-Cole, 1969.

Fine, Morton S., *Love, Sex and the Family,* New York: New American Library, 1971.

Fraser, Stewart E., *Sex, Schools and Society.* Nashville, Tenn.: Aurora Publishers, George Peabody College for Teachers, 1972.

Frazier, Nancy and Sadker, Myra, *Sexism in School and Society.* New York: Harper & Row, 1973.

Gersoni-Stavn, Diane, *Sexism and Youth.* New York: Bowker, 1974.

Goldman, Gloria, and Hunter, Lisa, *In All Fairness.* Far West Laboratory for Education Research and Development, 1974.

Goldstein, Eleanor C.; Morrissett, Irving and Cousins, Jack, (eds.), *Population.* Washington, D.C.: Exotech Systems, Inc., 1972.

Goldstein, Michael Joseph, *Pornography and Sexual Deviance.* Berkeley, California: University of California Press, 1973.

Gordon, Sol, *Facts About Sex.* New York: John Day Company, 1973.

_____ , *Facts About Sex for Today's Youth.* New York: John Day Company, 1973.

_____ , *Facts About VD For Today's Youth.* New York: John Day Company, 1973.

_____ , *On Being the Parent of a Handicapped Youth.* New York: New York Association for Brain Injured Children, 1973.

_____ , *The Sexual Adolescent: Communicating with Teenagers About Sex.* North Scituate, Mass.: Duxbury Press, 1973.

_____ , *Sexual Rights for the People Who Happen to be Handicapped.* Syracuse, New York: Syracuse University, 1974.

Grams, Armin, *Sex Education: A Guide for Teachers and Parents.* 2nd ed., Danville, Ill.: Interstate Printers and Publishers, 1970.

Green, Richard, *Sexual Identity Conflict in Children and Adults.* New York: Basic Books, 1974.

Guttmacher, Alan Frank, *Understanding Sex: A Young Person's Guide.* New York: Harper & Row, 1970.

Haims, Lawrence J., *Sex Education and the Public Schools.* Lexington, Mass.: Lexington Books, 1973.

Hamilton, Eleanor, *What Made Me?* New York: Hawthorn Books, 1970.

Hardin, Garrett, *Mandatory Motherhood: The True Meaning of "Right to Life."* Boston: Beacon Press, 1974.

Harrington, John, ed., *Male and Female: Identity.* John Wiley and Sons, Inc., 1972.

Harrison, Barbara Grizzutti, *Unlearning the Lie: Sexism in School.* New York: Liveright, 1973.

Haughton, Rosemary, *The Mystery of Sexuality.* Paramus, New Jersey: Paulist-Newman Press, 1972.

Henslin, James, *Studies in the Sociology of Sex.* New York: Appleton-Century-Crofts, 1971.

Hettlinger, Richard Frederick, *Living With Sex: The Student's Dilemma.* New York: Seabury Press, 1966.

Hinton, Gertrude D., *Teaching Sex Education.* Palo Alto, Calif.: Fearon Publishers, 1969.

Hite, Shere, ed., *Sexual Honesty.* New York: Warner Books, 1974.

Johnson, Eric. W., *Love and Sex and Growing Up.* Philadelphia: Lippincott, 1970.

_____ , *Love and Sex in Plain Language.* Philadelphia: Lippincott, 1974.

Jongeward, Dorothy, *Winning With People.* Reading, Mass.: Addison-Wesley Publishing Co., 1973.

Julian, Cloyd J. and Jackson, E.N., *Modern Sex Education.* New York: Harper & Row, 1972.

Karlin, Muriel Schoenbrun, *Administering and Teaching Sex Education in the Elementary School.* New York: Parker, 1975.

Katchadourian, Herant A., and Lunde, Donald T., *Fundamentals of Human Sexuality.* 2nd ed. New York: Holt, Rinehart and Winston, 1975.

Kelly, M. Ray, ed., *Participating Teacher's Guide.* Cambridge: Ealing Corporation, 1969.

Kempton, Winifred, *Love, Sex and Birth Control for the Mentally Retarded.* 2nd revised ed. Planned Parenthood Association and Family Planning and Population Information Center, 1972.

Kirkendall, Lester A., *You're Maturing Now.* Chicago: Science Research Association, 1968.

_____ and Thumbleson, William C., *Understanding The Other Sex.* Science Research Associates, 1973.

LeMasters, E.E., *Parents in Modern America.* Homewood, Illinois: Dorsey Press, 1974.

Lerrigo, Marion O., and Cassidy, Michael, *A Doctor Talks to 9-to 12-Year-Olds.* Chicago: Budlong Press, 1974.

_____, *A Story About You.* Chicago: American Medical Association, 1966.

LeShan, Eda J., *Sex and Your Teenager.* New York: Warner Books, 1973.

Levine, Milton I., *A Baby Is Born.* New York: Simon and Shuster, 1949.

Lieberman, E. James, and Peck, Ellen, *Sex and Birth Control: A Guide for the Young.* New York: Thomas Y. Crowell Company, 1973.

Lipke, Jean Coryllel, *Conception and Contraception.* Minneapolis: Lerner Publishing Co., 1971.

Love—The Concerns of Man. Evanston, Ill.: McDougal, Littell and Company, 1972.

Luthman, Shirley Gehrke, *Intimacy: The Essence of Male and Female.* Los Angeles: Nash Publishers, 1972.

Masters, William H. and Johnson, Virginia E., *Human Sexual Response.* Boston: Little, Brown, 1966.

May, Julian, *Living Things and Their Young.* New York: Follett, 1969.

_____, *Man and Woman.* New York: Follett, 1969.

Mayle, Peter, *Where Did I Come From?* New York: Lyle Stuart, Inc., 1973.

McBride, Will and Fleischhauer-Hardt, Helga, *Show Me!* New York: St. Martin's Press, 1975.

Meeks, Esther K. and Bagwell, Elizabeth, *How New Life Begins.* Chicago: Follett Publishing Company, 1969.

Meilach, Dona Z., and Mandel, Elias, *A Doctor Talks To 5-to-8 Year Olds.* Chicago: Budlong Press, 1974.

Miller, Benjamin F., *Masculinity and Femininity.* Boston: Houghton Mifflin, 1971.

_____, *Masculinity and Femininity.* Instructor's Guide. Boston: Houghton Mifflin, 1971.

Minor, Harold W., *Sex Education—The Schools and the Churches.* Richmond, Va.: John Knox Press, 1971.

Mooney, Elizabeth, *The School's Responsibility for Sex Education.* Bloomington, Ind.: Phi Delta Kappa Education Foundation, 1974.

Morrison, Eleanor Shelton, and Borosage, Vera (eds.), *Human Sexuality: Contemporary Perspectives.* Palo Alto, Calif.: Mayfield Publishing Co., 1973.

_____ and Underhill, Price, *Values in Sexuality: A New Approach to Sex Education.* New York: Hart Publishing Co., 1974.

Nelson, Jack L., *Teenagers and Sex: Revolution or Reaction?* Englewood Cliffs, N.J.: Prentice-Hall, 1970.

Pattulo, Ann, *Puberty in the Girl Who is Retarded.* National Association for Retarded Children, 1969.

Paul, Leslie Allen, *Eros Rediscovered: Restoring Sex to Humanity*. New York: Associated Press, 1970.
Pomeroy, Wardell Baxter, *Boys and Sex*. New York: Delacorte Press, 1968.
_____, *Your Child and Sex: A Guide for Parents*. New York: Delacorte Press, 1974.
Power, Jules, *How Life Begins*. New York: Simon and Schuster, 1965.
Reiss, Ira L., *The Social Context of Premarital Sexual Permissiveness*. New York: Irvington Publishing Co., 1967.
Rogers, Rex S., ed., *Sex Education: Rationale and Reaction*. Cambridge: University Press, 1974.
Rubin, Isadore, *Sex in the Adolescent Years*. New York: Association Press, 1958.
_____ and Kirkendall, Lester, *Sex in the Childhood Years*. New York: Association Press, 1970.
Sarvis, Betty, and Rodman, Hyman, *The Abortion Controversy*. New York: Columbia University Press, 1974.
Schiller, Patricia, *Creative Approach to Sex Education and Counseling*. New York: Association Press, 1973.
Schulz, David A., and Wilson, Roberta (eds.), *Readings On the Changing Family*. Englewood Cliffs, N.J.: Prentice-Hall, 1973.
Seaman, Barbara, *Free and Female: The Sex Life of the Contemporary Woman*. New York: Coward, McCann and Geoghegan, 1973.
Sexton, Patricia Cayo, *The Feminized Male*. New York: Random House, 1969.
Sexual Encounters Between Adults and Children. New York: Sex Information and Education Council of the U.S., 1972.
Sexual Latitude, For and Against. New York: Hart Publishing Company, 1971.
Sexuality and Human Values: The Personal Dimension of Sexual Experience. SIECUS Conference on Religion and Sexuality, St. Louis, 1971. New York: Association Press, 1974.
Shay, Arthur, *How A Family Grows*. Chicago: Reilly and Lee, 1968.
Southard, Helen Elizabeth, *Sex Before Twenty*. New York: Dutton, 1971.
Stacey, Judith; Beareaud, Susan; and Daniels, Joan (eds.), *And Jill Came Tumbling After: Sexism in American Education*. New York: Dell Publishing Co., 1974.
Sundgaard, Arnold, *The Miracle of Growth*. Urbana, Ill.: University of Illinois, 1967.
Thomas, Lydia A., ed., *Perspective on Sex and Sexuality, Life Values To Weigh, Judge and Discuss*. New York: Readers' Digest, 1970.
Tomorrow's Children, Perennial Education Films, Inc., 1971.
Trussell, James and Hatcher, R., *Women in Need*. New York: Macmillan, 1972.
Uslander, Arlene, et al., *Their Universe: A Look into Children's Hearts and Minds*. New York: Delacorte Press, 1973.
Westlake, Helen Gum, *Children: A Study in Individual Behavior*. Lexington, Mass.: Ginn and Company, 1973.
Willke, Jack C. and Willke, Mrs. J.C., *Sex Education: The How-To For Teachers*. Cincinnati: Hiltz and Hayes Publishing Company, 1971.
Yorburg, Betty, *The Changing Family: A Sociological Perspective*. New York: Columbia University Press, 1973.
Zolotow, Charlotte, *William's Doll*. New York: Harper & Row, 1972.

※ *Chapter Thirty-Four*

Evaluating Sex Education Programs

Derek L. Burleson, Ed.D.*

In any program or experiment in sex education, evaluation is crucial, yet frequently neglected. Accountability is, in fact, a watchword in American education today. In school systems across the country, citizens are asking: "What are we getting for our education dollar?" and they are making themselves heard at the ballot box, turning down school budgets because they cannot reconcile increased tax rates with the results they see in schools. We are plainly seeing a spirit of consumerism in American education that has put educators at all levels on the defensive. Reputations of school administrators are made or lost, especially in our large cities, on the basis of reading and math achievement scores. One need only browse through a sampling of our education journals to see how the demand for accountability has created a whole new vocabulary in the field: competency-based teaching, performance contracting, the voucher system, behavioral goals, programmed instruction, computer-based teaching, and more and more testing. Frankly, such terminology applied to the field of sex education concerns me.

On the other hand, we hear equally strong voices in American education calling for relevancy, for opening up the curriculum in terms of the needs of children and youth, for individualizing instruction, for recognizing alternative styles of learning, for opening classrooms, and for humanizing the educational process. This kind of terminology is more comforting for those of us in the field of sex

*Managing Editor, *Medical Aspects of Human Sexuality*; formerly Director, Educational and Research Services, SIECUS.

education. Yet let us also admit that this kind of terminology is vague, simplistic, and highly conducive to the type of teaching that says: "Let's throw out the textbooks and get the kids together to rap for a while." The field of sex education is caught in this dilemma of trying to meet these competing and frequently contradictory demands. I am very dubious about choosing one over the other. We are going to have to do both if we expect to assure the legitimacy of sex education in the curriculum and get the kind of community support to both initiate and maintain programs in our schools.

But how effective have we been in communicating to the public at large our conviction of the necessity for sex education? What kinds of data and what types of research do we have? The requests for evaluation of programs that have come to the SIECUS office are numerous. For example, a journalist writes: "I am doing a story on the controversy of sex education in the schools. Can you tell me what systems have the best sex-education programs?" In attempting to respond, I am confronted by two unknowns. What does a program mean? What criteria do I use with the value-laden term "best"? I could probably list some criteria for programs one could label "weak," "adequate," and "superior," but I have great difficulty in pointing to specific schools. Other than firsthand knowledge of a few programs, the literature on evaluation of sex education is nonexistent.

A school superintendent writes: "I need hard facts to justify to my community and school board that sex education really works." Behind that question is a plea for evaluative information that he can use to justify his program. What does he have in mind when he says "sex education really works"? Masturbation without guilt? A few dozen fewer pregnancies in the senior class? This superintendent obviously needs help on formulation of goals and objectives, with methods of achieving those goals. These are all very legitimate concerns of evaluation.

A parent writes: "Can you help us organize a sex-education program in our school to control the increasing number of teenage pregnancies and VD cases?" This parent has identified two very real problems in our society. She expresses unlimited faith in the educational process in the schools to solve these problems. Is this faith justified? Are her expectations realistic? Can the schools really do this? What evidence do we have to make this claim? Or are we asking the wrong questions?

A government agency grant officer writes: "All our grant applications must have clearly stated behavioral objectives before we can consider them. Can you provide me with the most important

performance objectives of sex education?" This one drew a chuckle or two around our office, but if you want that grant you have to pay attention to those requirements of bureaucracy.

These examples I have given of different requests for evaluation information emphasize the kind of work that needs to be done in the field. A survey of literature would show that there has been an abundance of articles attacking or defining sex education, promoting or discussing sex-education theories and models, and giving hints to teachers and help to troubled parents. What we do not find is any large body of evaluative research.

The fact must be faced that evaluation of sex education is difficult. Partially this is because the concept of sex education is rather nebulous, rarely having clearly defined goals that lend themselves to precise measurements. More important, since many of us feel that the essence of good sex education is in the process itself, we are dealing with such matters as the interaction between teachers and students and between students and students. No two experiences are the same. Therefore, most studies reported deal only with a specific program, and there is little or no replication. Another problem for researchers is not only that sex education itself is controversial or political, but any research surrounding it is likely to be even more so.

Research that has been reported tends to fall into three broad categories: changes in knowledge, changes in attitudes or values, and changes in behavior. By far the most frequently reported programs are those dealing with knowledge acquisition. This is understandable as it is the easiest kind of research to conduct. Some of the findings include the investigation of basic sex information requested by a large sample of children and youth in the state of Connecticut, *Teach Us What We Want to Know*.[1] A variety of studies shows that students can achieve significant increases in basic information about sex-related topics.[2] If you are teaching for information and knowledge, then it is reasonably certain that students will know more after they have taken the course than they did before.

This kind of information can best be used to establish the guidelines for grade placement of subject matter, to investigate children's questions about sex for establishing readiness for certain topics, and to guide us in developing materials with publishers and audiovisual producers.

The second body of evaluation research deals with changes in sexual attitudes and values as a result of sex-education programs. This is much more difficult to validate. While we stress the importance of developing positive and healthy attitudes about sex, there is little research to document that we are doing so. One small study

with elementary grade students showed that gains in knowledge do not, *per se*, produce significant changes in attitudes. A small study with junior-high-school students involved in a program with a heavy emphasis on small group process showed significant changes from lesser to greater permissiveness in their sexual attitudes. Depending on how permissiveness is defined, one may or may not like the results of that study. At the college level, studies showed that there were significant changes in sexual attitude resulting from a marriage and family course.[3] Such research efforts are a beginning, but I suggest extreme caution in generalizing from any of them, and avoid the temptation to quote those that agree with what you think is right and proper.

Our research tools to measure attitude change over a short period of time are crude, and of course, the determinants of attitudes go far deeper than would be affected simply by exposure to a sex-education program. Instead of devoting more and more effort to this type of before-and-after study, would it not make better sense to begin to scrutinize the process through which attitudes and values are confronted, challenged, and clarified?

A fairly common experience now in professional training of sex educators is to view explicit sex films depicting all sorts of sexual behavior, followed by small group discussions with trained group process people. This process is referred to as "sexual attitude reassessment or restructuring." It is one example of the kind of specific experience that has been designed to generate all kinds of feelings and attitudes about sex, and it is an opportunity for research into the process of attitude change and modification.

The third category of evaluation research is changes in behavior as a result of school programs in sex education. This is clearly the most difficult area to assess and, in some researchers' viewpoint, the most sensitive kind to conduct. Neither parents nor school administrators are particularly receptive to having teachers or outside researchers interviewing their children about their sexual behavior, even in the interests of science. A few studies have identified behavioral change associated with involvement in sex-education programs,[4] but these are modest changes. They include such things as increased ease and openness in talking about sex, and greater satisfaction in parent-child communication about sex. This kind of change cannot be termed dramatic, but it is nevertheless the fundamental aspect of behavior that must be nurtured before anyone, children or adults, can begin to deal with the many topics and issues in this area. It is also a realistic goal that the school might hope to accomplish.

Parents often express a great concern about behavioral effects of

sex education in relation to sexual activity. Some of us, in our zeal to win acceptance for sex education, have too often held up teenage pregnancy and mushrooming VD rates as the sole justifications for such programs. This simplistic approach to such complex issues can only hurt the field, because it builds up expectations that we cannot possibly meet at this time. My plea is that we begin to balance our rhetoric with some realism about what we can and cannot accomplish.

In spite of lack of research, there is nevertheless a sense of progress and positive direction in the field of sex education. Because the field is fairly new and somewhat controversial, we may become so engrossed in getting programs established and accepted that we are ultrasensitive to criticism. But if the criticism comes from within the family of professionals, and is combined with some constructive directions for the future, then this indicates that the field is reaching some level of maturity.

Descriptions of three programs follow, each representative of models that are worthy of study and replication. One such program is in the youth correctional institutions of California, and the other two are church sponsored. These choices are something of an anachronism to the general public's view of where sex education is conducted. The common thread of all three of these programs is their attention to process, although content is not neglected.

The Family Life Education Program developed by the California Youth Authority[5] was intended for use in youth correctional institutions. It was designed, keeping in mind the background of life styles of these high-risk young people who make up the population of these institutions. The published curriculum guide contains a veritable storehouse of good teaching techniques, group process exercises, and other suggestions for communicating with youth that are a far cry from the traditional classroom instruction methods. It recognizes that many, if not most, of these young people are or have been sexually active. It is open, flexible, and deliberately geared to concerns, interests, and needs of young people in this program. It calls for warm, sensitive, and mature adult leadership, with proven skills in group techniques. The teaching model is built around gathering and sharing information, exploring attitudes and values, and being creative with what is learned. There is a minimal use of commercial material. Young people are involved in making posters, developing a graffiti board, and drawing pictures of the opposite sex. Since these youngsters have come up against the law, there is provision in the program for learning about the sex laws of the state. In my opinion this represents a realistic and relevant program designed for those we euphemistically refer to as "hard to reach."

The second program is a high-school course developed by the United Methodist Church, called "Christians and the Meaning of Sexuality."[6] This is an intensive weekend workshop experience involving youth and their parents. In fact, one of the requirements to participate in the course is the presence of at least one parent or guardian for each young person. The youth and the parent have both separate and joint sessions. These are similar, but the youth sessions include more content. The sessions for both youth and parents are group centered, covering such areas as cultural images of masculine and feminine roles, different cultural models and the meaning of sex, communication among sexual beings, sex attitudes in the Bible and in Christian tradition, and wisdom and responsibility in being sexual. These courses are led by leaders trained by the United Methodist Church and by group facilitators who have also had special group process training. Worship is frequently worked into the program and is usually conducted in a spirit of reverent exuberance. There is a great deal of flexibility in the program which allows it to be adapted to the needs and wishes of the local community. Perhaps the essence of the program might be summed up in one of its stated objectives: the ability to affirm one's sexual being through a wide range of mystical, esthetic, festive, meditative, and dramatic modes of experience.

The third program, "About Your Sexuality," was developed by the Unitarian-Universalist Association.[7] Its use of some explicit film strips has been the focus of some titillating interest by the press. However, the broad scope of the program employs a wide variety of creative and investigative approaches in three areas: developing communications skills, building attitudes and values, and making responsible decisions. The course is usually taught by a male-female team who have received special training. There are nine units in the program which may be used optionally as the local group prefers. Its philosophical stance is: (1) sex is a positive and enriching force in life; (2) some expression of sexual outlet is normal and is to be expected at all ages, but this expression is influenced now by earlier reproductive maturity and faster pace in the total socialization process; (3) there are no automatic or inevitable physical or psychological consequences of any form of sexual behavior, but rather a wide range of possible outcomes; (4) sexual behavior and its consequences are determined and conditioned by family background, concept of sex-role, prior experience, geography, and opportunity to a much greater degree than intellectualized presentations and instructions; and (5) there is no one established or universally accepted norm of sexual behavior. The form varies with class, religion, education, and life style.

The strength of all three of these programs is their attention to methodology and the insight they bring to the process of value clarification and decisionmaking. They stand as models worthy of serious study for anyone interested in the development of a sex-education program.

NOTES TO CHAPTER THIRTY-FOUR

1. Ruth Byler, ed., *Teach Us What We Want to Know* (New York: Mental Health Materials Center, 1969).

2. Frederick E. Bidgood, The Effects of Sex Education: A Summary of the Literature, *SIECUS Report* 1 (4) March, 1973, 11.

3. *Ibid.*

4. *Ibid.*

5. State of California Documents Section, P.O. Box 20191, Sacramento, California 95820.

6. Graded Press, Nashville, Tenn., 1972.

7. Beacon Press, Boston, Mass., 1973.

Chapter Thirty-Five

Barriers and Strategies:
A Panel Discussion

Diane Brashear, Ph.D.;
Walter Smithey, M.A.;
Joseph Bodovitz;
Joyce Evans, M.A.

Moderator:

Diane Brashear, Ph.D.; Director, Brashear Center for Personal and Sexual Health, Indianapolis, Indiana.

Participants:

Walter Smithey, M.A., Psychologist; Administrative Staff Member, San Mateo County Office of Education

Joyce Evans, M.A., Fifth-Grade Teacher, Marin Country Day School; Corte Madera, California

Joseph Bodovitz, Former Chairman, School Board, Mill Valley School District; Mill Valley, California

Brashear: One of the gaps in the field of human sexuality is the gap between the knowledge base that is growing and the application of such knowledge. This is in reference not so much to curriculum development, but to application in the sense of developing and delivering programs to systems and agencies which have heretofore not experienced any kind of sex education. By systems, I mean the family as well as social systems and institutions in general.

Individuals concerned with delivering programs and educational information about sexuality, although frequently having the knowledge and commitment required, often appear naïve. The resulting programs may fail to become established because naïveté prevented adequate recognition that adult responses to sexual material are preset, especially to programs being planned for young children. In one group of parents considering sex education for their school

system, a father openly voiced concern that explicit sex films would be shown to the second grade. Actually, the curriculum specified only growing beans to illustrate the growing process. Adults, whether they are teachers, parents, or administrators, react to sex education discussions from their particular perspectives, and this may obstruct developing programs.

Another anxiety frequently encountered arises when we attempt to talk about sex in nonseductive social situations, that is in settings not meant to produce any specific sexual behavior. It is difficult to keep in mind that the proposed programs, though uncomfortable for the educator, parent, or administrator, usually are acceptable in a rather matter-of-fact way by the children.

We have to be constantly mindful of the power of attitudes and experiences, and what the anxieties attendant on introducing sex education programs can do to a school and/or family system. If we are going to introduce programs, we must be responsive to reactions. We need to prepare our communities, our families, and our schools so that our attempts to establish and present programs will be positive for all concerned.

A COMPARISON OF EXPERIENCES

Smithey: My background is as a classroom teacher. For the past twelve years, however, I have been in administration, working in the area of school psychology, guidance, and curriculum. Eight years ago I became a coordinator of family life education in the San Mateo County Office of Education, where we had earlier developed several family-life-education pilot programs.

I have a concept about the role of "gatekeeper" that we have within the educational system. We have a hierarchy of people who open and close gates, allowing or disallowing things to happen within education, starting with the board of education, the superintendent, the principal, the assistant principals, the assistant superintendents for instruction, directors of curriculum, the individual teachers, and, of course, the parents. To me, these interacting structures represent the most difficult and challenging barrier to implementing any kind of new program in education.

My efforts in instituting family life and sex education programs have been in the direction of bringing about an individualization of such education, including establishing multicultural, bilingual programs. Each time a new subject or a new issue is proposed for the curriculum, we have to gain the support of the entire hierarchy of gatekeepers, as well as the community as a whole. While there is

value in having this structure, often the systems have horrendous detail and echelons to which we must present, and from which we must expect, challenges.

To illustrate, our county has seventeen elementary school districts, three unified school districts, and three secondary school districts, besides our community college system. Each one is autonomous with its own board and its own superintendent hired by the board. We have to go through this process with each one of these separate entities before we can bring about any kind of change within the county educational structure.

The process is much more highly charged when it has anything to do with sexuality. It mobilizes fears about what is going to be done to the children. Administration becomes fearful that it is going to be attacked and will have to spend all its time trying to defend the programs. It is widely recognized that the more the parents are involved in the development of programs, the stronger the supporters they become and the more they will mobilize efforts to make them work.

Yet the difficulties cannot be overestimated. Our countywide committee on family life education was developed in 1964. Its composition includes representatives from all the significant groups that we could find in the community—the churches, the Medical Society, the League of Women Voters, and others with political influence. We organized about eighty representatives from these different groups who met and agreed to our proceeding to develop a curriculum of family life education and teachers' resource guides for grades kindergarten through twelve.

During this period, the *Time of Your Life* film series was developed as a result of a decision by the Bay Region Instructional Television Consortium, itself made up of representatives from the various school districts in the area. Shortly after the films were begun on television, people who were opposed to family life and sex education in schools started attending one school board meeting after another, making accusations and inciting anxieties among community members. Finally, a suit was instituted against our office and against five of the districts in our county, which still has not been resolved. This has been a shadow over the program for seven years. There is still fear that new or augmented programs in sex education will ignite more turmoil within the community. It takes conviction and self-assurance to proceed. I feel we proceeded carefully, thoroughly, and from a base of wide support. Yet our experience was on the whole negative.

Bodovitz: As a member of the school board in Mill Valley in Marin County, California, a suburban county north of San Francisco, it became my dubious pleasure to be chairman of the board while we went through a major controversy about instituting a program of sex education. It was quite an experience in that there exists in our community strong public interest in the public schools, with lively controversies about sex education or almost any other topic.

The *Time of Your Life* series, mentioned by Mr. Smithey, was begun in our district in a very quiet way, as part of the courses presented. As these films became a major item in the news media, with reports of people protesting their use in several districts in the area, a group of parents came to our school district board meeting, demanding to know why we were showing these movies to their young children.

The board reacted by creating a citizen's committee of twenty-one people to represent the broad range of views on this topic so that the matter could be fully studied. The citizen's committee recommended that we continue using the films. The problem was that the citizen's committee made that recommendation by a vote of eleven in favor and ten violently opposed.

The board's conclusion after we ourselves viewed the entire film series was that the material describing the facts of life was very well and sensitively prepared. The problem was the moral value discussion that preceded. Some felt some parts of that were objectionable, yet many in the community felt those parts were very well done. We also recognized that the television film series forced us to focus on whether sex education was a good idea or not. The films had drawn the fire, but of course the real issue was whether there should be sex education in the schools at all.

We concluded that a consensus of the community thought there should be such a program. With regard to those who were not in favor, we reminded them that the California state law requires that parents who feel concerned about this may choose not to have their children participate in the course. We realized, however, that this is not as simple a solution as one might think, for there is potential for stigmatizing the children of those parents; this, to my mind, would be a very unwholesome circumstance.

We also decided that if we expected teachers who, after all, had been hired to teach math, history, and science, to undertake this kind of a program, then a fair basis for decision would require our considering if the teachers liked the film series and wanted to use it. The teachers' response was that the films were a pioneering effort, and though they assumed that better teaching aids would become

available, the films were the best available. at the moment. They also said that if we expected them to do a creditable job in this emotionally charged field, we should not substitute our judgment for theirs, nor unreasonably limit the materials they could use.

Of interest is the fact that there was much public involvement and debate on this issue in our community. I think the key to our success was the full and widespread public understanding of what was being done. Our experience underlines the fact that teachers must let parents know what is happening and must give parents opportunities to inspect materials being used. In our district, on our "Meet the Teacher Night," which we have shortly after the beginning of school each year, most of the teachers display all of their classroom materials and texts, including the sex education materials. Questions are welcome on all topics.

Another important aspect of resistance to these programs has to be considered. Parents who have concerns about their children mastering general academic courses feel that sex education takes time that could better be spent on the general curriculum. We had to make clear from the beginning that sex education is in addition, and not instead of, other subjects.

It is essential for a board to understand both the people who support the programs and those who don't. There is a tendency to feel that all the "good" people want sex education programs, and everybody who doesn't is an obstructionist. I'm not suggesting that we be naïve about the opposition to these issues; however, we must realize that among them are some parents who are deeply troubled that the schools, by entering an area that used to be solely the concern of the home, are undermining parents' authority and influence over their children.

Evans: From a teacher's point of view, I would be dismayed by the kind of battling that Mr. Smithey and Mr. Bodovitz describe.

I have been privileged to develop a sex education program for the fifth grade of Marin Country Day School, a private suburban elementary school. (See pp. 197-207.) Mine would have been a difficult task were it not for the remarkable support I received from the headmaster and the board of trustees. Even with their support, though, I find that it is very important that they and the parents be informed as fully as possible in an ongoing way about what the program entails. I feel I have been involved in a cooperative partnership with the parents and the board.

The question I am most often asked by parents is: "What can I do to help?" The parents I deal with appreciate my sharing what is

happening in the class, so that they can continue the education at home. They are grateful for the school's creating an opportunity that they, as parents, can carry further. Many times in our interchanges, I recognize that the parent is also learning, making up for limitations in the sex education of the current adult generation.

I must emphasize, however, that mine is a small, rather homogeneous, cohesive group, which is definitely an advantage. Yet, even in the Parkrose School District, a public school district in Oregon, with the kind of hierarchical system Mr. Smithey outlined, the same kind of planning and procedure was successful.

Brashear: I had some experience with the State School for the Handicapped in Indiana, where a grant was received to develop a sex education program. The program was initiated because of a crisis within the system when there was a rise in the occurrence of VD and pregnancy. The school was alarmed as it was a residential institution with, therefore, the greatest responsibility for the children's sex education.

We developed a program which included a series of five meetings on human sexuality for the administrative staff, house parents, teachers, and secretaries. This program was compulsory for the staff. A study following the series revealed that eighty-nine of the ninety participants wanted a sex education program within the system. Essentially our technique was to have the staff, rather than outsiders, make the decision and have them identify what kinds of content they wanted taught in what grade.

Our next step was to have a parent education program in three sessions, very similar to the staff program. The parents' postcourse response was also affirmative. At that point, a joint committee of parents and house staff was developed.

As an aside, many sex education programs have been sold on the high pregnancy and VD rate in a community. I would warn against selling sex education programs on this basis. Cause and effect here is, at best, nebulous. However, Dr. Philip Sorrell, of the Department of Obstetrics and Gynecology at Yale University, suggests that where sex problems such as VD, pregnancy, and sexual dysfunction are at a low ebb, often there is a comprehensive sex education program.[1]

VALUES AS A CONCERN

Smithey: There is a great deal of concern on the part of the parents as to teaching values in the school. I was recently at a PTA meeting to explain values clarifications,[2] a concept closely associated with

drug education and sex education. Attending was a group from one of the religious communities who wanted no values clarification program in the schools. I believe they were not feeling very secure about their own ability to convey values to their children; however, values clarification is a powerful tool, and its misuse can bring about difficulties.

Brashear: The National Council on Family Relations did a survey of teachers of family life education.[3] The general agreement was that most teachers perceived themselves as reinforcing, rather than as directly teaching, values. Further, if one considers only a cognitive, developmental approach, it follows that one is not able to alter values even if one wanted to. The problem in terms of strategy in the community, though, is that parents and the community have deep and *multiple* concerns in this area.

Evans: I don't feel that any teacher teaching anything, nor anyone connected with the child in a teaching-learning exchange, is value free. In our attempt to be value free, we may end up giving the children nothing. In discussing this with the headmaster and the board, they concluded that the children should know my beliefs and values if I felt free in presenting these. They stipulated that the children be helped to understand that there are many other value bases. Values clarification exercises are important in that they do not stress a value; rather, they give the children opportunities to examine their own feelings and begin forming their own value systems.

We need to be sensitive to individual reactions, yet if I had to be value free, to offer the material and nothing more, I don't think I would be teaching.

PERSONNEL TO TEACH THE SUBJECT

Brashear: Another important consideration is who is to teach sex education to the young child. Some schools engage a person who travels from school to school to present sex education like art and music. It may be someone chosen in that he or she is a warm, comfortable human being, or someone who simply teaches biology.

Smithey: The California State Board of Education recommends that people have proper in-service training in family life education or sex education before they teach it. Although certification is not yet a general practice, the American Association of Sex Educators and Counselors has begun certification. Our office offers in-service

training continually as do Planned Parenthood organizations and others. Most administrators refer specific teachers to "a course" to enable them to teach sex education.

(An additional barrier was indicated in discussion by Richard Foster, Ed.D., former superintendent of schools, Berkeley, California. Dr. Foster indicated that research on certain school projects has shown that teachers who had been trained in new processes, on returning to their schools, found difficulties with their peers, their fellow teachers, not with the upper echelons in the hierachy. In general, he commented, discussions in teachers' rooms urge conservative approaches to avoid difficulties for all.)

Evans: Dr. Calderone, SIECUS director, feels that teachers should *want* to teach the material,[4] which I think is an important factor. Additionally, Dr. Calderone suggests that sex education ideally should be integrated into the total program. This can be challenging and effective. In that I primarily teach English, there are many interesting ways I integrate the sex education information into the curriculum through stories and novels. Dr. Calderone holds, and I agree, that the specialist who visits from outside the school is probably better than none at all, but far less than the ideal.

(Derek Burleson, Ed.D. of SIECUS commented that "in the elementary school, the integrative approach we recommend is through science, health and social studies. It seems to me bringing in an outside person has unfortunate connotations. If we accept the assumption that sex is a part of life, manifested in different ways, then it should be within the regular curriculum, and not with the 'outside specialist.' This is not to say that most teachers don't need some special help.") A psychiatrist, for instance, as a visiting sex education lecturer, might connect it in some children's minds with some disorder. A minister might bring up responses regarding judgmental and moralistic questions. However, such community leaders may legitimize the program.

Someone who is dealing with the children on a regular basis in a variety of contexts is ideal. An added advantage to having the "on campus" sex educator is the additional opportunity for conveying to other teachers on the staff what the children are learning and helping them integrate their special topics with the sex education material. This may be difficult when a teaching staff, reflecting the greater outside community, holds extremely diverse opinions with regard to such programs; but at least their awareness can be enhanced.

Brashear: In summary, the teacher or administrator who takes on the responsibility for delivering sex education content has to be a

somewhat politically able person. It is often a lonely job requiring not only knowledge and comfort with one's own sexuality but also knowledge of and comfort with the community and systems in which we are functioning. He or she must be able to present his or her views in a variety of contexts and anticipate that the process is not going to happen smoothly. We all know of many programs that have been watered down because of opposition. It is hoped that now is the time to begin to look at new ways to enrich programs.

NOTES TO CHAPTER THIRTY-FIVE

1. Personal communication.

2. Sidney Simon, Leland Howe, and Howard Kirschenbaum, *Values Clarification: A Handbook of Practical Strategies for Teachers and Students* (New York: Hart, 1972), 13-22.

3. Richard K. Kerckhoff, Value Stance in Family Life Education, *The Family Coordinator* 19 (3), 1970, 253.

4. Mary S. Calderone, Planning Programs of Sex Education, National Association of Independent Schools, 1967.

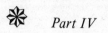 *Part IV*

Values and Conclusions

Chapter Thirty-Six

Society's Values and the Educator's Dilemma

Neil Smelser, Ph.D.*

A consideration of sex and gender identity from a social and cultural perspective requires that we focus on what we consider some of the most salient social, cultural, and political issues regarding educational institutions, and their relationship to the development of gender differentiations. An overview of the significance of societal values and the sorts of consequences that we may expect when societal values begin to break down or change provides a perspective for understanding the complexity of the issues.

There is first the notion of development as a "program" in which certain structures are generated in the personality as a result of the interaction of internal and external environments, which limit the alternatives at critical points and provide a structural base on which further development proceeds. Dr. Money has described the "programmed" quality of chromosome and endocrine influence that establishes sex, (see pp. 27-33) which can be diverted at certain critical intervals; however, once the structure is established, a certain irreversibility of development is established. He uses as an analogy the acquisition of a native tongue; psychoanalysts also utilize similar concepts in detailing the emergence of personality, emphasizing sequential emergence of structures in the various phases of psychosexual development.

We can extend the same logic of program from "above" as well, that is with respect to culture, values, and norms. For what are

*Professor of the University, Department of Sociology, University of California, Berkeley

values, if not evolved devices on the part of society to *limit* the endless variety of behaviors that are possible in social life? Consider, for example, the traditional American value of free enterprise; that is a statement of *preference*, of selection, that certain types of economic activity are preferable, better, more desirable than others, and, therefore, others ought not be institutionalized. Values are given "bite," moreover, by the institutionalization of *norms*, or more specific standards, that are meant to apply to situations of human exchange and interaction. Continuing with the economic example, the vast complex of property law (including laws of contract, exchange, partnership, and incorporation) make specific the rules that govern the workings of the economy under the values of free enterprise, or any other value system, including those of a mixed economic system. Norms further *limit* the range of behaviors that are possible, by sanctioning the preferred behaviors positively and those undesirable ones negatively.

Finally, norms are given "teeth" by the establishment of *agencies* or *organizations*—law-enforcement agencies, informal agreements among economic agents, and collective-bargaining agencies—that actually wield the sanctions and attempt to shape human behavior in line with the programmed scheme of values and norms.

It is possible to identify certain traditional *values* relating to what men and women should be like: men as aggressive, dominant, competitive, and independent; women as passive, submissive, soft, and dependent. *Norms* relating what kinds of behavior, and what kinds of attitudes, and what kinds of symbols—such as modes of dress—signify that the masculine and feminine values are being lived up to; and certain agencies are dedicated to seeing to it, in a general way, that these values and norms are implemented. In particular, these are the family, the school, the mass media, the church, and parts of the legal system, which continuously monitor and propagate the desirable character of social life, and mete out various types of sanctions to bolster these messages.

We mustn't oversimplify by suggesting that values and norms are a straitjacket. I have more in mind a general program, a gyroscope that sets society and social life on its course; there is a degree of flexibility in all sorts of value systems and normative systems. Nor do I mean to suggest that the program of culture suppresses all else. What I do suggest is that the human condition can be represented by two sets of programs, moving toward one another and ultimately meshing: the program of individual development, as determined by biological and other exigencies, and the program of culture that constitutes a statement of preferred channels of development. It is in

the articulation of these two programs that individuals are moulded, and it is in the articulation of these programs that we meet the resistances, the vulnerabilities, and the conflicts between nature and culture.

What happens when the cultural program, including the values, norms, and agencies, undergoes processes of rapid change, or even deterioration and disintegration? The question is important, for indeed, that is what has been happening to our values concerning gender identification, as demonstrated by numerous studies and observations in this volume.

When culture is not there, people are forced to fall back on their own resources and invent culture anew. This alone is a mighty demand, but it is made more difficult by the fact that because values are in change and conflict, the cultural milieu no longer provides even general guidelines as to how that improvisation is to be made.

These are the consequences of rapid cultural change: First, there is sense of loss, anxiety, and disorientation, with a feeling that we know what's wrong, but we don't know what's right. Most of our current discourse on sex-roles is almost entirely negative, pointing out what men and women shouldn't be, with the strong implication that the old values are irrelevant or mischievous. Such thoughts help, to be sure, but result in a very high level of anxiety and sense of loss of moorings or loss of direction.

This anxiety reaches into the intimate social settings, for it leaves the parent and teacher floundering, unable to know what to do, condemned if they attempt to develop conventional little boys and girls, for that is wrong, and condemned if they attempt some new experiment in nonsexist development, for the old values are far from dead. Another frequent phenomenon that accompanies periods of uncertainty are enormous prophesies of gloom, that this or that or another institution is going to break down totally if we permit certain changes to continue. Concomitantly there is the all-pervasive cry of conservative protest.

As a result of these diverse responses, there arises a high level of conflict, for any time a new solution or new attempt to invent culture is introduced, it meets not only the conservative response, but also the voices of others who have invented a new bit of culture on their own. The uncertainty, the anxiety, the floundering gives birth to a babble of voices, a multitude of missionaries who have something they think is novel and helpful, and a battlefield on which the army of innovators attempt to impose their inventions on one another.

A third consequence is a lingering hope for a leader, a voice who

will in fact come forth with a general invention that will give new guidance, provide a new program or gyroscope for us to get our bearings. But actual changes that generally occur after the establishment of some new arrangement are often quite modest. Finally, the sum response is that we all attempt to improvise in our own ways, with all the attendant anxiety and uncertainty; we attempt to devise new arrangements. One of the most discomforting things about this is that in making new arrangements, we often think we are inventing something new, but because we are so bound by our old values, we discover that it is a subtle version of the old program. We see repeatedly, for example, that attempts to eradicate racism and to integrate schools end in segregation by the informal processes within schools. Similar consequences frequently result from experimental efforts to alter sex-role discrimination. Inventors are enormously ingenious in temporary self-deception.

A final comment. In the issues under discussion in this book, I believe we ought to maintain an attitude of humility, with respect to the exactitude of the knowledge we possess and the precise impact of the actions we take on the basis of that knowledge. We must conclude that there are really no final answers, but profit from explorations into a number of different factors that can be seen as developing those crucial bases of identification along sexual and gender lines that constitute such an important part of the self. We have learned a great deal about the biological and chemical determinants of patterns of growth. We have been reexposed to, and I think to some degree consolidated, the kinds of psychological processes that develop as the individual strives to master the exigencies that continuously crop up in different form during the course of development. We have also looked more closely into the interpersonal processes and, in particular, the larger structural and cultural factors that impinge continuously and in sometimes unrecognizable ways on the process of development. The most crucial aspect of our problems is how does this all fit together. What is the organization of these known points of impingement on the developmental process?

Professor Erik Erikson reminded us that we may, within our individual professions and professional work, develop refined tools and isolate refined factors for tracing development. We have to always keep in mind that the individual puts these together in a system and that the course of development is the systematic incorporation of the varieties of different things in a unique pattern.[a] It is the patterning of the kinds of forces that we have been identifying that is the agenda for the future.

---

[a]From symposium discussion, The Sexual and Gender Development of Young Children, San Francisco, 1974.

Chapter Thirty-Seven

The Tide of Change

John Money, Ph.D.*

Change, any kind of change, is a threat to human beings, not only to their value systems but to their state of health.

Even change that is happily embarked on, like a happy marriage, increases the statistical chance of a breakdown in health.[1] It is, therefore, not surprising that many people today feel threatened by the change in stereotypes of gender identity/role that is taking place in our midst.[a] Some, indeed, are outraged, for gender identity is so intimately bound to self-identity that one's very sense of self may be imperiled by a change in gender stereotypes. Those who feel most threatened are likely to contend that the very idea of changing the gender stereotypes is a perverse whimsy, and that it defies immutable biology. Those who feel less threatened, or not threatened at all, are more inclined to see the change in gender stereotypes as part of a tide of history that is sweeping over the world.

There are five biosocial currents that flow with this tide. The first is the invention of labor-saving and augmenting devices of the industrial and automation revolution. It is no longer necessary or

*Professor of Medical Psychology and Associate Professor of Pediatrics, the Johns Hopkins University

aThe double-barrelled term sounds clumsy, but it is the only one available to signify the unity of what one personally feels and knows to be one's gender, on the one hand, with, on the other hand, evidence manifested in both body language and vocal language from which an observer makes his own inference. Ideally, either term, identity or role, would signify both the inner and the outer aspect as a unity, but usage in the English language favors not such a unity, but a dichotomization, which is precisely what I wish to avoid.

expedient to capitalize on or maximize the brute differences between the sexes. Dimorphism of physique, size, and strength are no longer as important as in generations past; nor is woman's lactation, in an age of infant food substitutes.

The second biosocial current is a result of medical and public health advances, namely the extension of life expectancy from the mid-forties at the beginning of this century to the mid-seventies now, with women, on the average, outliving men. Thus, women have a long period after the menopause when child bearing and rearing are not primary preoccupations.

The third is the lowering of the age of puberty which is known to have been taking place at the rate of four months every ten years for a century and a half. Thus, woman may either begin her child-bearing years earlier and later have a longer period free of family duties; or she may need an early career while postponing the onset of child rearing.

The fourth is the population explosion and the need for a couple to reduce the number of child-bearing years in their lives despite the extended life span and earlier age of puberty, thus freeing the woman for a long-term nondomestic career. One might argue that the woman who has completed her own family might become the caretaker of other people's children, say her own grandchildren, but such a program would simply release other, younger mothers for non-maternal work.

The fifth is the invention of birth control, which has been truly effective, cheap, and mass-distributed only since the late 1920s. Birth control for family limitation provides an easy way for society to regulate its size, relative to the lower age of puberty and the population explosion.

I lived in Arnhem Land on the north coast of Australia, on three different occasions in the 1960s, among the aboriginal people who, within the living generation, had come in from a nomadic Stone Age way of life to settle down and send their children to school, use the facilities of the clinic and the local store, and to begin an agricultural and industrial working culture.

As nomadic hunters, these people were actually living in the age that we have lost in our history of transition, for under their former wandering way of life, the only way to feed a newborn baby until it grew up to accept tougher foods was at the breast. It made great survival sense for woman to stay on a quieter nomadic circuit with the babies. The women collected shellfish and plant foods around the shore, while the men went on long distance sea-fishing and hunting trips.

There is something to be learned here with respect to change of sex stereotypes, for there is a limit to how much they can change by slow evolution instead of abrupt revolution. The limit is set by the fact that gender identity/role, from its very plastic undifferentiated beginnings at birth, differentiates by early childhood to have great tensile strength and resistance to reshaping. It is in infancy and early childhood that dimorphic stereotypes of gender identity/role are set for another generation, in the same way that, at the same stage of development, continuity of a native language is set for another generation. Break the continuity for one generation, as the Arnhem Land aborigines have done, and the old stereotypes (or the old language) may be gone forever.

Today those adults who feel most at ease with change in the sex stereotypes, or those who advocate overthrowing them, are those whose early childhood more or less fortuitously prepared them for unorthodoxy. If as a society we decide to commit ourselves to change everyone, then the program must, of necessity, begin with child rearing. It could be that we must abolish the taboo on infantile sexuality and, learning a lesson from the other primates as well as from anthropology, *reinstate* the natural legitimacy of coital rehearsal in the play of young children. Then our children would grow up to have no uncertainties about the irreducible sex differences that underlie dimorphism of gender identity/role. They would get the "givens" established and be free to develop options according to individual opportunity and disposition. Today we do it the other way round: we develop in children our own cultural version of the options and hide the givens from them. We do not exercise the option of footbinding as part of the feminine stereotype, a custom still publicly visible in the tiny feet and hobbled walk of a few adult women in China. Our options are, however, equally arbitrary and just as stultifying, not only for women, but for men as well.

Change of the gender stereotypes or other attitudes regarding sex is not a matter of fashion or whimsy, but an inevitable tide of history. The conservative response to the waxing tide of gender stereotypic change is one of apprehension. Conservatives fear that the proponents of change may be overestimating the power of nurture over nature. They experience their own gender identity, expressing itself as gender role, as so utterly fixed and indelible that they cannot envisage a time in personal development history when it was not fixed, but open to options of developmental differentiation.

The lesson to be learned from historical change is that people in their most convinced ideology sometimes are wrong, and there have to be some on the other side who are willing to say that they are

Chapter Thirty-Eight

The Role of Ideology in the Education of Young Children

Lilian G. Katz, Ph.D.*

It is a reasonable assumption that for any academic discipline, the less dependable its data base, the more dependent its members are upon ideologies.[1] There are many definitions of "ideology." Typically the term is used disparagingly. However, in this discussion I want to emphasize positive uses of the term: namely, as a network of beliefs concerning the things of which we are least certain, and about which we are most passionate. In addition, ideologies usually have a utopian component. We can generally tell when discussions intrude upon ideologies; in such cases arguments over ideas and even facts are taken personally—challenging a fact or a proposition is experienced by the ideologue as an attack on the person.

Those of us in the field of early childhood education working directly with young children are especially dependent on ideologies because our data base is weak. It is difficult to develop dependable data for several reasons. First, the object of our inquiry, the young child, is immature; thus, we cannot tell whether the changes we observe are due to maturation, development, or data-gathering-instrument insufficiency. Furthermore, the data base must remain weak because critical or definitive experiments that might settle empirical or even theoretical issues would be unethical.

Ideologies are highly resistant to change. They die out with the generation that cherishes them. As Thomas Kuhn has shown, in the light of new evidence old paradigms are not discarded.[2] We have to wait, for their adherents have to retire or pass away.

*Professor, Early Childhood Education and Director, Educational Resources Information Center; University of Illinois

At present we seem to be in an era characterized by what DeLissovoy calls the "interregnum," a period of uncertainty or between certainties, marked by stridently competing values or value pluralism.[3] How are teachers to deal with value-laden problems encountered on a day-to-day basis during this period of change and pluralism?

The ideas and information presented in this volume suggest a "crackup of consensus"[4] and an implicit message that we learn to accept and respect a wide variety of alternative life styles. We are told of young families in communes who are committed to a "humanistic organic ideology." These families endeavor to be close to nature and to do, as families, what is natural (as opposed to what?). However, does pursuing a course which seems to be natural mean to be without guidance at all? After all, polio is natural, the drought in Ethiopia is natural. A back-to-nature movement is no simple path to simplicity and beauty. It may include going back to smallpox and diphtheria or, in a behavioral context, to human sacrifice and infanticide.[5]

We have heard a report of one "intentional" community in which children and adults are treated as equals and in which children were said to be given complete freedom of choice and indeed complete freedom (see pp. 159-163).[6] It seems to me that by virtue of their immaturity, children need to have values transmitted to them. Adults' responsibility for deliberate transmission of values would seem to require some process of selection from among alternatives. (It may be that even the refusal to select values constitutes a value position in and of itself.) Do intentional communities that avow "free choice for children" want their children to choose racism or materialism, for instance? Adults' abdication of their responsibility to define what is worthwhile and to assert what is good would seem to threaten young childrens' rights to be socialized by dependable and authoritative (not authoritarian)[7] elders. Young children need adults who are more experienced and wiser than they are, who are willing to make decisions, and who will act upon those decisions in terms of the crucial question of what is valuable. Questions of value cannot be settled empirically; their answers are embedded in ideologies that fill the vacuum created by the absence of reliable data. Issues of sexual and gender development are as refractory as other central issues in child rearing.

In discussions of issues of sex, there is often insufficient focus on intimacy, privacy, love, and the matter of sex within a context of deeper and fuller relationships. In general there seems to be a decline of interest in helping the young to develop their capacity to care for

each other and ultimately for their own young. Harry Broudy reminds us that it is characteristically human to transform instrumental acts into aesthetic expression: we transform our capacities to move into dance, to shout into song, to grunt into words and poetry, eating into dining, and sex into love.[8] Dance and song, poetry and love are distinctively human elaborations of the givens. It is, after all, our *minds* that distinguish us from all other living things.

Given then that issues in sexual and gender development cannot be settled empirically and are thus ideology bound, how can we arrive at a stance that makes sense and is defensible? Some of the issues are easy. I agree with those who say that neither children nor adults should be treated prejudicially on the basis of their sex. For instance, estimates or judgments of intellectual competence should not be linked to the individual's sex. Norms concerning such personality attributes as passivity and assertiveness, and certainly esteem, should not be linked to the sex of the individual. Given these agreements, it seems reasonable to accept the proposition that change is in order.

What is not so clear is the answer to the question: Change to what? If it is "only natural" for boys to be active, fidgety, restless, and mischievous, do I want girls to acquire these attributes in equal proportions? Do I now want, on the other hand, boys to become as passive and docile as girls? Is it simply a matter of every child, regardless of sex, being "free" to acquire any of these attributes without fear of sanction?

Surely neither of these alternatives is desirable. We seem to be in need of a new norm, a new stereotype, a new "ideal" type for all of us. But who is to create the new norms? The new ideal types for all of us? What are the rights and responsibilities of teachers in norm development? A great deal of contemporary discussion seems to focus more on rejection of the old norm of maternal nurturance than on a new norm of paternal nurturance. Until the focus shifts toward the latter we may be encouraging young adults to perceive the nurturance of children as unsatisfying, unesteemable, or undesirable.

In the field of preschool education, in which nurturance is, as it were, professionalized, we seem to suffer from what appears to be a universal correlation: The younger the child you work with is, the less training you have, the less pay and other job benefits you have, and the less status or prestige you have. It would be very disheartening if the movement to change sex-role stereotypes strengthened and contributed to that correlation.

It has been pointed out that, in our society and in others, self-esteem is intimately linked to gender. However, one cannot have self-esteem in a vacuum. Self-esteem is derived from the assignment

288 Values & Conclusions

of value (from positive to negative) to oneself *based on some criterion*. Whatever criteria one uses to evaluate oneself, one's worth and lovability are learned early in life within the context of the family. The criteria by which an individual's worth or acceptance is evaluated vary from family to family, from community to community. Children have no opportunities to choose the criteria against which their lovability is established. They are more or less victims of family criteria circumstances. In some families physical attractiveness or beauty is a criterion; in others, toughness is a criterion; in others, intellectual precocity is required for acceptability. Similarly, conventional or traditional masculinity and femininity may constitute one of the central criteria for a given family. Whose responsibility is it to set the criteria against which self-esteem is to be assessed? Answers to these questions are not to be found in research or theory. They are essentially moral and philosophical assertions. In moral and philosophical issues there are no experts.

In this discussion I have been talking not so much about changing behavior, as about changing the meaning we assign to behavior. It is probably true that the deeper the meaning something has for us, the longer it has been "in the learning" and the longer it will take to unlearn. We seem to need new norms, to reassign meanings to such behaviors as nurturance of the young, regardless of the sex of the nurturer. We need some help with questions like: What is the good life? What makes our lives worth living? What is the good person, man and woman? What are the proper relations between humans? In short, we need a new social philosophy built upon the transformation of our recent and contemporary experiences rather than the imaginings of times long gone by.

NOTES TO CHAPTER THIRTY-EIGHT

1. Lilian G. Katz, Early Childhood Education and Ideological Disputes, *Educational Forum* 39 (3), 1975, 267-271.

2. Thomas Kuhn, *The Structure of Scientific Revolutions*, Second edition (Chicago: University of Chicago Press, 1970).

3. Vladimir DeLissovoy, Child Rearing in a Society of Contradictory Values, *Dimensions* 2 (4), June, 1974.

4. *Ibid.*

5. William L. Langer, Infanticide: A Historical Survey, *History of Childhood Quarterly* 1 (3), Winter, 1974, 353-365.

6. John Rothchild and Susan B. Wolf, *The Children of the Counterculture* (New York: Doubleday and Co., 1976).

7. Lilian G. Katz, Perspectives on Early Childhood Education, *Educational Forum* 37 (4), 393-398.

8. Harry S. Broudy, *The Real World of the Public School* (New York: Harcourt Brace Jovanovich, 1972).

Chapter Thirty-Nine

Guidelines for Teachers
Lilian G. Katz, Ph.D.*

In one of my recent graduate classes at the University of Illinois my students and I became involved in a lively discussion of the pros and cons of an approach to early childhood education called *open education*, or *informal methods.* I suggested to the students, most of whom were also teachers in local schools, that many parents do not prefer these "open" or child-centered methods for their children and are more comfortable with conventional pedagogy. I tried to encourage the students to respect and understand parents' preferences. The students responded by suggesting that we just have to explain to parents what the newer methods are about and convince them that the conventional schooling is not best for children. I then asked these teachers: How many of you prefer to teach according to the principles and with the methods of *open education*? The response was unanimous: all seventeen teachers in the group preferred the newer open methods. Then I asked: How many of you who have children want your children taught by these methods? Nine of them said no. Various reasons were given, all captured in the comment of one mother-teacher: "I cannot take chances with my son. He's got to know how to make it in the system the way it really is now." She could see the urgency of socialization into existing norms for her own child. But as a teacher, in her own professional role, she wanted to apply newer and more "progressive" methods.

A subsequent discussion with the same group centered on issues

*Professor, Early Childhood Education, and Director, Educational Resources Information Center; University of Illinois

related to sexism in early childhood programs. Everyone in the class agreed that it is necessary to change traditional sex stereotypes, eliminate sexism in the curriculum, in books, and television for children. Again when I asked the mothers in the group how many wanted their own children to have nonsexist curricula in the schools, mothers of sons said no. The causes of rejection of nonsexist practices were expressed as follows: "I cannot put my son in the situation where he might be teased by his friends" or "His father is already anxious over his development as a man" or "I have enough trouble with my in-laws—all I need is for my son to come home from school with an interest in cooking or sewing."

This difference between an individual's professional preferences and her maternal preferences exemplify very well the Parsonian[1] distinction between universalistic and particularistic standards. One of the basic characteristics of professionalism is a commitment to universalistic standards of performance with respect to the welfare of *all* clients; the standards of performance are expected to be applied universally to all cases, and personal involvement with the client is minimized in order to preserve the rational or principled aspects of professional service.[2] In contrast, parents—in this case, mothers—are particularistic; they are deeply emotionally involved in the child's welfare, biased in favor of their child, and champion the welfare of their own children, if necessary, at the expense of other people's children.

I have often had occasion to ask teachers: Who is your primary client? Invariably they answer: The child. But the appropriateness of this answer is doubtful. It is probably wiser to think of the parent as the primary client. To agree to the proposition that parents are the primary client of the teacher of young children redefines the problems, but does not eliminate them. In any given group, parents do not necessarily agree with each other just by virtue of their common roles. Suppose a parent comes to you, as the teacher, and says: "Don't let my son play with dolls." What is an appropriate response for you to make? Teachers often assert that the appropriate response is to "educate" the parent to the developmental value of doll play for boys. But parent education is not that easy. Nor is the evidence supporting the developmental value of doll play available.

The basic first guideline seems to be: Do not encourage children to engage in behavior that will increase the likelihood of conflict with their parents' preferences or wishes. I believe that it is more important to increase a mother's confidence in her child's future than to be pedagogically correct. This implies that a teacher's responsibility is to encourage children to engage in activities and

behaviors that strengthen parental confidence in their children. The only exceptions to this guideline might be when the contraindicative evidence is overwhelming or when the parentally preferred behavior may harm other children.

A second guideline is: Value your own values. Values do not have to be held forever. They can be examined and reexamined in the light of new knowledge, evidence, and experiences.

Third: Decide for yourself, and as a staff, what is worth making an issue over. If *you* want to make an issue over coital rehearsal, masturbation, or sex-role equality, do so. Think through as fully and deeply as you can what *you* really believe; refine your understanding of what the behavior and the issue means; and then take your stand with clarity and courage. But do not have too many issues, because you will spend too much time in contention and neglect your real assignment.

Fourth: Make a point of exploring and learning of the resources available to you. You are not a therapist yourself. However, some clinical skills that therapists use are useful for teachers to acquire. Skills in conversing with children are especially useful, because they help to increase the information we have of how a child constructs reality. We can use this information to help the child make more or better sense of his experiences. These processes of uncovering childrens' constructions of reality are the essence of teaching.

Fifth: Treat parents' positions, preferences, and views as valid even when you disagree with them. But keep it in mind that respect for parents does not require you to downgrade or devalue your own expertise. It can never be helpful to a child to undermine his respect for his own home.

Sixth: Keep it in mind that children need adults. They need adults who are willing to take stands on what is worth doing, what is worth knowing, what is worth loving and caring about. If you abdicate that responsibility, you teach children that everything is equally worth while and equally worthless.

Seventh: Never underestimate the power of ideas. I agree fully that the whole realm of experience that we call affective—feeling, touching, etc.—is important. But it is our ideas that give those sensations meaning. Ideas are characteristically human and are enormously powerful—whether good or bad.

Eighth: I recommend that in your own educational setting, you develop a code of ethics. Ethics are propositions concerning what are good or right (versus expedient) actions; they help us cope with the temptations of our occupations. Our ethics are usually embedded in our ideologies. I think it is a general principle that the less power the

client has with respect to the professional, the more important the ethics of the professional are. Similarly, the younger the child is, the more important your ethical position is. Take some time, as an individual and as a staff, to formulate your ideas concerning what is right rather than expedient, what your temptations on the job are, and what actions you might be asked to take by parents, administrators, or colleagues which may violate your ethical principles.

Finally, remember that every solution to every problem creates new problems. The definition of what constitutes a problem is constantly changing. The contemporary definition of child abuse and neglect is different from the definition of one hundred years ago. If we strive to make all children "happy" we can only fail. I think we must concern ourselves with how to help children to experience their lives as meaningful, satisfying, interesting, and worth living.

Social change requires generations. It may help to see ourselves as participants in a very small portion of the total tide of history. I take the trend of history to be the continuous, although slow, development of humaneness and human-ness.

NOTES TO CHAPTER THIRTY-NINE

1. Talcott Parsons, *The Social System* (Glencoe, New York: Free Press, 1964), 61-63 and *passim*.
2. G. McPherson, *Small Town Teacher* (Boston: Harvard University Press, 1972).

※ *Chapter Forty*

Conclusions

Jerome D. Oremland, M.D.*

From the vantage point of being chairman and co-editor of this complex project, a number of observations seemed to typify some of the major dilemmas of the topic. As chairman it was my privilege to be with the various panels as they labored to prepare their agendas and formats, to attend portions of all the meetings, and to hear some of those most interesting after-panel discussions, regretting that the symposium as a whole was unable to benefit from them, but hoping that my notes would recapture their tone and essential ideas. It was striking that in nearly every discussion the same central concerns emerged, and in the responses to them was an easily detectable, strong partisanship on the part of the various disciplines involved.

The main issues of the symposium tended to revolve around: the imparting of physiological-anatomical information with regard to sexual development and sexual activities; the imparting of a concept of responsibility for, information regarding the implications of, and ways of deepening the meaning of sexual activities and the evolving sexual life; and concern about the variety of origins of and the range of feelings and behaviors associated with the developing sense of maleness and femaleness.

There was unanimity that children, even very early, can be taught a great deal about the development of sexual organs, of sexual feelings, and of various aspects of copulation and birth, and that the information is helpful. In general, those who observed from a

*Chief of Psychiatry, San Francisco Children's Hospital and Adult Medical Center; Chairman, Extension Division, San Francisco Psychoanalytic Institute

comparative sociological perspective, be it another country, a chosen alternative culture (a commune), or economically disadvantaged children (a ghetto), or from a physiological, evolutionary perspective tended to be impressed with how much information and experience children, even very young children, can be exposed to without apparent evidence of disturbance and with potential benefit. In this regard, the observations in Sweden were most telling, putting into the broadest relief the difference between culturally condoned and governmentally endorsed highly liberal attitudes and our much more inhibited, puritanical society.

Those involved with the study of development and particularly the dynamics of personality, such as the psychoanalysts with their elaborate schematic concept of a variety of coexistent, phase-sequential developments, were most concerned about dosage and age-appropriateness of information and experience. Rather than relying on apparent disturbance as criteria, they repeatedly raised questions regarding the potential for engendering hidden or latent symptoms.

The educators, as practitioners, consistently reflected concerns about application. They questioned how far we should go in curriculum development, illustrating the range of choices by such sensitive and practical questions as how explicit should the genitalia of dolls be, to discussions of the advantages of—if not initiating, at least allowing—coital rehearsal among very young children.

In the symposium, clear examples were offered as to how much information can be given to even very young children, and a seemingly equal number of significant examples illustrating how distorted or unacknowledging of the information the child at all ages can be. The unanswerable question was how much these distortions are idiosyncratic to the particular child, a reflection of children's limited though developing capacities, or related to the general cultural inhibition motivated by a need to maintain the fantasy of the innocence of childhood, perhaps because of society's fear of activating unbridled emotions and ideas in children.

Despite the unanswered questions, a number of specific programs have evolved and were described, and excellent materials of a wide variety were presented. By most measures the programs and the materials were deemed successful, though generally incomplete. In this regard, a very interesting panel developed on the barriers to and strategies for implementing programs. A number of experiences suggested that the development of programs is far less difficult than implementing them. A telling comment was made that the turmoil of school boards, personnel, and communities as each program is anticipated far exceeds the difficulties among the children once they

are implemented. It was suggested that it is the adults rather than the children who have difficulty in discussing sexual matters in "non-romantic or impersonal settings."

In general, it was concluded that the keystone to the acceptance of the programs is widespread involvement of the community in their development, with extensive discussions of purpose and content. Scare tactics for having programs accepted were unanimously discouraged. However, despite best efforts toward obtaining widely based endorsement, programs may fail because of what might best be called the local ecology: strong religious orientations, with concerns that the school is usurping and/or undermining family authority; unfortunate timing, such as schools still strongly affected by large-scale reorganizations to improve racial imbalance; or nearby communities involved in upheaval because of family life programs.

An area where there was wide agreement but considerably increased breadth of concern was the school's role in the development of attitude and meaning regarding developing sexuality and evolving sexual life. There was unanimity of opinion that this was a necessary if not essential concomitant in any sex-education program. In fact, one of the most experienced persons at the symposium openly suggested a moratorium on the development of materials on the former topic, which he feels is already well, if not overly, developed, with maximal attention given to the latter topic.

This area, loosely called *values* in the symposium, highlighted a major dilemma of compulsory education. The schools reflect and support the society that has created them, and at the same time the schools propagate and lead into new directions that very society. The straightforward values, such as consideration for others, importance of a sense of fulfillment and enjoyment, tenderness, and the like, were readily agreed upon. Even there, however, one realized that this represented but one spectrum of values, which the symposium tended to elevate to being the best values, betraying the underlying liberal humanitarian view that seemed common to all the disciplines.

The more difficult areas, such as attitudes towards homosexuality, premarital intercourse, and the wide variety of sexual activities and attitudes which are often called *alternative life styles*, the symposium tended to regard as acceptable evidences of the plurality of our culture. Yet one could not help but sense that though there was an acknowledgement and endorsement of plurality, actually the idealized standard of the symposium was the eventual attainment of monogamous, heterosexual, loving (often described with such words as open, giving, and honest) marriage relationships with variants being acknowledged, tolerated, but not condoned or encouraged. In

general, proponents of homosexuality, parenthood without a partner, sexual communal living, and the like, although forced to support
the public schools, will find their proposals not given equal treatment
or time in the overt and hidden curricula unless they militantly
demand it, which, (as was also apparent in the symposium) is no
longer only a theoretical possibility.

In this regard, there seemed to be one significant change from
what might be called the standard American ethic in the implied
idealized standard of the symposium. Strikingly, there was a lack of
emphasis on having or rearing children as a societal value or as a most
important path to personal fulfillment. This certainly reflected a
change from what might have been expected in similar discussions
ten years ago.

The essential conflict between the libertarian position and society's tendency, if not responsibility, to perpetuate itself, reached a
clarity of discussion a number of times throughout the symposium,
but a particularly clear perspective was put on it by a representative
of the legal profession in the *values* discussion. He cautioned against
overestimating and overrelying on the law as the effective agent to
bring about social change. At the same time he upheld the importance of the law in allowing parents to perpetuate their own values in
their children even when these values are at wide variance, and
perhaps contradictory, to the values of the society as a whole. He
referred to the significance of the legal discussions resulting in the
Supreme Court decisions regarding the Amish people and the public
schools as an example of the law's protecting and preserving an
idiosyncratic belief system. His discussion in broad terms focused on
the rights of individuals and small groups (minorities) to maintain
themselves, and indicated the law's responsibility not to allow the
public school to represent and perpetuate *solely* any minority,
including the *powerful* one.

The subtlety of the concern about values is well illustrated in the
detailed presentation of a course that a young married woman offers
in a private school to relatively homogeneous white, upper-middle-
class fifth-graders. She asserted that she must present values in order
to teach any subject, but especially family life, and had discussed this
with the board of trustees of her school. In keeping with current
precepts, they agreed that it would be allowed as long as she
indicated that hers was but one set of values, all others also to be
respected and acknowledged. In the conference, she didn't specify
her values, but one couldn't help but wonder if the board would have
been so accepting were she identifiably lesbian or an open advocate
of free love. One wondered if it could be possible that the teacher's

professed values would not have more of an impact on the children than the other values alluded to even though the teacher was attempting to promote a tolerance towards pluralism.

In general, the developmentalists and the legal expert felt that a self-selection system does take place and that it should be encouraged with increasing alternatives so that parents, presumably, could find the school that most closely represents those values they wish engendered. It was also pointed out that this offers teachers the advantage of being able to choose systems in which they could teach the values that are most harmonious with their own views.

Although this proposal superficially seemed agreeable, it was quickly sensed that it might be contrary to the tradition of compulsory education, which implies that parents should not be allowed to have total say with regard to their children in matters that also involve the welfare of the society. Essentially, the state doesn't trust to the judgment of parents the decision of whether or not to go to school, and one wondered if the state would be willing or should be willing to trust totally to the good judgment of parents the kind of school. Such a proposal should also create a range of artificially homogeneous school situations with all the limitations that come with attempting to teach living skills from a homogeneous prospective in a homogeneous environment which have to be applied in a pluralistic culture.

The complexity of the situation from a different standpoint was fully evident as we heard the report of a commune which demanded equal rights for children, including full and unhampered access to sexual activity among themselves and with adults. This easily could be seen as a chosen life style with its adherents rigidly demanding that the public school system support and promulgate such a view. However, at the same time, the more clinically oriented participants of the symposium questioned that society's promotion of such a view could be tantamount to failing to protect children from overstimulation and psychological abuse and that society must not be any less cognizant or any less willing to intervene in situations involving psychological abuse than it is regarding physical abuse. The question of the emerging concern for the rights of children and who is to be their advocate when parents and society disagree was acknowledged as a highly controversial area in which progress is only beginning.

In summary, generally, it was agreed that a great deal of education can be imparted about the importance of tolerating difference, the importance of recognizing individuality, the importance of respect in relationships, and the general concept that with varying degrees of

intensity of relationship comes varying attendant degrees of responsibility. It was felt that these were important *values* to instill in children and that the sex education courses and family life series are particularly well suited for making these ideas explicit; however, to be effective these ideas must be implicit in every course in the curriculum and in the milieu of the school.

In this regard, the important point was made that sexual education and the development of values, though often concentrated in a course or a series, should not be taught in isolation and should be integrated into the complete curriculum and functioning of the school. As specific examples, it was suggested that the social studies series, history, and literature also particularly well lend themselves to this purpose. Developing such a curriculum and school carries with it the added implication felt unanimously advantageous by the symposium that sexuality not be considered an isolated phenomena but regarded as an important component of the fabric of relationship and of life.

Probably the greatest interest and controversy in the symposium centered around the discussion of gender and its development. Although it was difficult to find a conclusive word or phrase (and a number of participants tended to use *sexual identity*, *sexual-role* or *gender identity*) in general, it seemed convenient to use *gender* to cover the sense of maleness and femaleness with its concomitant feelings and behavior.

The symposium emphasized that throughout history there has been a continual redefining of gender directly and indirectly reflecting expedient survival needs of the culture. However, it was felt that probably at no other time has there been as much overt consideration of gender or as wide an availability of options and potential for confusion than at present. One could not help but be astonished on hearing the clinical descriptions at the enormity of the present capabilities dramatically to alter surgically, physiologically, and psychologically sexual appearance and gender behavior, and it was clear that the potential is ever increasing with indications already that basic alterations can be made intrauterinely and eventually genetically.

However remarkable are the developments for inducing direct change, it was equally remarkable, as various research studies were reported, how different the environment influencing the female is from that of the male from birth and even prior in terms of parental expectation. Studies demonstrated that, indeed, newborn males are different from females, and mothers (perhaps more than others) treat the newborn males differently from their newborn females. These

differences ever increase into an essentially dimorphic environment reflecting the sexual stereotypes. Throughout the symposium there was the overriding concern that the dimorphic quality hampers development in general. Implicit in this concern is the concept that becoming a person is of a higher order representing fuller development, transcending the concept of man or woman. In this regard, the symposium tended to see a similarity between sexism and racism, using at times an almost political rhetoric as the two were seen as equal evils of society. There seemed to be the implication, not clearly explored, that because we have erroneously stigmatized blacks and that this has had a far-reaching deleterious effect on their development with vast unfortunate social consequences, our attitudes towards maleness and femaleness are equally stigmatizing with an inevitably similar negative effect.

Examples of direct and indirect dimorphic influences within the schools were amply demonstrated in the various surveys presented including direct observations of classrooms, interviews with the school staff, and reviews of curricula material. In the discussion, the concern always seemed to be that the female has been more stigmatized and is therefore more blunted than the male. Although many discussions were thoughtful, there was a tendency to equate person with male and to advocate the enhancement of the female by allowing and encouraging her to participate in things traditionally male, with the exception of disruptive behavior (considered largely a male "contribution" to the classroom).

In general, there was less concern that males be allowed to participate in or are systematically excluded from situations traditionally female. For example, artistic activity was never mentioned or studied in any of the reports even though there is a traditional tendency to see artistic activity as being more related to the female (and the male homosexual); yet there was little concern expressed that boys may be deprived of opportunity for, or reinforcement of, artistic endeavor. Though there was some discussion about the significance of boys being deprived of the opportunity to express feelings other than anger, such as crying or fear, and some discussion of the importance of doll play for boys, in general, the concern centered on allowing girls access to male territory.

It was difficult to know if there was but another expression of continuing depreciation of those areas associated with the female or whether it reflected presumed advantages of the male and a demand for equal opportunity. Nonetheless, when it came to such crucial considerations as attitudes towards child care and mothering, in general there seemed to be more concern that girls were traditionally

pushed into these and actively discouraged from pursuing professions rather than concern whether the challenges, rewards, and
special attributes of child care and mothering were being accorded
high enough value. These discussions seemed to reflect the general
tenor regarding gender, which with few exceptions failed to find and
endorse significant female values and characteristics and which
tended toward a unisexual view that largely seemed imitative of the
culturally defined male. Psychoanalysts easily could see this as the
age-old denial of things feminine; and the sociologists, the age-old
tendency of the have-nots to replace the haves.

In the vital area of child rearing, most felt that eventually infant
and child care will and should be equally divided between the sexes
with an increasingly important role for the professional child-care
worker. In short, more and more children will be reared by parents
equally sharing tasks, and children will be spending increasingly
larger proportions of their lives in child care centers with nonparental
persons of both sexes.

Some felt that shared child care was essential to enhance the
importance of fatherhood; some saw it as essential in order to free
the female for other pursuits; and some saw it as an important
vehicle to enhance the mutual respect of each sex for the other.
Unfortunately, the implications of this style of child care on the
developing infant were not sufficiently considered; available data
regarding the effects on development of young children, especially
infants, of being cared for by multiple persons is meager. It seemed
that the possible effects of single vs. multiple caretakers might be a
factor of greater import with regard to personality development and
societal change than the question of male vs. female infant caretakers.

One of the experimental education programs presented was predi-
cated on the concept that the primary problem underlying sexism
(and racism) was the competitive structure of our society, with its
tendency to instill as a value *striving* with concomitant super-
ordinate/subordinate relationships. In that regard, it was interesting
that a research report from one of the commune alternative life
styles, a commune that emphasizes subordination of the individual to
the commune, indicated that communal living with multiple early
caretakers decreases the aggressive competitive strivings in young
children, male and female alike. In that their findings, though only
suggestive at the moment, are in agreement with observations on
youngsters reared in other commune situations such as the kibbut-

zim, the question is raised whether there is an intrinsic relationship between competitive strivings and the nuclear (triangular) family. Competitive strivings are then subsequently reinforced in the culture as a whole, including the schools, which in gender terms affect male-female relationships. Such findings suggest that alteration of the triangular family pattern, as we know it, by equal division of child care tasks between parents, may have more effect on personality development including gender expression because of the shift from single caretaker to multiple caretakers than because of the effects of having the male interacting earlier and in more significant ways, with corresponding changes in the female's relationship with the infant.

In general, in the discussions of gender, educators seemed particularly concerned about stereotyping and the response to stereotyping, seeing children's behavior as tending to become what is anticipated for them. In this regard, they seem close to the classical *tabula rasa* model often referring to a self-fulfilling prophesy concept of behavior. For example, in one study one investigator suggested that the reason more boys than girls were sent to the principal's office for misdemeanors was that it was expected that boys act in a disruptive way. As she studied her results further, she wondered if the fact that boys are less mature at the same age level than girls made them more prone to misdemeanor and that this proneness to misdemeanor then becomes mislabeled and reinforced by regarding it as masculine because boys are expected to misbehave.

It was not surprising that the educators were highly respectful and concerned about the consequences of the environment they create for children, for most educators conceptualize development from an operant-conditioning viewpoint. This, however, led them at times to overemphasize the school's impact as both an instigator and director of children's behavior. From the standpoint of external influences, however, one could not but wonder about the impact of television, which probably in terms of hours of influence outdistances the school and probably the family.

From a different viewpoint, the developmentalists, particularly the psychoanalysts, generally felt that children take out of their environment that aspect that has particular meaning for them in terms of their most pressing developmental needs and in terms of the significant antecedents in their development. They tended to emphasize less the primacy of attitudes in inducing behavior, especially the major differences in gender, and were most inclined to see attitudes as giving form, to varying degrees, to emerging behavior at various

times. They also seemed more aware of the small groups, the subsocieties, that develop in each class as children find what they need and obtain reinforcement for it from peers and teachers.

In summary, there was little question that there is a sexual dimorphic environment for the male and female, and that that dimorphism is intensely reflected in the schools, even though there was a wide range of opinion as to the sources of the dimorphic tendency. Nonetheless, everyone, on hearing the description of the curricula and the atmosphere of the school, was impressed by how early and ubiquitously these phenomena find their way into the overt and covert activities of the school, with most seeing these as deleterious inhibitors on developing potentials.

There were a number of areas discussed during the symposium less directly related to the role of the school in the sexual and gender development of young children, yet relevant in that they detailed for the participants the highly divergent personal and cultural backgrounds of the children in their classrooms. The descriptions also reminded us of how remarkably differing schools are.

In considering the effects of disruption in the family, one of the most interesting findings was that young (latency age) girls seem to be the group most at risk psychologically when a divorce is in process and subsequently. Heretofore, the concern in divorce had been largely for the effects on boys of being reared in father-absent households. The implications of the finding with regard to girls is far-reaching, underlining the importance of the father at every stage of development for boys and girls.

In this regard, a very sensitive account by a highly experienced educator of young children reminded teachers that they provide something special to children by maintaining their professional distance. She cautioned teachers, especially in circumstances of family disruption, of the dangers of the teacher subtly and/or unwittingly displacing or replacing the parent. Among other things she reminded teachers that this can only result in an inevitable, needless second loss for that child. She warned teachers about the dangers of attempting to meet, without additional professional help, the demands that parents at times make on the teacher during family disruption. Further, she reminded the symposium that with the increasing divorce rates, all too frequently the teacher's family itself may be in a disruptive process as he or she deals with children and parents in similar circumstances.

In considering children who are being reared in *alternative life styles* be they formalized into microcommunity, a commune, or be they idiosyncratic to a family living in an otherwise conventional

neighborhood, it was clear that the range of experiences that children are having and bring to the classroom is extraordinary and increasing. Throughout the symposium there was a feeling of concern about the consequences for children of these often radical departures and at the same time an interest in them as natural experiments in child rearing.

In the research reports on a variety of these situations, it was clear that the variables being studied are multiple, not the least of which is the significance of the fact that the parents of these young children are themselves young, transitional, and inexperienced. Most of them were reared in, and often were reacting overtly against, traditional and disruptive family circumstances. There was a general feeling of compassion as we heard of highly courageous young people attempting to be different. Unfortunately, all too frequently the being different seemed to be a *going back*, an idealization of times of yore, with longed for idyllic simplicity that never really existed.

However, thousands of children are being reared in ways that reflect radically changing views. It was clear that there will be an increasing heterogeneity in the classrooms in a way never before encountered, with increasing demands and challenges for teachers (most of whom came from rather conventional child-rearing experiences) who must sort out those aspects conducive from those aspects destructive to children, so that they as teachers and schools can most advantageously respond.

Several interesting circumstances were described in which sexual disturbance in the schools and classrooms were but symptomatic of home life disruption, particularly homes marked by excessive sexual exposure by uncaring and unknowledgeable parents. In a panel somewhat related, the question of the advisability of parental nudity with young children was discussed. Again the symposium polarized, with the more sociologically inclined pointing to its widespread occurrence, and the more clinically oriented emphasizing the risks of overstimulation. Some advocates indicated that it allows children to see what they are to become and learn what they are not, which they term identification and complementation. In a most sensitive discussion, one of the developmentalists evolved the concept that the act cannot be separated from the motivation. He felt that the lack of spontaneity and the quality of forcing which tends to characterize, especially, those parents who, in a sense, are in transition and reacting against inhibitory upbringings, is in itself transmitted to children, contributing to a sense of being overwhelmed.

However, little of what was described compared with the description of a primary school in an urban ghetto. In this school the

children's sexual and aggressive behavior was extreme in almost every way and clearly reflected the lack of protection and dosing by parents who themselves seemed, because of extensive sociological and psychological disturbance, barely able to deal with their own sexual and aggressive feelings. The description by this black principal of a "walk around the school yard" was convincing evidence of the extensive sexuality of young children and how it, in concert with other disruptive activity, seems antithetical to education. His observations reminded us that Freud's latency period was intended as a schematic concept to represent the relative repression of sexual-aggressive feelings and impulses by the positive identifications of the oedipal period. Rather than latency, Freud referred to the *ideal* of latency, full well recognizing that it was a relative concept and implying that the degree that it is achieved during those years indicates the degree to which the identifications have been consolidated. He saw its relative attainment as essential in order for certain types of imitative learning, learning at the behest of the parental substitutes, the teachers, to take place. One could not help but realize that in this school, there was learning but of a different type from what the curriculum committee had intended, and with compassion we heard how teachers, rather than being facilitators and directors, were forced into being referees and wardens.

An area which seemed to receive little attention was the discussion of masturbation of young children. All unanimously agreed that it is "normal" and that guilt associated with masturbation, especially as induced by adults, is deleterious. However, there seemed to be little concern that masturbation can be a repetitive attempt, unsuccessfully, to master excessive stimulation. There seemed to be little discussion of the significance of masturbation as symptomatic of regressive trends, a relying on oneself and reestablishing one's own sense of intactness out of fear of trusting *involvement* with others. Further, the quality of masturbation (excessive and/or compulsive) provides us with important additional information indicating that those essential progressions away from the self as a unit into a more social self are not taking place and are too laden with anxiety. It seemed that though there is now widespread agreement that the inhibition of masturbation is harmful, especially inducing guilt in order to inhibit masturbation, there seemed to be an overacceptance with little acknowledgement that masturbation has to be viewed, as any other activity, in terms of its significance. In short, we can be so accepting of masturbation as being normal, and so aware of the importance of not inducing guilt, that we lose sight of its complexity in the various developmental progressions.

Throughout the symposium there was a good deal of discussion of the role of the English language itself in reinforcing unfortunate connotations with regard to gender. This was to become a monumental problem for the editors of this volume as we struggled with how best to deal with the third-person singular pronoun, references to mankind, and the like, in that conventional (and grammatically correct) usage gives undue affirmation to maleness.

After much discussion, the editors decided that the primary consideration and, in fact, the truly underlying principle that evolved during the symposium was the full recognition of the potential advantages that accrues for all in respecting individuality and the full acknowledgement of the great risks to all inherent in forcing preconceived patterns, including the nonsexist language. In keeping with this, we tried to use the form that the presenter felt most comfortable with and used most naturally in the spontaneous discussions. Yet it was clear throughout the symposium that language is changing in response to the new awarenesses and sensitivities that have developed to gender issues. Although it was doubtful that the symposium as a whole saw unmitigated advantages to adopting the uni- or non-sexist language that some advocated, it was interesting to note the absence of references to the *opposite* sex. Referring to the *other* sex as opposed to *opposite* sex seems evidence of the decreasing need to polarize with all its defensive and derisive connotations and a more realistic acceptance, respectfulness, and appreciation of the similarities and the differences. It seems clear that when language changes, we can have confidence that true and significant shifts in concepts are taking place.

The symposium closed with a general feeling that though we know much, there is a great deal more to learn, and though we can do much, there is a great deal more to do. In general, I feel that the noneducators achieved increased respect for the educators as they heard firsthand the challenges they face. In a sense, the noneducators, as the theoreticians and researchers, more fully realized that the educators as the practitioners are the ones who really put to test what we know and from whom we can best learn what we need to know.

References

References

Abelin, Ernest. The Role of the Father in the Separation-Individuation Process. In *Separation-Individuation, Essays in Honor of Margaret S. Mahler*, ed. John B. McDevitt and Calvin F. Settlage, 229-52. New York: International Universities, Inc., 1971.

Ainsworth, Mary D. The Development of Infant-Mother Interaction Among the Ganda. In Brian Foss, *Determinants of Infant Behavior*, 2nd ed., 67-104. London: Methuen, 1963.

_____. Patterns of Attachment Behavior Shown by the Infant in Interaction with his Mother. *Merrill-Palmer Quarterly* 10 (1964): 51-58

Almy, Millie. *The Early Childhood Educator at Work*. New York: McGraw-Hill, 1975.

Alpert, Augusta. The Latency Period. *American Journal of Orthopsychiatry* 11 (1941): 126-32.

Andray, Andrew. *How Babies Are Made*. New York: Time-Life, 1968.

Athanasiou, Robert; Phillip Shaver; and Carol Travis. Sex. *Psychology Today*, July 1970, 37-52.

Balint, Michael. Individual Differences of Behavior in Early Infancy and an Objective Way of Recording Them. *J. Genet. Psychol.* 73 (1948): 57-117.

Bandura, Albert, and Richard H. Walters. *Social Learning and Personality Development*. New York: Holt, Rinehart and Winston, 1963.

Baratz, Stephen, and Joan C. Baratz. Early Childhood Intervention: The Social Science Base of Institutional Racism. *Harvard Educational Review* 40 (1970): 29-50.

Barclay, J.R. Changing the Behavior of School Psychologists: A Training Rationale and Method. Final Report for 1967 NDEA Institute in Advanced Counseling for School Psychologists at California State College, Hayward, October 1968.

Barry, Herbert; Margaret K. Bacon; and Irvin I. Child. A Cross-Cultural Survey of

some Sex Differences in Socialization. *Journal of Abnormal and Social Psychology* 55 (1957): 327-32.

Baruch, Dorothy. *New Ways of Sex Education.* New York: McGraw-Hill, 1959.

Baumrind, D., and A. Black. Socialization Practices Associated With Dimensions of Competence in Preschool Boys and Girls. *Child Development* 38 (1967): 291-328.

Beach, Frank A. Characteristics of Masculine "Sex Drive." In *Nebraska Symposium on Motivation*, 1-32. Lincoln: University of Nebraska, 1956.

Bell, Richard Q., and Naomi Costello. Three Tests for Sex Differences in Tactile Sensitivity in the Newborn. *Biologia Neonatorum* 7 (1964): 335-47.

Bell, Richard Q., and Joan F. Darling. The Prone Head Reaction in the Human Neonate: Relation with Sex and Tactile Sensitivity. *Child Development* 36 (1965): 943-49.

Bem, Sandra L. The Measurement of Psychological Androgyny. *Journal of Consulting and Clinical Psychology* 42 (1974): 155-62.

Bender, Lauretta, and Abram Blau. The Reaction of Children to Sexual Relations with Adults. *American Journal of Orthopsychiatry* 7 (1937): 500-18.

Benjamin, Harry. *The Transsexual Phenomenon.* New York: The Julian Press, 1966.

Berest, Joseph J. Report on a Case of Sadism. *The Journal of Sex Research* 6 (August 1970): 210-19.

Berger, Bennet M., and Bruce Hackett. The Decline of Age-Grading in Rural Hippie Communes. *The Journal of Social Issues* 30, 2 (Winter 1974): 163-83.

Berlin, I.N. Learning Mental Health Consultation; History and Problems. *Mental Hygiene* 48 (1964): 257-66.

_____. Preventive Aspects of Mental Health Consultation to Schools. *Mental Hygiene* 51 (1967): 34-40.

_____. Transference and Countertransference in Community Psychiatry. *Archives of General Psychiatry* 15 (1966): 165-72.

Bernstein, Anne C., and Philip A. Cowan. Children's Concepts of How People Get Babies. *Child Development* 46 (1975): 77-91.

_____ How Children Learn About Sex and Birth. *Psychology Today*, January 1976, 31-36.

Bieber, Irving. A Discussion of Homosexuality: The Ethical Challenge. *J. of Consult. and Clin. Psych.* 44, 2 (1976): 163-66.

Bieber, Irving et al. *Homosexuality—A Psychoanalytic Study of Male Homosexuals.* New York: Basic Books, 1962.

Bidgood, Frederick E. The Effects of Sex Education: A Summary of the Literature. *SIECUS Report* 1, 4 (March 1973): 11.

Biller, H.B., and D.L. Singer. Sex Role Development and Creative Potential in Kindergarten-Age Boys. *Developmental Psychology* 1 (1969): 291-96.

Bindman, A.J. Mental Health Consultation; Theory and Practice. *Journal of Consulting Psychology* 23 (1959): 473-82.

_____. The School Psychologist and Mental Health. *Boston University Journal of Education* 146 (1964): 2-10.

The Black College: A Continual Progression of "Community-Family Guided

Education—A Process Toward Afro-American Continuity." In *The Black College in an Age of Ferment*, ed. James Hudson, 105-28. Tallahassee: Florida A & M University, 1974.

Blos, Peter. *On Adolescence: A Psychoanalytic Interpretation*. New York: The Free Press of Glencoe, 1962.

————. The Second Individuation Process of Adolescence. *Psychoanalytic Study of the Child* 22 (1967): 162-86.

————. *The Young Adolescent; Clinical Studies*. New York: Free Press, 1970.

Boadella, David. *Wilhelm Reich: The Evolution of His Work*. New York: Dell Publishing, 1973.

Bornstein, Berta. On Latency. *Psychoanalytic Study of the Child* 6 (1951): 279-85.

Bowlby, John. Childhood Mourning and its Implications for Psychiatry. *Am. Journal of Psychiatry* 118 (1961): 481-98.

————. *Childhood Mourning and its Implications for Psychiatry in Childhood Psychopathology*, ed. Saul I. Harrison and John F. McDermott, 263-89. New York: International Universities Press, 1972.

Brecher, Ruth, and Edward Brecher, eds. *An Analysis of Human Sexual Response*. Boston: Little, Brown & Company, 1966.

Bridger, Wagner H. Ethological Concepts and Human Development. *Rec. Adv. Biolog. Psychiat.* 4 (1962): 95-107.

Broderick, Carlfred B. How the Sex Drive Develops. *Sexology* 30 (June 1964): 780-84.

————. Sexual Development Among Pre-Adolescents. *The Journal of Social Issues* 22 (April 1966): 6-21.

Broderick, Carlfred B., and Stanley E. Fowler. New Patterns of Relationships Between the Sexes Among Preadolescents. *Marriage and Family Living* 23 (February 1961): 27-30.

Broudy, Harry S. *The Real World of the Public Schools*. New York: Harcourt Brace Jovanovich, 1972.

Brown, Daniel G., and David B. Lynn. Human Sexual Development: An Outline of Components and Concepts. *Journal of Marriage and the Family* 28 (May 1966): 155-62.

Butler, C. The Influence of Parents' Emotional Attitudes Concerning Sex on the Sex Education of Their Children. Masters thesis, University of Chicago, Committee on Human Development, 1952.

Byler, Ruth, ed. *Teach Us What We Want to Know*. New York: Mental Health Material Center, 1969.

Caine, Augustus. A Study and Comparison of the West African Bush School and the Southern Sotho Circumcision School. Masters thesis, Northwestern University, 1959.

Calderone, Mary S. Planning Programs of Sex Education. National Association of Independent Schools, 1967.

California Youth Authority. Family Life Education Program. State of California Documents Section.

Caplan, G. Concepts of Mental Health and Consultation; Their Application in Public Health and Social Work. Washington, D.C.: Children's Bureau, 1959.

Caplan, G. Opportunities for School Psychologists in the Primary Prevention of Mental Disorders in Children. *Mental Hygiene* 47 (1963): 525-39.

_____. Types of Mental Health Consultation. *American Journal of Orthopsychiatry* 33 (1963): 470-81.

Chasen, Barbara. Sex Role Stereotyping and Pre-Kindergarten Teachers. *Elementary School Journal* 74 (January 1974): 225-30.

Christians and the Meaning of Sexuality. Nashville, Tenn.: Graded Press, 1972.

Clay, Vidal S. The Effect of Culture on Mother-Child Tactile Communication. *The Family Coordinator* 17 (July 1968): 204-10.

Clower, Virginia L. The Development of the Child's Sense of his Sexual Identity. *J. Am. Psychoanal. Assoc.* 18 (1970): 165-76.

Cohen, J., and B.T. Eiduson. Changing Patterns of Child Rearing in Alternative Life Styles. In *Child Personality and Psychopathology: Current Topics*, ed. Anthony Davids. New York: Wiley, 1975.

Conn, Jacob H. Children's Awareness of the Origins of Babies. *Journal of Child Psychiatry* 1 (1947): 140-76.

_____. Children's Reactions to the Discovery of Genital Differences. *American Journal of Orthopsychiatry* 10 (1940): 747-55.

Cowan, E.L. Emergent Approaches to Mental Health Problems: An Overview and Directions for Future Work. In *Emergent Approaches to Mental Health Problems*. ed. E.L. Cowan, E.A. Gardner, and M. Zax, 389-455. New York: Appleton-Century-Crofts, 1967.

Cowe, E.L., and R.P. Lorion. Changing Roles for the School Mental Health Professional. *J. School Psychology* 14 (1976): 131-38.

Davison, Gerald. Homosexuality: The Ethical Challenge. *Journal of Consulting and Clinical Psychology* 44, 2 (1976): 157-62.

DeCecco, John; F. Minnigerode; M. Adelman; M. Shively; M. Hall; and D. Knutson. Research on the Violations of Civil Liberties of Homosexual Men and Women. *J. of Homosexuality* (1977): in press.

DeCecco, John P., and Michael G. Shively. A Study of Perceptions of Rights and Needs in Interpersonal Conflicts in Homosexual Relationships. *Journal of Sex Roles* (1977): in press.

deLissovoy, Vladimir. Child Rearing in a Society of Contradictory Values. *Dimensions* 2, 4 (June 1974).

Delora, JoAnn S., and Jack R. Delora, eds. *Intimate Life Styles: Marriage and Its Alternatives*. Pacific Palisades, Calif.: Goodyear Publishing, 1972.

Deutsch, Helene. *Psychology of Women; A Psychoanalytical Interpretation* 1. New York: Grune & Stratton, 1944.

Dreitzel, H. Peter. *Childhood and Socialization*. New York: Macmillan Publishing Co., Inc., 1973.

Dubignon, J.; D. Campbell; M. Curtis; and M. W. Partington. The Relation Between Laboratory Measures of Sucking, Food Intake, and Perinatal Factors During the Newborn Period. *Child Development* 40 (1969): 1107-20.

Ehrensaft, Diane R. Sex Role Socialization in a Preschool Setting. Doctoral dissertation, University of Michigan, 1974.

Eiduson, Bernice T.; Jerome Cohen; and Janette Alexander. Alternatives in Child Rearing in the 1970's. *American Journal of Orthopsychiatry* 43 (1973): 720-31.

Elias, James, and Paul Gebhard. Sexuality and Sexual Learning in Childhood. *Phi Delta Kappan* 50 (March 1969): 401-405.

Elkind, David. *Children and Adolescents, Interpretive Essays on Jean Piaget.* New York: Oxford University Press, 1970.

Engel, R.; D. Crowell; and S. Nishijima. Visual and Auditory Response Latencies in Neonates. In *Felicitation Volume in Honour of C.C. DeSilva.* Ceylon: Kularatne & Company, Ltd., 1968.

Erikson, Erik. *Childhood and Society.* New York: W.W. Norton and Co., Inc., 1950.

_____. The Theory of Infantile Sexuality. In *Childhood and Society,* 44-92. New York: Norton, 1950.

Fagot, Beverly. Sex Differences in Toddlers' Behavior and Parental Reaction. *Developmental Psychology* 10 (July 1974): 554-58.

Fenichel, Otto. *The Psychoanalytic Theory of Neurosis.* New York: Norton, 1945.

Finch, Stuart M. Sex Play Among Boys and Girls. *Medical Aspects of Human Sexuality.* September 1969, 58-66.

Firestone, Shulamitt. *The Dialectic of Sex; The Case for Feminist Revolution.* New York: Bantam, 1971.

Fisichelli, Vincent R., and Samuel Karelitz. The Cry Latencies of Normal Infants and Those with Brain Damage. *J. Pediat.* 62 (1963): 724-34.

Ford, Clellan S., and Frank A. Beach. *Patterns of Sexual Behavior.* New York: Harper, 1951.

Fox, J.R. Sibling Incest. *British Journal of Sociology* 13 (June 1962): 128-50.

Fraiberg, Selma. *The Magic Years; Understanding and Handling the Problems of Early Childhood.* New York: Charles Scribner's, 1959.

Frank, Lawrence K. *On the Importance of Infancy.* New York: Random House, 1966.

Freud, Anna. The Concept of Developmental Lines. *Psychoanalytic Study of the Child* 18 (1963): 245-65.

_____. The Role of the Teacher. *Harvard Educational Review* 22 (1952): 229-34.

Freud, Sigmund. Beyond the Pleasure Principle. *Standard Edition* 17 (1922): 7-64. London: Hogarth Press, 1955.

_____. Three Contributions to the Theory of Sex. In *The Basic Writings of Sigmund Freud,* ed. and trans. A.A. Brill, 553-629. New York: Modern Library, 1938.

_____. Three Essays on the Theory of Sexuality. *Standard Edition* 7 (1905): 125-245. London: Hogarth Press, 1953.

Friedman, Stanley M. An Empirical Study of the Castration and Oedipus Complexes. *Genetic Psychology Monographs* 46 (1952): 61-130.

Furth, Hans G. *Piaget and Knowledge; Theoretical Foundations.* Englewood Cliffs, N.J.: Prentice-Hall, 1969.

Gagnon, John H. Sexuality and Sexual Learning in the Child. *Psychiatry* 28 (August 1965): 212-28.

Gagnon, John H., and William Simon. The Sociological Perspective on Homosexuality. *The Dublin Review* (Summer 1967).

Galenson, Eleanor, and Herman Roiphe. The Impact of Early Sexual Discovery

on Mood, Defensive Organization, and Symbolization. *Psychoanal. Study of the Child* 26 (1972): 195-216.

Garai, Josef E., and Amram Scheinfeld. Sex Differences in Mental and Behavioral Traits. *Genet. Psychol. Monogr.* 77 (1968): 169-299.

Gessell, A.; H.M. Halverson; H. Thompson; F.L. Ilg; B.H. Costner; L.B. Ames; and C.S. Amtruda. *The First Five Years of Life: A Guide to the Study of the Preschool Child.* New York: Harper and Row, 1940.

Gibbs, James. *Peoples of Africa.* New York: Holt, Rinehart and Winston, 1965.

Glick, Paul C. Some Recent Changes in American Families. *Current Populations Reports, Special Studies Series 52.* Washington, D.C.: U.S. Government Printing Office, 1975.

Goldberg, Susan, and Michael Lewis. Play Behavior in the Year Old Infant; Early Sex Differences. *Child Development* 40 (1969): 21-31.

Goldstein, Michael, and Harold Kant. *Pornography and Sexual Deviance.* Berkeley: University of California, 1973.

Good, L. Thomas; J. Sikes; and J. Brophy. Effects of Teacher Sex and Student Sex on Classroom Interaction. *Journal of Educational Psychology* 65 (1973): 74-89.

Goodwin, D.L. Consulting with the Classroom Teacher. In *Behavioral Counseling,* ed. J.D. Krumholtz and C.E. Thoresen, 260-66. New York: Holt, Rinehart & Winston, 1969.

Gould, Lois. X: A Fabulous Child's Story. *Ms.* 1, 6 (December 1972): 74-76, 105-106.

Grant, Ewan C. Human Facial Expression. *Man* 4 (1969): 525-36.

Green, Richard. *Sexual Identity Conflict in Children and Adults.* New York: Basic Books Inc., 1974.

_____. One-Hundred Ten Feminine and Masculine Boys: Behavioral Contrasts and Demographic Similarities. *Archives of Sexual Behavior* 5 (1976): 425-46.

Green, Richard, and John Money, eds. *Transsexualism and Sex Reassignment.* Baltimore: The Johns Hopkins University Press, 1969.

Greenacre, Phyllis. Early Physical Determinants in the Development of the Sense of Identity. *J. Amer. Psychoanal. Assoc.* 6 (1958): 612-27.

_____. Special Problems of Early Female Sexual Development. *Psychoanalytic Study of the Child* 5 (1950): 122-38.

Greenfield, Patricia M. *What Can We Learn from Cultural Variation in Child Care.* San Francisco: American Association for the Advancement of Science, November 1974.

Greer, Germaine. *The Female Eunuch.* New York: McGraw-Hill, 1971.

Handbook on Sex Instruction in Swedish Schools. Stockholm: National Board of Education, 1957.

Hannerz, Ulf. Soulside: Inquiries into Ghetto Culture and Community. In *The Best of Simple,* ed. L. Hughes. New York: Hill and Wang, 1961.

_____. What Ghetto Males Are Like: Another Look. In *Afro-American Anthropology,* ed. Norman Whitten and J.F. Szwed, 313-25. New York: The Free Press, 1970.

Harlow, Harry F. The Heterosexual Affectional System in Monkeys. *American Psychologist* 17 (1962): 1-9.

Harlow, Harry et al. The Maternal Affectional System of the Rhesus Monkey. In

Maternal Behavior in Mammals, ed. Harriet Rheingold, 268. New York: Wiley, 1963.

Hartley, Ruth E. A Developmental View of Female Sex-Role Definition and Identification. *Merrill-Palmer Quarterly* 10 (January 1964): 3-16.

Hattendorf, Katharine W. A Study of the Questions of Young Children Concerning Sex: A Phase of an Experimental Approach to Parent Education. *Journal of Social Psychology* 3, 1 (1932): 37-65.

Henry, George A. *Masculinity and Femininity*. New York: Macmillan, 1973.

Herzog, Elizabeth, and Cecelia E. Sudia. Boys in Fatherless Families. U.S. Department of Health, Education and Welfare, Office of Child Development, DHEW Publication No. (OCD) 72-33, Children's Bureau, reprinted 1971.

Hetherington, E. Mavis. Effects of Father Absence on Personality Development in Adolescent Daughters. *Developmental Psychology* 7, 3 (1972): 313-26.

Hetherington, E. Mavis; Martha Cox; and Roger Cox. Beyond Father Absence: Conceptualization of Effect of Divorce. Denver: Society for Research in Child Development, April 1975.

Hoffman, L.W. Early Childhood Experiences and Women's Achievement Motives. *Journal of Social Issues* 28 (1972): 129-55.

Honzig, M.P., and J.P. McKee. The Sex Difference in Thumbsucking. *J. Pediat.* 61 (1962): 726-32.

Hutt, C., and W.C. McGrew. Effects of Group Density Upon Social Behavior in Humans. Symposium on Changes in Behavior with Population Density, Assoc. Study Animal Behav., 1967.

Jacklin, Carol N.; Eleanor E. Maccoby; and Anne E. Dick. Barrier Behavior and Toy Preference: Sex Differences (and Their Absence) in the Year-old Child. *Child Development* 44 (1973): 196-200.

Jacobs, Carol, and Cynthia Eaton. Sexism in the Elementary School. *Today's Education* 61 (1972): 20-22.

Jerome, Judson. *Families of Eden*. New York: Seabury Press, 1974.

Johnson, M.H. Sex-Role Learning in the Nuclear Family. *Child Development* 34 (1963): 319-33.

Jones, Blurton. An Ethological Study of Some Aspects of Social Behavior of Children in Nursury School. In *Primate Ethology*, ed. D. Morris, 347-68. Chicago: Aldine Publishing Co., 1967.

Jones, Ernest. The Early Development of Female Sexuality. In *Papers on Psychoanalysis*, 438-51. London: Bailliere, Tindahl and Cox, 1950.

_____. *The Life and Work of Sigmund Freud* 2. New York: Basic Books, 1955.

Kagan, Jerome, and Howard A. Moss. *Birth to Maturity*. New York: Wiley, 1962.

_____. The Emergence of Sex Differences. *School Review* 80 (1972): 217-28.

Kanter, Rosabeth. *Commitment and Community*. Cambridge, Mass.: Harvard University Press, 1972.

Karlsson, Hans-Jorgen. Sex Education in Swedish Schools. Stockholm: National Swedish Board of Education, May 5, 1974.

Kasanjian, V.; S. Stein; and W.L. Weinberg. *An Introduction to Mental Health Consultation*. Public Health Monograph No. 69. Washington, D.C.: U.S. Government Printing Office, 1962.

Katz, Lilian G. Early Childhood Programs and Ideological Disputes. *Educational Forum* 39, 3 (1975): 267-71.

Katz, Lilian G. Perspective on Early Childhood Education. *Educational Forum* 37, 4 (1973): 393-98.

_____. Teaching in Preschools: Roles and Goals. ERIC Document No. 70706-E AO-U-26, 1969.

Katzman, Marshall. Early Sexual Trauma. *Sexual Behavior*, February 1972, 13-17.

Kelly, Joan B., and Judith S. Wallerstein. The Effects of Parental Divorce: Experiences of the Child in Early Latency. *Am. J. of Orthopsychiat.* 46 (January 1976): 20-32.

Kerckhoff, Richard K. Value Stance in Family Life Education. *The Family Coordinator* 19 (1970): 253-60.

Ketcher, Allan. The Discrimination of Sex Differences by Young Children. *Journal of Genetic Psychology* 87 (1955): 131-43.

Kinsey, Alfred C. *Sexual Behavior in the Human Female.* Philadelphia: W.B. Saunders Co., 1953.

Kinsey, Alfred C.; Wardell B. Pomeroy; and Clyde E. Martin. *Sexual Behavior in the Human Male.* Philadelphia: W.B. Saunders Co., 1948.

Klapper, Zelda S. The Impact of the Women's Liberation Movement on Child Development Books. *Amer. J. Orthopsychiat.* 41 (1971): 725-32.

Kleeman, James A. Genital Self-Discovery During a Boy's Second Year: A Follow-up. *Psychoanalytic Study of the Child* 21 (1966): 358-92.

Kohlberg, Lawrence. A Cognitive-Developmental Analysis of Children's Sex-Role Concepts and Attitudes. In *The Development of Sex Differences*, ed. E. Maccoby. Stanford: Stanford University Press, 1966.

Korner, Anneliese F. Individual Differences at Birth: Implications for Early Experience and Later Development. *Am. J. Orthopsychiat.* 41 (1971): 608-19.

_____. Neonatal Startles, Smiles, Erections and Reflex Sucks as Related to State, Sex and Individuality. *Child Development* 40 (1969): 1039-53.

_____. Sex Differences in Newborns with Special Reference to Differences in the Organization of Oral Behavior. *Journal of Child Psychology and Psychiatry* 14 (1973): 19-29.

Korner, Anneliese F., and Helena C. Kraemer. Individual Differences in Spontaneous Oral Behavior. In *Third Symposium on Oral Sensation and Perception: The Mouth of the Infant*, ed. James F. Bosma. Springfield: Charles C. Thomas, 1972.

Korner, Anneliese F., and Evelyn B. Thoman. The Relative Efficacy of Contact and Vestibular-Proprioceptive Stimulation in Soothing Neonates. *Child Development* 43 (1972): 443-53.

_____. Visual Alertness in Neonates as Evoked by Maternal Care. *J. Experiment. Child Psychol.* 10 (1970): 67-78.

Kreitler, Hans, and Shulamith Kreitler. Children's Concepts of Sexuality and Birth. *Child Development* 37 (1966): 363-78.

Kuhn, Thomas. *The Structure of Scientific Revolutions.* 2nd ed. Chicago: University of Chicago Press, 1970.

Lambert, N.M. A School-based Consultation Model. *Professional Psychology* (1974).

Langer, William L. Infanticide: A Historical Survey. *History of Childhood Quarterly* 1 (Winter 1974): 353-65.

Langworthy, Orthello R. Development of Behavior Patterns and Myelinization of the Nervous System in the Human Fetus and Infant. *Contributions of Embryology* 24 (September 1933): 1-57.

Lansky, Leonard M. The Family Structure Also Affects the Model: Sex Role Attitudes in Parents of Preschool Children. *Merrill-Palmer Quarterly* 13 (1967): 139-50.

Lansky, Leonard M.; Sheila Fling; and Martin Manosevitz. Sex Typing in Nursery School Children's Play Interest. *Developmental Psychology* 7 (1972): 146-52.

Lee, Patrick C.; and Nancy Gropper. Sex Role Culture and Educational Practice. *Harvard Educational Review* 44 (August 1974): 369-410.

Lerner, Gerda, Ed. The Myth of the "Bad" Black Woman. In *Black Women in America.* New York: Vintage Books, 1973.

Lester, J. My Daughter the Quarterback, My Son the Bellydancer. *The Civil Liberties Review* 2 (1975): 76-80.

Levit, Eugene E., and Albert Klassen Jr. Public Attitudes Toward Sexual Behavior: The Latest Investigation of the Institute for Sex Research. Fiftieth Anniversary Meeting, American Orthopsychiatric Association, June 1973.

Levy, David M. Finger Sucking and Accessory Movements in Early Infancy. *American Journal of Psychiatry* 7 (1928): 881-918.

Lewis, Michael. State as an Infant-Environment Interaction: An Analysis of Mother-Infant Interactions as a Function of Sex. *Merrill-Palmer Quarterly* 18, 2 (1972): 95-121.

Lewis, Michael, and Howard A. Moss. Sex, Age, and State as Determinants of Mother-Infant Interaction. *Merrill-Palmer Quarterly* 13 (1967): 19-35.

Liley, A.W. The Foetus as a Personality. *Australian and New Zealand Journal of Psychiatry* 6 (1972): 99-105.

Linnér, Birgitta. *Sex and Society in Sweden.* New York: Harper & Row, 1973.

Lipsitt, Lewis P., and Nissim Levy. Electrotactual Threshold in the Neonate. *Child Development* 30 (1959): 547-54.

Litin, Edward M.; Mary E. Griffin; and Adelaide M. Johnson. Parental Influence in Unusual Sexual Behavior in Children. *The Psychoanalytic Quarterly* 25 (1956): 37-55.

Lynn, David B. *The Father: His Role in Child Development.* Belmont, Calif.: Brook/Cole, 1974.

_____. *Parental and Sex Role Identification.* Berkeley: McCutchen, 1969.

Maccoby, Eleanor E., ed. *The Development of Sex Differences.* Stanford, Calif.: Stanford University Press, 1966.

Maccoby, Eleanor Emmons, and Carol Nagy Jacklin. *The Psychology of Sex Differences.* Stanford: Stanford University Press, 1974.

_____. Stress, Activity and Proximity-Seeking: Sex Differences in the Year-Old Child. *Child Development* 44 (1973): 34-42.

Mahler, Margaret S. *On Human Symbiosis and the Vicissitudes of Individuation* 1. New York: International Universities Press, 1968.

_____. *The Psychological Birth of the Human Infant: Symbiosis and Individuation.* New York: International Universities Press, 1975.

Mahler, Margaret; Fred Pine; and Anni Bergman. *The Psychological Birth of the Human Infant*. New York: Basic Books, 1975.

Marmor, Judd. Orality in the Hysterical Personality. *J. Am. Psychoanal. Assoc.* 1 (1953): 656-71.

Martinson, Floyd M. Eroticism in Infancy and Childhood. *Journal of Sex Research* (November 1976).

_____. *Infant and Child Sexuality: A Sociological Perspective*. St. Peter, Minn.: The Book Mark, 1973.

_____. *Marriage and the American Ideal*. New York: Dodd Mead and Co., 1960.

_____. Sexual Knowledge, Values, and Behavior Patterns. A Study by Department of Sociology, Gustavus Adolphus College and Lutheran Social Service of Minnesota, 1966.

Masters, William, and Virginia Johnson. *Human Sexual Inadequacy*. Boston: Little, Brown, 1970.

McDermott, John C. Parental Divorce in Early Childhood. *Am. J. Psychiat.* 124 (April 1968): 118-26.

McGrew, W.C. *An Ethological Study of Agonistic Behavior in Preschool Children*. New York: Karger, 1969.

McPherson, Gertrude. *Small Town Teacher*. Boston: Harvard University Press, 1972.

Mead, Margaret. *Sex and Temperament in Three Primitive Societies*. New York: Dell, 1963.

Melville, Keith. *Communes in the Counter Culture*. New York: William Morrow, 1973.

Meyer, John W., and Barbara J. Sobieszek. Effect of a Child's Sex on Adult Interpretations of its Behavior. *Developmental Psychology* 6 (1972): 42-48.

Minuchin, Patricia. Sex-Role Concepts and Sex-Typing in Childhood as a Function of School and Home Environments. *Child Development* 36 (1965): 1033-48.

Mischel, Walter. Sex-Typing and Socialization. In *Carmichael's Manual of Child Psychology*, 3rd ed., ed. Paul H. Mussen, 3-72. New York: John Wiley and Sons, 1970.

Missakian, Elizabeth A. Genealogical and Cross-Genealogical Dominance Relations in a Group of Free-Ranging Rhesus Monkeys (Macaca mulatta) on Cayo Santiago. *Primates* 13 (1972): 169-80.

Mohr, J.W.; R.E. Turner; and M.B. Jerry. *Pedophilia and Exhibitionism*. Toronto: University of Toronto, 1964.

Money, John. Ablatio Penis: Normal Male Infant Sex-Reassigned as a Girl. *Archives of Sexual Behavior* 4, 1 (1974): 65-71.

_____. Gender Role, Gender Identity, Core Gender Identity: Usage and Definition of Terms. *J. Amer. Acad. Psychoanalysis* 1, 4 (1973): 397-403.

_____. Psychosexual Differentiation. In *Sex Research*, ed. John Money. New York: Holt, Rinehart and Winston, 1965.

_____. *Sex Errors of the Body: Dilemmas, Education, Counseling*. Baltimore: Johns Hopkins University Press, 1968.

_____. Sexology: Behavioral, Cultural, Hormonal, Genetic, etc. *The Journal of Sex Research* 9 (February 1973): 1-10.

Money, John, and Anke A. Ehrhardt. *Man and Woman, Boy and Girl: The Differentiation and Dimorphism of Gender Identity from Conception to Maturity.* Baltimore: Johns Hopkins University Press, 1972.

Money, John, and H. Musaph, eds. *Handbook of Sexology.* Amsterdam and New York: Elsevier/North Holland, 1977.

Money, John, and Patricia Tucker. *Sexual Signatures: On Being a Man or a Woman.* Boston: Little, Brown, 1975.

Moore, James, and Diane Kendall. Children's Concepts of Reproduction. *J. of Sex Research* 7 (1971): 42-61.

Moore, R.S., and K. Sanner. Helping Teachers Analyze and Remedy Problems. In *Behavioral Counseling,* ed. J.D. Krumholtz and C.E. Thoresen, 250-59. New York: Holt, Rinehart & Winston, 1969.

Moss, Howard A. Sex, Age and State as Determinants of Mother-Infant Interaction. *Merrill-Palmer Quarterly* 13 (1967): 19-35.

Mungo, Ray. *Total Loss Farm.* New York: E.P. Dutton Co., 1970.

Murdock, George P. *Africa, Its Peoples and Their Cultural History.* New York: McGraw-Hill, 1959.

Mussen, P., and E. Rutherford. Parent-Child Relations and Parental Personality in Relation to Young Children's Sex-Role Preferences. In *The Causes of Behavior* II, ed. J.F. Rosenblith and N. Allensmith. Boston: Allyn and Bacon, 1966.

Neuman, F., and W. Elgee. Permanent Changes in Gonadal Function and Sexual Behavior as a Result of Early Feminization of Male Rats by Treatment with an Antiandrogenic Steroid. *Endokrinologie* 50 (1966): 209-24.

Newman, L. Transsexualism in Adolescence. *Arch. Gen. Psychiat.* 23 (1970): 112-21.

Nisbett, Richard E., and Sharon B. Gurwitz. Weight, Sex and the Eating Behavior of Human Newborns. *J. Comp. Physiol. Psychol.* 73 (1970): 245-53.

Parker, W. The Emerging Homosexual Minority. *The Civil Liberties Review* 2 (1975): 136-44.

Parsons, Talcott. The American Family: Its Relations to Personality and Social Structure. In *Family, Socialization and Interaction Process,* ed. T. Parsons and B.F. Bales. Glencoe, Ill.: Free Press, 1955.

_____. The Social Class as a Social System: Some of its Functions in American Society. *Harvard Educational Review* 29 (Fall 1959): 297-318.

_____. *The Social System.* New York: Free Press, 1959.

Pederson, F.A., and P.Q. Bell. Sex Differences in Preschool Children Without Complications of Pregnancy and Delivery. *Developmental Psychology* 3 (1970): 10-15.

Pederson, Frank A., and Kenneth S. Robson. Father Participation in Infancy. *American Journal of Orthopsychiatry* 39 (1969): 466-72.

Piaget, Jean, and Bärbel Inhelder. *The Growth of Logical Thinking From Childhood to Adolescence.* New York: Basic Books, 1958.

Pizzo, Peggy Daly. *Operational Difficulties of Group Day Care.* Washington, D.C.: Day Care and Child Development Council of America, 1972.

Prescott, James. Early Somatosensory Deprivation as an Ontogenetic Process in the Abnormal Development of the Brain and Behavior. *Medical Primatology* (1970).

Prescott, James. Maternal-Social Deprivation as Functional Somato-sensory Differentiation in the Abnormal Development of the Brain and Behavior: A Developmental Neural-Behavioral Theory of Socialization. American Psychological Association Proceedings, September 8, 1970. Pp. 866-67.

_____. Developmental Neuropsychophysics. National Institute of United Health and Human Development, 1972.

Prescott, James W., and Cathy McKay. Human Affection, Violence and Sexuality: A Developmental and Cross-Cultural Perspective. Philadelphia: Society for Cross-Cultural Research, February 1973.

_____. Somatosensory Deprivation and the Pleasure Principle: Neurobiological and Cross-Cultural Perspective of Sexual, Sadistic, and Affectional Behavior. Dallas: Society of Biological Psychiatry, April 1972.

Prince, Virginia, and P.M. Bentler. Survey of 504 Cases of Transvestism. *Psychol. Rep.* 31 (1972): 903-17.

Proposed Guidelines for Sex Education in the Swedish School System. Stockholm: State Commission on Sex Education, 1974.

Rahe, Richard; Jack L. Mahan; and Arthur J. Ransom. Prediction of Near Future Health Changes from Subjects' Preceding Life Changes. *J. Psychosomat. Res.* 14 (1970): 401-406.

Rahe, Richard; Merle Meyer; Michael Smith; George Kjaer; and Thomas Holmes. Social Stress and Illness Onset. *J. Psychosomatic Research* 8 (1964): 35-44.

Ramsey, Glenn V. The Sex Information of Younger Boys. *American Journal of Orthopsychiatry* 13 (1943): 347-52.

Rath, Robert A., and Douglas J. McDowell. Coming Up Hip; Child Rearing Perspectives and Life Style Values Among Counter Culture Families. *Sociological Symposium* 7 (Fall 1971): 49-60.

Raths, Louis; Merrill Harmin; and Sidney B. Simon. *Values and Teaching: Working with Values in the Classroom.* Columbus, Ohio: C.E. Merrill Books, 1966.

Rayder, Nicholas F.; John C. Larson; and Allan I. Abrams. The Effect of Socio-Contextual Variables on Child Achievement. Unpublished manuscript, 1976.

Ribble, Margaret A. *The Personality of the Young Child; An Introduction for Puzzled Parents.* New York: Columbia University Press, 1955.

Roiphe, Herman. On An Early Genital Phase: With An Addendum on Genesis. *Psychoanal. Study of the Child* 23 (1968): 348-65.

Rothbart, Mary K., and E.E. Maccoby. Parents' Differential Reactions to Sons and Daughters. *Journal of Personality and Social Psychology* 4 (1966): 237-43.

Rothchild, John, and Susan B. Wolf. *The Children of the Counterculture.* New York: Doubleday and Company, 1976.

Saario, Terry; Carol N. Jacklin; and Carol K. Tittle. Sex Role Stereotyping in the Public Schools. *Harvard Educational Review* 43 (1973): 386-416.

Sade, D.S. Determinants of Dominance in a Group of Free-Ranging Rhesus Monkeys. In *Social Communication Among Primates,* ed. S.A. Altmann, 99-114. Chicago: University of Chicago Press, 1967.

Safilios, Constantine-Rothschild; Barbara Bovee Polk; and Robert B. Stein. Sex

Role Socialization and Sex Differences. In *Early Child Development*, ed. V. Ethenakis. Munich: Institute for Early Socialization, 1975.

Saghir, Marcel, and Eli Robins. *Male and Female Homosexuality; A Comprehensive Investigation*. Baltimore: Williams and Wilkins, 1973.

Sale, June. *I'm Not Just a Babysitter*. Pasadena: Pacific Oaks College, 1971.

Sandler, Joseph. The Background of Safety. *Int. Journal of Psychoanalysis* 41 (1960): 352-56.

Sarason, S.B.; M. Levine; I.E. Goldenberg; D.L. Cherlin; and E.M. Bennet. *Psychology in Community Settings*. New York: John Wiley and Sons, 1966.

Sarnoff, Charles. *Latency*. New York: Jason Aronson, Inc., 1976.

Sarvis, M.A. *Collaboration in School Guidance*. New York: Brunner/Mazel, Inc., 1970.

Schafer, Roy. The Loving and Beloved Superego in Freud's Structural Theory. *Psychoanalytic Study of the Child* 15 (1960): 163-88.

Schwab, George. *Tribes of the Hinterland*. Papers of the Peabody Museum of Am. Arch. and Ethnography 31, 161-63. Harvard, 1947.

Serbin, Lisa A.; K. Daniel O'Leary; Ronald N. Kent; and Ilene J. Tonick. A Comparison of Teacher Response to the Pre-academic and Problem Behavior of Boys and Girls. *Child Development* 44 (1973): 796-804.

Sears, Robert R.; Eleanor E. Maccoby; and Harry Levin. *Patterns of Child Rearing*. New York: Harper and Row, 1957.

Settlage, Calvin F. Danger Signals in the Separation-Individuation Process: The Observations and Formulations of Margaret S. Mahler. In *The Infant at Risk*, ed. Daniel Bergsma. New York: Stratton Intercontinental Medical Books Corp., 1974.

―――――. Introduction to the Panel on the Psychology of Women: Late Adolescence and Early Adulthood. *J. Am. Psychoanal. Assoc.* 24 (1976): 631-45.

―――――. On the Libidinal Aspect of Early Psychic Development and the Genesis of Infantile Neurosis. In *Separation-Individuation: Essays in Honor of Margaret S. Mahler*, ed. John B. McDevitt and Calvin F. Settlage, 131-54. New York: International Universities Press, 1971.

Sexton, Patricia C. *The Feminized Male*. New York: Vintage Books, 1969.

Shagass, Charles, and Marvin Schwartz. Age, Personality and Somatosensory Cerebral Evoked Responses. *Science* 148 (1965): 1359-61.

―――――. Somatosensory Cerebral Evoked Responses in Psychotic Depression. *Br. J. Psychiat.* 112 (1966): 799-807.

―――――. Visual Cerebral Evoked Response Characteristics in a Psychiatric Population. *Am. J. Psychiat.* 121 (1965): 979-87.

Shively, Michael. Sexual Orientation Survey. San Francisco State University, unpublished manuscript, 1976.

Simon, Sidney B.; Leland W. Howe; and Howard Kirschenbaum. *Values Clarification: A Handbook of Practical Strategies for Teachers and Students*. New York: Hart Publishing Co., 1972.

Simon, William, and John Gagnon. Psychosexual Development. *Transaction* 6 (March 1969): 9-17.

Skolnick, Arlene, ed. *Rethinking Childhood*. Boston: Little, Brown, 1976.

Skolnick, Arlene, and Jerome Skolnick. *Family in Transition: Rethinking Marriage, Sexuality, Childrearing and Family Organization.* Boston: Little, Brown, 1971.

Soltan, H.C., and S.E. Bracken. The Relation of Sex to Taste Reactions. *J. Heredity* 49 (1958): 280-84.

Spitz, Rene A., with Katharine Wolf. Autoeroticism: Some Empirical Findings and Hypotheses on Three of its Manifestations in the First Year of Life. *Psychoanalytic Study of the Child* 3-4 (1949): 85-120.

Stoller, Robert J. *Sex and Gender; On the Development of Masculinity and Femininity.* New York: Science House, 1968.

Stunkard, A. Anorexia Nervosa. In *The Science and Practice of Clinical Medicine*, ed: J.P. Sanford. New York: Grune & Stratton, 1972.

Stunkard, A., and J. Hirsch. Obesity. In *The Science and Practice of Clinical Medicine*, ed. J.P. Sanford. New York: Grune & Stratton, 1972.

Thoman, Evelyn B.; P. Herbert Leiderman; and Joan P. Olson. Neonate-Mother Interaction during Breast-Feeding. *Development Psychol.* 6 (1972): 110-18.

Toman, Walter. *Family Constellation; Theory and Practice of a Psychological Game.* New York: Springer, 1961.

Ullerstam, Lars. *The Erotic Minorities.* New York: Grove Press Inc., 1966.

Unitarian-Universalist Association. *About Your Sexuality.* Boston: Beacon Press, 1973.

Valenstein, Elliot S.; Jan W. Kakolewski; and Verne C. Cox. Sex Differences in Taste Preferences for Glucose and Saccharin Solutions. *Science* 156 (1967): 942-43.

Vesey, Lawrence. *The Communal Experience.* New York: Harper and Row, 1973.

Wade, George N., and Irving Zucker. Hormonal and Developmental Influence on Rat Saccharin Preferences. *J. Comp. Physiol. Psychol.* 69 (1969): 291-300.

_____. Taste Preferences of Female Rats: Modification by Neonatal Hormones, Food Deprivation and Prior Experience. *Physiol. and Behav.* 4 (1969): 935-43.

Wallerstein, Judith S., and Joan B. Kelly. The Effects of Parental Divorce: The Adolescent Experience. In *The Child and His Family; Children at a Psychiatric Risk* 3, ed. E.J. Anthony and C. Koupernik. New York: Wiley and Sons, 1974.

_____. The Effects of Parental Divorce: Experiences of the Child in Later Latency. *Am. J. of Orthopsychiat.* 46 (1976): 256-69.

_____. The Effects of Parental Divorce: Experiences of the Preschool Child. *Journal of the Am. Academy of Child Psychiatry* 14, 4 (Autumn 1975): 600-16.

Ward, Ingeborg L. Prenatal Stress Feminizes and Demasculinizes the Behavior of Males. *Science* 175 (1972): 82-84.

Whiting B., and C. Pope. A Cross-Cultural Analysis of Sex Differences in the Behavior of Children Aged Three to Eleven. *Journal of Social Psychology* 91 (December 1973): 171-88.

Wilson, T. Lightfoote. Notes Toward a Process of Afro-American Education. *Harvard Educational Review* 42 (1972): 374-89.

_____. *Toward Equitable Education; A Handbook for Multicultural Consciousness for Early Childhood, a Bicentennial Revolution?* Redwood City, Calif.: Ujamaa Developmental Education Publications, 1976.

_____. A View of Developmental Education and the "Disadvantaged" in a National Perspective: Implications for International Education. *J. of Negro Education* 41 (Summer 1972): 276-90.

Wolff, Peter H. The Causes, Controls and Organization of Behavior in the Neonates, Monograph 17, *Psychological Issues* 5, 1 (1966): 1-105.

_____. The Natural History of Crying and Other Vocalizations in Early Infancy. In *Determinants of Infant Behavior* 3, ed. Brian M. Foss, 113-38. London: Methuen, 1969.

Wortis, Rochelle P. The Acceptance of the Concept of the Maternal Role by Behavioral Scientists: Its Effects on Women. *Amer. J. Orthopsychiat.* 41 (1971): 733-46.

Zablocki, Benjamin. *The Joyful Community*. Baltimore: Penguin Books, 1972.

Index

About the Editors

Evelyn K. Oremland, M.S.W. is a social worker with wide experience in many aspects of early childhood development. As co-editor of *The Effects of Hospitalization on Children*, and as consultant and lecturer on the emotional considerations of child care in the hospital, she has worked with the various and complex responses of the normal child to his environment, stressful and palliative. As a consultant to projects on preventive psychiatry and early remedial intervention, she is remarkably qualified to review, organize, and coordinate the many divergent observations, experiences, and research about children, their families, and their schools which constitute this volume on the sexual and gender development of young children.

Jerome D. Oremland, M.D., a psychiatrist and psychoanalyst, is Chief of Psychiatry at the San Francisco Children's Hospital and Adult Medical Center. He has authored many papers on various aspects of personality development, particularly the development of relationship and the sense of self and other. A member of the faculty of the San Francisco Psychoanalytic Institute and of the Graduate School of Social Welfare, the University of California, Berkeley, Dr. Oremland has taught extensively on various aspects of creativity, borderline personality, and early phases of personality development. As Chairman of the Extension Division of the San Francisco Psychoanalytic Institute, he has organized numerous important multi-disciplinary symposia on various aspects of personality development, the child, and his environment.

About the Contributors

Millie Almy, Ph.D. Professor of Education, University of California; Berkeley, Calif.

Richard Baugh. Former Assistant Principal, John Muir School; Berkeley, Calif.

Bennett Berger, Ph.D. Professor of Sociology, University of California; San Diego, Calif.

Joseph Bodovitz. Former Chairman, School Board, Mill Valley School District; Mill Valley, Calif.

Diane Brashear, Ph.D. Director, Brashear Center for Personal and Sexual Health; Indianapolis, Indiana.

Gale J. Brownell. Teacher, Family Life Education, Martin Luther King Jr. High; Berkeley, Calif.

Derek L. Burleson, Ed.D. Managing Editor, *Medical Aspects of Human Sexuality*; formerly Director, Educational and Research Services, Sex Information and Education Council of U.S. (SIECUS).

Betty Cohen, M.S.W. Bananas (Child Care Information and Referral Service); Berkeley, Calif.

John P. DeCecco, Ph.D. Professor of Psychology, San Francisco State University; Director, Center for Homosexual Education, Evaluation, and Research, San Francisco State University.

Diane Ehrensaft, Ph.D. Department of Education, University of California; Berkeley, Calif.

Bernice T. Eiduson, Ph.D. Professor, Department of Psychiatry, University of California; Los Angeles, Calif.

Joyce Evans, M.A. Fifth Grade Teacher, Marin Country Day School; Corte Madera, Calif.

Richard Green, M.D. Professor, Departments of Psychiatry and Behavioral Science and Psychology, State University of New York at Stony Brook; Stony Brook, New York.

Joseph Gutstadt, M.D. San Francisco Psychoanalytic Institute, Marin Community Mental Health Service.

Dorothy S. Huntington, Ph.D. Child Development Specialist, Peninsula Hospital and Medical Center; Burlingame, Calif.

George C. Kaplan, M.D. Faculty, San Francisco Psychoanalytic Institute.

Lilian G. Katz, Ph.D. Professor, Early Childhood Education and Director, Educational Resources Information Center; University of Illinois.

Anneliese F. Korner, Ph.D. Adjunct Professor, Dept. of Psychiatry, Stanford University; Stanford, Calif.

Ronald D. Lee, M.S.W. Clinical Social Worker and Director, The Center for Special Problems, San Francisco Community Mental Health Services.

Floyd M. Martinson, Ph.D. Professor of Sociology, Gustavus Adolphus College; St. Peter, Minn.

Elizabeth A. Missakian, Ph.D. Research Associate, Synanon Research Institute; Marshall, Calif.

John Money, Ph.D. Professor of Medical Psychology and Associate Professor of Pediatrics, The Johns Hopkins University; Baltimore, Maryland.

Jerome D. Oremland, M.D. Chief of Psychiatry, San Francisco Children's Hospital and Adult Medical Center; Chairman, Extension Division, San Francisco Psychoanalytic Institute.

Susan Parker, M.S.W. Vice-principal, Tyrrell Junior High School; Hayward, Calif.

Morris Peltz, M.D. Director of Training, Children's Hospital, San Francisco; Faculty, San Francisco Psychoanalytic Institute.

June Sale, M.S.W. Family Day Care Project; Pacific Oaks College; Pasadena, Calif.

Calvin F. Settlage, M.D. Chief, Child Psychiatry, Mt. Zion Medical Center; Faculty, San Francisco Psychoanalytic Institute.

Michael G. Shively. Co-investigator, Civil Liberties for Homosexuals Project; Research Associate, Center for Homosexual Education, Evaluation, and Research, San Francisco State University.

Rosalind Singer, M.A., M.P.H. Health Education Consultant, Albany Unified School District; Albany, Calif.

Neil Smelser, Ph.D. Professor of the University, Department of Sociology, University of Calif.; Berkeley, Calif.

Walter Smithey, M.A. Psychologist/Coordinator Family Life Education, San Mateo Office of Education.

Albert J. Solnit, M.D. Director, Child Study Center, Yale University; New Haven, Conn.

Philip M. Spielman, M.D. Faculty, San Francisco Psychoanalytic Institute.

Judith S. Wallerstein, M.S.W. Lecturer, School of Social Welfare, University of California; Berkeley, Calif.

Charles Walton, M.D. Faculty, Extension Division, San Francisco Psychoanalytic Institute.

Harriette Block Wasser, M.A. School Psychologist, Berkeley Unified School District; Berkeley, Calif.

Thomasyne Lightfoote Wilson, Ph.D. Consultant, Ravenswood School District, East Palo Alto, Calif.; Faculty, San Jose State University.